Practical Intuition for Therapeutic Practices

Rosa Castro, Psy. D.

Rosa Castro

Copyright© 2018 Rosa Castro

No part of this book may be reproduced or transmitted in any form or by any means, electronic or mechanical, including photocopying, recording, or by any information storage or retrieval system, except in the case of excerpts by a reviewer, who may quote brief passages in a review.
All rights reserved
ISBN-13: 978-1719181310

Contents

Acknowledgment vi
Preface 1
Chapter I Introduction 7
Chapter II Understanding Intuition 17
Chapter III Integrating Intuition in Therapy 25
Chapter IV Reviewing Treatment Modalities 42
Chapter V Exploring Intuitive Techniques 67
Chapter VI The Sensory System 78
Chapter VII The Benefits of Aromatherapy 100
Chapter VIII Utilizing Meditation in Therapy 109
Chapter IX Developing Intuitive Skills 139
Chapter X - Aura Scanning 161
Chapter XI Therapeutic Chakra Techniques 177
Chapter XII Healing Regressive Techniques 216
Chapter XIII Intuitive Tarot and Psychotherapy
.... 241
Chapter XIV Using Reiki in Therapy 249
Chapter XV Professional Integration 270
Chapter XVI Ethics and Intuitive work 285
Conclusion 291
Reference 292

Acknowledgment

I would like to thank Lars Nohrstedt for his patience, faith, and encouragement through the process of developing this book. I would like to also thank Raycine Lavan and Virginia Stewart Avalon for their editorial help and encouragement during the writing of this book. I would like to express my gratitude to Dr. Elena Michaellidou for her professional guidance and enthusiasm.

Preface

When I let go, I listen, and when I listen, I know. – R. Castro

Why this book?

This book was inspired by my healing journey, which began in 2017, shortly a month after I turned 57. In 2017, April 27th I had a brain tumor removed. In truth, I never imagined I would have had the capacity to remember enough to write beyond a few words. After surgery, my ability to focus was so bad that when I started a sentence halfway through I would forget what I was writing or saying.

Not being able to function made me realize I needed to heal. Lucky for me, I had more than 36 years of experience working as a substance abuse therapist. Which meant I understood how to create positive habits. My work experience, as well as my education in psychology and alternative techniques, allowed me to develop ways to heal myself. I managed to combine my professional training with my intuition to bring myself back.

My healing journey began after I was released from the hospital May 2nd, 2017. As a result of my healing journey, this book was born.

This book, however, is not about my recovery from brain surgery, but about how mental health clinicians and alternative health care practitioners can use intuitive techniques in helping individuals obtain psychological stability and optimum health. I will eventually write about my healing journey upon completing my healing year since currently, I am still healing.

Professional Background

My career as a therapist is rooted in my own need to understand the complicated relationship between people, specifically couples and family. I read books on psychology as early as the 5th grade, in hopes of understanding my family dynamics. Though the books never helped me in resolving my issues at home; they paved the way for my career in the field of mental health.

While I was getting my degree in psychology, from Fordham University, I began working as a drug therapist in a Methadone Maintenance program in the 80's. I took the job as a counselor as an experiment, to see if I would enjoy working with people. What had begun as an experiment, became a lifelong career of 30 years. Though I started in a

Methadone maintenance program, throughout the years, I worked in various types of treatment modalities from inpatient to outpatient, prison system, school system, and fee for service, to name a few. My work experience exposed me to different styles of treatment and work philosophies. In addition to my work history, I also took the time to study and develop my intuitive skills and learn about various alternative healing systems.

Intuitive Background

My intuitive background is a patchwork of workshops and personal inquisitiveness. The beginning of my intuitive training was fluid and consisted of curiosity and family influence. On my mother's side of the family, being intuitive and spiritual was a considered a natural and healthy phenomenon.

The ability to recall dreams and decipher them was a skill that developed as the result of ongoing discussions between my grandmother and mother. It was considered reasonable to talk about one's dreams and pay extra attention to the symbols and messages that revealed. I understood dreams held a particular role way before I encounter any books on psychoanalysis or dream interpretations. In fact, the books I read only validated the facts I knew regarding the value of symbols in dreams.

Aside from being introduced to dream interpretation, I also learned about the wonders of the tarot deck. My grandmother used to have a friend who would read the cards for her periodically. I was always curious and would ask a lot of questions. Eventually, I got my first deck at age three from my grandmother's friend, Don Pedro. Of course, I did not know how to read the tarot deck but would pretend anyway.

Throughout the years, I would find myself using regular playing cards and pretend to read like a tarot reader. I had no clue how to read the tarot and no way to find out how. I grew up with no access to Google, YouTube or for that fact the internet. So, learning was a matter of trial and error since there were very few metaphysical books or intuitive developments. The tarot cards spoke to me, but I didn't quite know how to trust what I experienced. It wasn't until I turned 19, that I got my first real lesson, which of course, was not based on traditional styles of learning. I learned to read the tarot reading entirely intuitively.

My initial tarot lesson occurred in a dream. While dreaming, I was instructed "to read the tarot deck; you need to get "inside" the cards." I had no idea what the message in the dream meant and how I was supposed to fulfill the instructions. It wasn't until I started to get interested in meditation that the process of reading the tarot became clear.

I picked up a card and imagined myself inside the card. I imagined myself inside the picture and allowed myself to merge with the image. What I did was enable the card to unveil its story. And that was how I began my journey of reading the tarot.

Many of my intuitive experiences occurred as I learned to pay attention and relax my mind. Meditation became my exploratory tool and the format I used for allowing my intuitive to expand. I allowed myself to deepen my connection to my gut and learn to trust my intuition. I did not let doubt silence my inner voice and as time passed I my intuitive sight became stronger.

Of course, being in the field of psychology did impact my intuitive development. Often, I encountered other therapists who dismissed my beliefs and thought I was rather strange. I recall discussing a dream with a therapist who stated that my dreams were wishful thinking. Honestly, I did not get discouraged by her lack of insight, but what I did learn was to repress my experience and keep silent. In many ways, I went back into the psychic closet and maintained my dream experiences and intuitive skills private. After all, working with psychologist and therapist meant constant scrutiny, which could contribute to career suicide.

Personal Reiki Background

The first introduction to Reiki, it was in the spring of 1992. It was during a period of when I had embarked on a conscious journey of self-improvement and discovery. During that period, I was taking a weekly class in Channeling taught by Diane Munez at the time. The teacher, Diane was also a student of the Barbara Brennan, a well-known Metaphysical Teacher, and Healer. Diane was also a student evolving and fine-tuning her innate talents. At the point, when Diana introduced Reiki to a few of her students, many had been taking Channeling classes with her for over two years. She was trusted for her methods and had positive results from all the techniques she taught. When Diane talked about offering a weekend workshop on the healing techniques of Reiki, no one hesitated to sign up for it.

The workshop scheduled for two weekends. It was held in Diane's home and taught by Dan Buffo, also a student of Barbara Brennan at the time. Dan had received his Reiki training from Phyllis Lei Furomoto at the Reiki Alliance back in 1989. Several students agreed to take the workshop on that particular weekend.

The class began with a brief introduction, which included a general discussion of the weekend agenda, as well as to each other. The teacher introduced himself and presented his background to the class. The introduction segment took about an hour in total. The next thing we did was continue with a grounding meditation, followed by lectures on the history of Reiki, its practical applications, attunements and practice sessions between students. The workshop took two entire weekends to complete and provided me with level I and level II attunements.

Two years after the attunements to Reiki level I and level II, I received my master's level in Reiki through Samantha Heitman. My practice with Reiki is often personal, but I have taught a few classes and have used Reiki on clients who were open to the idea. I have also had meditations groups, which also included reiki energy for individuals who were interested.

Intuition and Therapy

Though I worked as a counselor full-time, I managed to continue my intuitive work. Throughout the years I worked as a psychic reader, healer, and teacher. I also took many workshops and learned how to fine-tune my skills as a psychic and healer. There was a period in my life, from the late 80's until the late 90's where I attended and took as many workshops as possible. I was a full-time therapist and full-time seeker of intuitive knowledge. I learned about intuitive development as much as possible by learning, as well as by teaching others.

I also quietly used my intuition in my work. The reason for the silence had a lot to do with my line of work in the field of mental health. Conventional systems of therapy are partial to **evidence-based practices** and are not supportive of many **experienced-based methods**. There are many reasons for the rejection of intuitive techniques aside from lacking the viable research. Few therapists know how to intuitive techniques, and many agencies have a specific mission statement that adheres to particular treatment modalities and insurance payment restrictions.

Why this book

I decided to write this book since I wanted to share specifically how intuitive techniques can apply to therapy. Within this book, I review different methods that work best in the therapeutic environment along with the corresponding treatment modalities. This book covers some necessary information, the benefits, limitations, and applications of a few fundamental techniques.

Though this book is "not a how-to" it does provide some meditation exercises to help the person gain some perspective on how intuition works. The goal of this book is to help individuals achieve confidence in using their intuition, as well as learn about the practical applications of intuitive techniques.

Chapter I   Introduction

"Intuition is the key to everything, in painting, filmmaking, business - everything. I think you could have intellectual ability, but if you can sharpen your intuition, which they say is emotion and intellect joining together, and then knowingness occurs." - David Lynch

Intuitive Techniques

Throughout history, science had struggled to identify how intuition works yet there is no denying that it is an ability we as humans possess. In the process of exploring intuition, scientists have unveiled that humans maintain two separate operating systems, one is instinctual and produced by the subconscious, and the other system controls logical and conscious thoughts (Turner 2014).

It is important to note, that though the brain may dictate specific functions, it does not mean that the hemispheres of the brain create personality types. (Wanjek 2013). There is a tendency to use one side of the brain more than others, which is known as **lateralization,** which means specific areas of the brain manage mechanical activities like speech, walking and so forth, which do become impaired during brain injury. However, it takes more than one region of the brain to control physical activities or the ability to write, walk and so on.

The instinctual system functions through the ability to understand things intuitively, specifically emotions and natural reactions. Intuition offers insight into situations that conventional therapy may not always decipher correctly. There are situations in which intuition can be more effective than rational thinking. According to research, humans do not process their world only in a rational manner, but also intuitively. (Dane, Baer, Pratt & Oldham, 2011). When individuals face a crisis that requires immediate reactions, the brain is triggered into action as the heart races, sending signals that prepare the body for flight or fight responses. This behavior is instinctual and based on intuitive awareness of perceived danger. Only upon analyzing the situation will a person take appropriate actions. In summary, the intuitive mind gathers information, which becomes processed by rational thought and then converts it into proper behavior. (Dane et al.)

The intuitive mind is an integral part of the human mind and serves a vital role in how individuals function. Learning to work with intuition allows individuals to open realms that are limited to the rational mind. By incorporating intuition into the world of therapy, professional clinicians and healthcare practitioners are expanding their professional perspectives.

There is a potential partnership that can naturally grow between therapy and intuitive techniques. The combination of intuition and therapy allows both clinicians and healthcare practitioners to dive deeper into a client's internal world, permitting retrieval of vital information that will serve to resolve internal conflicts and restore balance. In a nutshell, the book is about exploring ways to combine intuitive skills in the mental health and healthcare field efficiently.

Who should use this book

This book is not intended for the cynic looking for loopholes or evidence to dismantle intuitive practices but for professionals looking for options to traditionally based practices. The material in this book comes from various sources such as psychoanalytical theories, philosophical ideas and a variety of natural alternative techniques. The contents of this book have been gathered from both personal experience and training taken while working in the field of substance abuse and mental health. This book is useful for professionals who provide mental health services or healthcare and often find that conventional therapy has some limitations when it comes to treating individuals.

The terms "clinicians and professionals" are used interchangeably throughout the book when referring to mental health therapists, and healthcare practitioners in general. The types of mental health professionals and healthcare practitioners that can benefit from this book include:

Art therapists
Chiropractors
Coaches
Counselors
Drug Counselors
Hypnotherapists
Massage therapists
Mental Health Counselors
Music Therapists
Nurses
Physical Therapist
Physicians
Physician Assistants
Psychiatrists
Psychologists
Psychotherapists
Social Workers

Most of the professions listed do require professional training in either medical, psychological, or counseling work, in addition to learning about intuitive development. This book is **not** for the layperson who wants to use therapeutic techniques in their alternative healing practice. It is for the professionals who want to use intuitive skills in their professional practice.

Psychic Abilities vs. Intuitive Skills

Before we begin, it helps to know that there is a difference between having psychic abilities and using intuitive skills. When it comes to psychic abilities, a person is tapping into a frequency that provides flashes of information that requires the use of interpretative skills. Intuitive skills rely on a sense of knowing and deep understanding. To understand the difference between psychic abilities and intuition, think of psychic abilities as natural, innate skills and the intuition as instinctive awareness and internal understanding that often defies logic.

The Value of Intuition

Individuals have been culturally trained to believe that being rational and scientific is the only means of obtaining information (Cholle 2011). Because of cultural influence, the field of psychology has evolved from a soft-science into the mindset that only evidence-based practices are acceptable means of developing mental health treatment. Ironically, though psychologists regard themselves as scientists, not everyone in the global scientific community regards psychology to be **hard science**. In fact, psychology is regarded as a **soft-science**, since not all its theories have evidence-based data to support them. (Pettijohn et al.).

The human mind is not solely a rational machine that can neatly be programmed to function in one manner. The mind is a combination of chemistry, social influences, and intuitive awareness. A comprehensive approach to therapy would include the trifecta of the body, environment, and emotional intelligence given the fact that they all play a role in a person's well-being. Therapists are trained to recognize the role of chemical imbalances and social influences on behavior and emotional well-being but seldom focus on intuitive awareness. (Cholle)

Anyone can develop intuitive abilities, but many dismiss personal experiences, which diminishes the potential of evolving intuitively. Individuals who utilize their abilities have learned to rely heavily on their inner voice and have learned not only to depend on it but also to decipher the many subtle messages that come forward from the hidden well of information. Keep in mind, that everyone has the natural ability to be a psychic, but many do not embrace it due to the fear of being ridiculed or rejected. To grasp the concept of intuition, think of regarding everyone having the ability to learn to dance, but some do not dance due to fear of looking foolish or being judged by others.

About this book

This book contains material for mental health professionals and alternative care practitioners who are looking to apply intuitive techniques effectively in their practices. The purpose of this book is to help systematically organize natural intuitive skills for professional use with evidence-based practices. This book will not replace evidence-based techniques but instead, serve as a secondary enhancement tool.

Traditionally, intuitive methods have been associated with charlatans and regarded poorly due to limited sources of evidence-based data. The fact is that historically, intuition was something not easily measured and gave the appearance of being somewhat subjective; however, it does not mean it is not useful or lacks merit. Though there is a limited amount of research, we do have studies that are ongoing and have increased throughout the years, demonstrating the value of intuitive skills. As of recent years, researchers have shown the importance of intuition regarding emotional intelligence as well as its function in a person's ability to make decisions. (Nierenberg 2016)

There several intuitive techniques that are useful when working with clients, both in therapeutic programs or private practice. Whether one is a substance abuse therapist, hypnotherapist, massage therapist, or coach, many of the intuitive techniques discussed are interchangeable and valuable therapeutically.

One can utilize intuitive techniques as part of the therapeutic session or in helping ourselves when we are trying to obtain mental clarity and insight. The techniques explored within this book will not only provide additional working tools but also assist in fine-tuning one's natural intuitive abilities to support going beyond the traditional evidence-based practices. Many of the techniques in this book do not require special intuitive skills. However, they are categories as intuitive because they function outside mainstream analytically driven systems.

Each of the chapters in this book will cover the following topics:

1. Introduction
2. Understanding Intuition
3. Integrating Intuition in Therapy
4. Reviewing Treatment Modalities
5. Exploring Intuitive Techniques
6. The Sensory Systems
7. The Benefits of Aromatherapy
8. Utilizing Meditation in Therapy
9. Developing the Intuitive skills
10. Aura Scanning
11. Therapeutic Chakra Techniques

12. Healing Regressive Techniques
13. Intuitive Tarot and psychotherapy
14. Using Reiki in Therapy
15. Professional Integration
16. Ethics and Intuitive Work

    This book provides informative material, as well as some basic meditations and exercises that are designed to assist in the exploration of intuitive techniques. Each meditation and training will offer an opportunity to learn firsthand how each method works and what areas would require further learning to integrate them into the therapeutic practice more successfully. Keep in mind the goal of this book is not to turn mental health professionals or any healthcare practitioner into psychic readers, but to allow them to understand the value of utilizing natural intuitive abilities in the therapeutic work they do and gain a little more confidence in the process of using those skills. Remember that the most significant barrier when it comes to using intuition is self-doubt and self-criticism.

    There are some references to resources that do include research on the benefits of intuitive work, for those looking to see precisely how intuition can be efficiently paired off with therapy. There are also meditations and exercises to try, as well as sources on various schools of psychology. This book is not written to replace traditional therapy, but to offer an additional tool for therapists, social workers, coaches and healing practitioners looking to expand their practice.

Intuitive Exercises

    Individuals should practice each exercise and meditation as often as possible if a therapist or practitioner wishes to fine-tune their skills and confidence levels. It is a fact that any skill anyone learns will only become finely tuned through practice and constant drills. According to research studies (Lufityanto, Donkin, & Pearson 2016) intuition is something that can improve over time with ongoing practice. Initially some methods may seem monotonous and repetitious; however, this is the most crucial part of learning. Regardless how tedious and repetitive it appears in the beginning; ongoing practice trains the brain to form a natural association which allows a task to become second nature. Think of it like this; remember when an individual wanted to learn how to ride a bike as a child? Initially, no one knows how to bike, but with practice, many were able to learn and manage to ride with ease. Most things in life require learning and practice before one can feel confident in their knowledge.

Though the lessons will provide valuable information, individuals should invest the time in reading other types of material available in the subjects discussed. Of course, it is entirely possible to develop one's intuition without reading any books. Reading is merely recommended to provide a comprehensive foundation with as much information and knowledge as possible. Aside from giving information, one of the goals will be to teach individuals how to relax and let go of intrusive self-doubts that may interfere with personal progress. Also, aside from learning to relax, the book will focus on topics that are designed to enhance one's focus and increase the ability to concentrate.

The book consists of **three sections**. Each section focuses on specific areas designed to gradually increase awareness and help improve the value of fine-tuning intuitive skills for therapeutic work.

The **first section** contains information on **brief descriptions** and outlines on how each intuitive technique works and its comparative therapeutic modality.

In the **second section,** there is a review of **practical applications** of several intuitive techniques to provide mental health clinicians and alternative healthcare practitioners with simple methods for implementation. There are also a few exercises throughout the different chapters in the book to help therapists and practitioners see how some methods developed.

The **third-section** covers **professional preparation** and **ethical issues** that impact professional development.

Though this book discusses how to incorporate intuition in therapeutic practice, it is not an intuitive development book, but rather a guide that helps provide some real perspective on how intuitive techniques could integrate with traditional treatment systems. Individuals are advised to explore the intuitive techniques they enjoy the most by reading other available material for more information and details. The more a person understands and fine-tunes their intuitive skills, the easier it will be to utilize them in a therapeutic session with complete confidence.

For the sections that have exercises, individuals are encouraged to take notes regarding the experience encountered, regardless of the number of details. The documented records will serve as a tracking system of the progress made constructively, which will help in determining which areas require further improvement. It is helpful to read each section and do all the exercises, even those that are familiar and simple. To prepare for the upcoming material, the following items will come in handy:

- A journal for documenting all experiences
- A recording device, if possible, use a cell phone
- A few candles for meditation
- Favorite crystals or even stones
- Tarot deck (whichever one has symbols that stimulate the imagination)
- Incense
- Any gadget or symbol that invokes a sense of calmness or peace of mind

Keep in mind that the supplies are mere suggestions, as well as the exercises, and there is no obligation in any way to document anything or participate in any of the suggested activities. The recommendations are designed to help maximize the personal experience within this book. The key to developing the capacity to utilize intuition efficiently lies in one's ability to understand precisely how intuition works, as well as learning how to use one's skills through recommended exercises.

Chapter Summary

Before moving forward, the next thing that is needed is to make a firm commitment to maintaining an open mind while reading this book. Realize that intuition is a natural process and though there has been some research, science has not been able to grasp its benefits fully. We all have had premonitions, gut feelings, or reactions to things that seem off or did not feel right. Many times, we ignored those gut feelings, only to regret it later. In this case, a person is learning to listen to the gut and allowing the self to explore beyond the scope of rational thinking and traditional limits. Though this book covers intuitive systems and helps guide individuals in the applications of the intuitive techniques, it is not a psychic training book.

"A man likes to believe that he is the master of his soul. However, as long as he is unable to control his moods and emotions, or to be conscious of the myriad secret ways in which unconscious factors insinuate themselves into his arrangements and decisions, he is probably not his own master. These unconscious factors owe their existence to the autonomy of the archetypes. A modern man protects himself against seeing his split state by a system of compartments. Specific areas of outer life and his behavior are kept, as it were, in separate drawers and are never confronted with one another."

— *Carl Jung, (1964)*

SECTION - I

Understanding Intuition

Chapter II
Understanding Intuition

It is through science that we prove, but through intuition that we discover- Henri Poincare

Psychological Reality

There is a world beyond our textbooks and the safety net of theory. It is a world that has no map or pre-rehearsed lines. It is where fears are real, and emotions run hand in hand with unknown factors and demons, yet the opportunity to understand this world of elusiveness is possible. Exploring this realm is feasible with intuitive techniques that offer a higher degree of information retrieval then verbal questioning.

Intuitive methods are not a new approach to therapeutic work, in fact, Freud's dream interpretation techniques and Jung's theories on symbolism are examples of intuitive approaches. Both Freud and Jung's psychoanalytical systems have scientific limitations since each evolved from theories and not evidence-based data. Freud's theories focused on the **Dream symbolism** and hidden sexual messages. (Schredl 2008) Jung focused his therapeutic ideas based on **Collective Unconscious.** (Moreno 1967)

Psychology is continuously growing as research attempts to validate new theories and develop **evidence-based systems**. Regardless of the evolution of psychology, the unconscious mind holds the key to many personal mysterious. The mind is continuously evolving and is not ruled by a logical pattern, which is why human behavior is often unpredictable. Unlike a computer or a piece of equipment, as much as humans can be trained or socially influenced, some factors contribute to unpredictable behavior patterns. In **hard sciences** like chemistry, math, or physics, there is a consistent, predictable order, while in psychology there are concepts that can be fuzzy, and unreliable, which is why its referred to as a **soft science**. (Ziegler, Kemper & Lenzner 2015)

In fact, both psychology and psychoanalysis are regarded as soft sciences, since they often utilize systems that are not evidence-based. Though many in the field of psychology regard themselves as scientists, many in the field of Biology, Chemistry, or Physics would disagree. There are different global views as to whether the field of psychology is science or not. (Pettijohn et al.)

"The unconscious mind is the matrix out of which conscious grows; for the consciousness does not enter the world as a finished product but is the result of small beginnings." (Jung 1964)

The Rejection of Intuition

One of the main reason intuition regarded with dismissal has a lot to do with the limited history of available research. Also, the term intuition is often misunderstood and mistaken for psychic work. Though psychic abilities and intuition go hand in hand, psychic skills refer to the skill or ability to perform specific tasks that go beyond the standard scope of the human senses. Intuition is a deep knowing and understanding of situations and occurrences. Cholle (2011) describes intuition as the ability to understand without analytical processing.

Before technology was considered a mainstream reality, folks had to rely on their intuition and personal trial and errors to make vital decisions. Intuition has been a topic of exploration for both philosophers and scientists since the era of the Ancient Greeks (Lufityanto et al.). Though intuition has been a topic of interest, many scientists have been challenged for decades in their abilities to demonstrate how it works. It is possible that one of the leading challenges in researching intuition has a lot to do with the types of scientific methods used.

Measuring intuition with a typical **rational approach** is very much like trying to cut water with a knife, which is why intuition has been a challenge to research and, as a result, its value diminished. It is essential to realize that lacking the skills to measure something does not keep it from existing or being useful. Our brain can collect data, both consciously and unconsciously, which in turn allows it to process information intuitively and rationally. (Lufityanto et al.)

As technology grew, the rational mindset, rather than intuition, became the preferred method for solving problems. The term intuition often gets dismissed and regarded as irrational feelings that need replacing with rational thoughts. The fact is intuition is not a feeling, but an innate awareness based on emotional intelligence. Intuition is our unconscious connection to our collective bank of emotional and mental activities complied over the years. Intuition is the bridge to our unconsciousness; while rational thinking is our mental processing of conscious activities

The Value of Intuition

Our intuition uses **emotional intelligence** to make sense of emotional impressions and reactions to personal constructs. Intuition allows individuals to gain access to the emotional mind, which retains a wealth of psychological data, perceptions, memories, and social awareness. Though historical data had struggled to prove precisely how intuition works, research has demonstrated it plays an influential role when it comes to working with a client. According to researchers, Chaffey, Unsworth & Fossey, (2011) intuition is a natural tool for processing emotional realities and gaining an understanding of delicate situations, which makes it a valuable tool in the development of empathy and understanding the emotional trials of our clients.

Our perception is continuously helping us process our world by gathering information and integrating it into our realities. Intuition becomes the small voice that many overlook and ignore due to self-doubt and poor self-image. Keep in mind; learning to listen to the inner voice does not have to come at the sacrifice of rational thinking. The decision to use one's intuition does not have to occur in a black and white spectrum since there is such a thing as balance.

The relationship between **rational thinking** and **intuitive awareness** can be a union of proper checks and balances, in which the logical mind can decipher initial impressions. Our rational mind helps sort out the false impressions from true inspirations since we are prone to misinterpretation due to random unhealthy beliefs and selective perception. Many individuals are eager to make sense of their world, so they often subject themselves to **psycho-mythological** concepts in hopes of sorting through all the confusion (Lilienfeld, Lynn, Ruscio & Beyerstein 2010).

The imbalance between rational thinking and intuitive awareness contributes to poor decision making and constant internal conflicts. Therefore, this book is not about eliminating rational thinking in favor of intuitive thinking, but rather about learning to combine the two sectors into one. When clinicians and practitioners adjust their ability to listen to their inner voice, the one that guides them through chaos and stressful periods, they develop their intuitive skills. The more that individuals fine-tune their listening skills, the better equipped they become in tapping into non-verbal cues and emotional intelligence that often eludes most people.

For a therapist, intuitive skills are valuable and offer a deeper understanding of the many issues their clients face. The therapist's intuitive abilities provide them with an empathetic ear that listens to the message between the lines and knows how to identify hidden problems of which the client may not always be aware of or is not comfortable disclosing. Intuition bridges the gap between emotional and logical realities.

It has been tradition to label and neatly fit patients into charts according to the limitations of DSM-V. Granted, any therapist who wishes to make money via insurance is required to abide by these labels. Through stagnated labels, patients have not only been diagnosed but also treated with a ready-made recipe that involves tons of questions and long periods of waiting for a breakthrough, which often takes years of expensive therapy to occur. In a world where hues of gray are the rule, versus the black and white neatness of labels, tradition has left the patient in the waiting room.

The need for Intuitive techniques has evolved because many clinicians and practitioners find themselves limited with therapeutic guidelines that do not always take the individual's culture, gender, and spiritual backgrounds seriously. Keep in mind, even without intuitive techniques; many therapeutic modalities are incapable of helping every client overcome many emotional and mental roadblocks, which is why professionals are continuously taking workshops and updating their skills. Both clinicians and practitioners take ongoing-workshops to keep their skills sharp and professionally relevant, as well as updated to the latest therapeutic developments. (Morgan 2018)

Intuitive Techniques in Therapy

Using Intuitive techniques in therapy might sound like something out of a wish book, but the fact is that intuition offers the therapist an opportunity to explore subtle realms, as well as techniques for fostering concrete changes. Intuitive techniques blend well with traditional therapy and health care modalities.

Innate intuitive **abilities help decipher** subtle issues that often get washed away in the over-analytical aspects of treatment. Keep in mind; theory and traditional practice are a substantial component of therapeutic work; however, they are not the only viable sources for helping clients overcome mental health issues and physical problems.

Intuitive techniques tap into the mind's symbolically-based style of storing information and personal experiences to provide awareness. The brain is a warehouse of data stored in codes and cryptic symbolism, and archetypes which can be difficult to decipher unless an individual is entirely aware of the meaning behind their symbolic world.

Retrieving **symbolic information** with Intuitive techniques provides an opportunity to obtain and extract data with tools that go beyond the typical verbal methods of traditional retrieval. Intuitive techniques provide various options for helping clients that vary depending on the training and specialty of each clinician or healthcare practitioner.

In the field of mental health, a therapist can obtain delicate information using noninvasive and minimally confrontational tools. Techniques that are used range from visualization, energy scanning, regressive methods, breathing exercises, object scanning (tarot decks, scrying, to name a few); Also techniques such as intuitive dialoguing (for example, channeling, hypnosis, to name a few.).

Initially, the idea of working with methods like tarot reading, channeling or even tea leaf reading might seem bizarre, illogical and dismissed as things only psychics can do. These techniques have been widely used by con artists and unscrupulous charlatans, which have reduced the validity of those methods. However, regardless if its psychic abilities or intuition, neither system has a component of being good or bad, since they are only techniques that help individuals obtain information. (King 2018)

Understanding Intuitive Skills

To fully understand intuitive skills, there is a need to define them accurately and separate them from psychic methods like fortune telling, channeling, or mainstream psychic work. For starters, intuition and psychic abilities are not mysterious or cryptic in their make-up but are highly misunderstood and poorly utilized. As strange and poorly understood these methods may appear, they have several things in common, which is that they work through symbolism, archetypes and a history of collective sensory experiences. In short, intuitive techniques, merely navigate through personal symbols and archetypes stored within the memory. (Adamski 2011)

Our brain recalls every event in simple text, which is then paired off with specific **symbolic associations** and **social archetypes** that help with memory recall. The sensory system can retain and record events as it gathers information through our senses, the most notable being olfactory, auditory, visual, and touch. (Miller 2006) For instance, certain smells, sounds, or colors make us feel cozy and relaxed, which usually reflects our initial experience with them. Blue is considered a relaxing color, but if the patient has a history of abused taken place in a blue room, s/he would invariably feel agitated in a room with a similar color.

There are various systems to help professionals and client **activate unconscious** thoughts or **memory recall**. Through intuitive methods, almost anything can serve as a memory activator for retrieving useful information. If a clinician wanted to help a client recall how they felt about a stressful job cycle, the client could randomly select a tarot card, free associate, until they got in touch with feelings or thoughts related to the cycle.

A coach could ask a client about a goal, then select a card to use as a guiding tool, which they can explore together. Alternatively, a counselor could use regressive meditation to trace the origins of anger and self-sabotaging in a therapeutic session. The possibilities that meditation offers are endless and only limited by imagination.

Intuitive Methods

Utilizing intuitive methods in therapy does require training, not only in the traditional aspects of therapeutic work but also in developing one's insights and perceptive abilities through a series of mental techniques. Though training might sound impossible, it is quite practical and straightforward once learned. The mind is capable of being trained to sharpen its ability to tap into the environment through the senses, and through introspective abilities. Learning to trust what one perceives through the senses does require trusting the process, and consistent training; however, the results enable one to tap into a realm otherwise left undetected through the logical mind.

There different types of intuitive techniques that clinicians or practitioners can select from, some rather simple that requires almost no training or much practice. However, some techniques require proper training and extensive dedicated practice. To help a person decide which methods to use, we will begin with the simplest, most comfortable types of techniques, and then gradually work our way up to more complicated systems

Regardless of how the clinician or a practitioner, decides to use this book, they should take time reviewing the material and allow themselves to enjoy it, rather than force themselves to excel in any subject. Inner criticism has a way of dismantling the intuitive voice.

Chapter Summary

To enter the realm of intuitive awareness requires trust and inner strength of conviction because our strongest opposition will come from traditionally trained peers and our inner critic. There might be no supportive voice to aid a person in handling the delicate transitions that they face with their clients. The therapist might be on their own when it comes to intuitive techniques. The rewards are as numerous as the doubts; nevertheless, stay tuned. It is always a new wave that sweeps tradition into a corner.

"All great men are gifted with intuition. They know, without reasoning or analysis, what they need to know. "
-Alexis Carrel

Chapter III
Integrating Intuition in Therapy

Intuition is nothing but the outcome of the earlier intellectual experience.- Einstein

Intuitive Techniques in Therapy

There are potential benefits to using intuitive techniques in therapy, yet due to the evidence-based preferences of many mental health professionals, it is an underdeveloped area. To determine precisely how intuitive tools can be useful, they need to be reviewed to determine their efficacy for treatment applications. Also, some of the more popular therapeutic modalities will be reviewed to help sort out which system will pair off best with the different intuitive techniques. This current chapter will briefly review a few intuitive techniques, selected explicitly due to their potential for enhancing the therapeutic session.

As mentioned before in the previous chapter, intuitive techniques will not replace therapeutic practices; many recommended techniques are only enhancements for therapeutic work. Also, please note, that not all methods are useful or appropriate in therapy since some do not produce favorable outcomes with specific mental health or physical issues.

In this chapter, we cover brief descriptions and elaborate further in the proceeding chapters; also, within this chapter, there are two charts provided for quick references. One chart provides a brief outline of different therapeutic modalities and the second chart a quick review of intuitive techniques and corresponding treatment modalities.

The Challenge of Integration

The process of integrating intuitive techniques in psychotherapy has mirrored the long battle between professionals who embrace **evidence-based practices** and **practice-based evidence.** (Barkham, & Mellow-Clark, 2003) In the efforts of obtaining scientific validation, psychology has relied heavily on evidence-based practices and avoided methods that potentially invalidate its scientific credence. Because of fighting to maintain the reputation of being scientifically valid, many in the field of psychology are quick to dismiss theories not validated through evidence-driven research.

Opportunities to expand the field of psychology are restricted because of firm competition with the scientific community and established research guidelines. To maintain professional integrity, many researchers in the field of psychology adhere to research guiding principles established by mental health organizations. One mental health organization that influences research in psychology is the US National Advisory Mental Health Council (NAMHC). According to guidelines established by NIH (1999), there are four specific guidelines required for delivering therapeutic services that meet the needs of clients which consist of the following protocols:

- **Efficacy Research** – The goal is to determine which therapeutic intervention has **measurable results.** (NIH)
- **Effectiveness Research** – This measure **the potential benefits** when applied to population samples
- **Practice Research** – Explores the implementation **of evidence-based practices** into treatment
- **Service systems** – This pertains to reviewing the **cost and the policies** involved in providing services

Though NAMHC has created research protocols, studies have indicated that evidence-based practices might indeed be lacking because of the number of limitations associated with research development. (Barkham & Mellow-Clark)

Research has influenced what practices are acceptable in psychotherapeutic applications and which ones get dismissed and regarded as implausible therapeutic tools. Barkham and Mellow-Clark, report evidence-based practices might not be enough when designing therapeutic systems. The fact is that mental health practitioners do not always adhere to evidence-based practices strictly by the book. According to Hellerstein (2008), many evidence-based practices are not sufficient since evidence-based recommendations typically derive from research settings and not real-time therapy.

Many clinicians and practitioners select their therapeutic techniques-based on **practice-based evidence** since they rely on techniques dictated by the needs of their clients, personal skills and not strictly research or textbook guidelines. (Hellerstein). Almost any new graduate coming out of school will encounter the harsh reality, what is taught by professors is often not used in the real working world.

Rational Thinking vs. Intuitive Ability

Intuition is frequently seen as a mysterious and unreliable ability. However, it is the most natural trait of all human beings. The natural role of intuition can be seen in the early stages of childhood cognitive development, as a child learns to navigate their environment through their instincts and sensory system. An infant relies on their intuition, and senses to connect to their environment before analytical abilities mature. (Oswalt 2008). As the individual matures, the different levels of intuitive abilities range from individual to individual, depending on personal awareness and acceptance. Many individuals have learned to ignore their intuition in favor of rational and analytical thinking since in many cultures insight is viewed as an inferior human attribute.

Though rational thinking serves us well in the technological and scientific realm, it fails to connect to the unconscious domain of the human mind. Rational thought works on analyzing and judging situations, which is significant for summarizing and diagnosing conditions. However, rational thinking can be subjective which tends to dismiss whatever does not fit the preassembled system it prefers, which means it will ignore and disqualify what appears to be inconsistent with its logical format.

Subjective beliefs do not only influence the rational mind, but they also created limitations because of cognitive biases. (MacDonald n.d.) Our logical skills are useful in sorting through situations that require consequential thinking and restraining inappropriate emotional outburst, but it has limits when it comes to retrieving unconscious memories and understanding hidden emotional issues.

The rational brain often fails to connect to the unconscious successfully since critical thinking often produces cognitive biases and overanalyzing. According to an article by Cherry (2018), cognitive bias generates an error in reasoning based on a history of adverse beliefs and poor judgment skills. It is essential to realize when it comes to the type of individuals seeking therapy; they often do so since they cannot resolve emotional and mental conflict, making it even harder for them to utilize rational thinking skills.

Because of faulty analytical thinking abilities, there is a struggle to obtain critical information from the unconscious realm. The fact is the unconscious it not formatted in a neat pattern, and the memory is a warehouse of bits and pieces of symbols representing the past. The best way to tap into the symbolism of the unconscious is by using intuitive methods since rational thinking is often influenced by a subjective reality which can impede judgment. (Fischer 2015)

The intuition allows a person to gain access to an emotional data bank of information; often experienced as intuitive understanding and awareness. Each person has the innate ability to interpret realities and experiences within their world, which contributes to their development and language skills. (Wood, Smith, & Grossniklaus, 2001) However, due to factors such as mental illness, social repression, cultural norms and poor self-image, individuals learn to ignore and dismiss their instincts and intuitive experiences. (Chaffey et al. 2012)

Intuitive Techniques

The intuitive techniques chosen in this book are simple to implement and modify to meet the requirements of traditional therapeutic practices. For instance, in psychoanalysis, the approach Jung used when discussing dreams and symbolism is compatible with the way imagery is approached in the tarot readings. When a tarot reader uses the tarot deck, they permit the symbolism, colors and various personal constructs to guide them in interpreting the tarot deck when doing a reading. For a tarot reader, the cards often hold symbolic meanings that trigger ideas and intuitive flashes that allow them to answer questions presented by the client.

In psychoanalysis, the symbolism in dreams or Rorschach test, reveal inner meanings and enable a psychoanalyst to uncover hidden meanings behind certain critical elements presented in therapy. The psychoanalyst plays a similar role to the tarot reader, in which they both get to interpret whatever symbolism is shared in session by the client either through dreams or selected tarot cards.

If we used the tarot deck in cognitive therapy or humanistic therapies like client-centered therapy or Gestalt, the client would be the one interpreting the tarot, rather than the therapist. The client would use the deck to develop awareness of specific issues and emotional roadblocks, using the various tarot cards. An example of using the tarot would be the following:

- A client is struggling with deciding career goals. To help decide the best case scenario, the client pulls out three cards; each card can allow them to review where their general focus is and what keeps them stuck. The cards can help the client see where they may be stuck, and how it impacts their life, or help them see how to resolve the current situation by viewing potential options.

Keep in mind the deck is a symbolic representation of the things we experience and helps reactivate us emotionally whenever there are vital visual reminders. The memory is easily triggered by images that retain personal meaning, very much like the Rorschach inkblot can trigger individualized reactions in patients.

Memory and Intuitive Techniques

Many of the methods used both with therapeutic and intuitive practices work by triggering the memories and emotional database within each person. Every person keeps a symbolic mental data bank of all the events that created emotional impressions throughout their lives. Though the individual may not think daily of every single situation they

encountered, they do retain those memories in their unconscious mind, which get triggered by the smallest symbol, which can be in the form of a color, geometric shape, image or scent, and so forth.

The memory contains tons of information collected through all our senses, and each one provides the mind with a symbol that can be activated at any moment to invoke emotional as well as mental recollections. Visuals and sensory stimulation easily trigger the memory. As a result, the images of the tarot are useful in triggering emotional memories and reactions. Of course, some symbols are more complicated and at times even profoundly buried depending on the number of incidents that occurred, the degree of intensity and physical impact on the body. (Miller) Situations that produce enormous reactions also create higher levels of responses in our bodies, often creating chemical changes that not only prepare the memory but engage us in an emotional response that is usually designed to protect us from perceived danger. Therefore, the more intense the situation, the harder the body works to defend itself, the higher the level of chemicals like cortisol are created to prepare us to run or fight.

Daily events produce memories on a regular basis, but since they tend to occur often, the reminiscence becomes one big pile of similar incidents, with slight nuances to distinguish them apart, such as a word, a sound, scent, a color, and so forth. It is easy to forget specific events took place because they do not create too many unique chemical signatures that help them become distinctive. We have a systematic and symbolic system of retaining memories; To activate memory retrieval, associated triggers are required to stimulate effective recall. In short, each significant memory gets anchored to a specific triggering element. To understand how memories become anchored to triggers, review the following scenario:

- It is a hot day, the sound of the ice cream truck is playing in the background. A person is reading their favorite superhero comic book as the ice cream is arriving. The ice cream truck has background music playing. There is a strong chance that the person will retain the ice cream truck music along with the pleasure of reading a comic book based on their favorite hero. In the present moment, the person will recall their favorite hero whenever an ice cream truck drives by playing music. Alternatively, in a different scenario, involving visual cues, a person selects a photo from a wedding they attended, and again memories come back making them relive some conversation or thought triggered by the picture.

When it comes to triggering the memory, the tarot deck is like looking at old photos since they will trigger thoughts or feelings often coded in the colors, shapes or pictures; Even without training, a person can still manage to interpret images using the tarot deck. When looking at the tarot cards, imagine being in an art gallery looking at the paintings and letting the images talk freely without censorship.

A tarot deck is a valuable tool for accessing unconscious information and bringing it into the conscious realm. The human conscious and unconscious have a working relationship, in which the unconscious attempts to maintain equilibrium within the psyche by balancing the one-sided tendencies of the ego consciousness. The unconscious mind attempts to communicate with the unconscious through dreams, personal symbolism, creative expressions and intuitive awareness. (Jung 1964).

There different intuitive techniques that provide individuals access to unconscious information, without interference from the critical mind; which is especially useful in memory retrieval work. The techniques in this book will guide mental health professionals, and alternative healthcare practitioners obtain the knowledge needed to help individuals access memories and unconscious realities by surpassing the roadblocks that stifle intuitive work. Intuitive techniques are valuable at retrieving memories and unconscious information for uncovering old patterns, as well as creating new realities

Required Training

The training necessary for the different intuitive techniques is a matter of personal preference. The idea is to always select tools that feel natural and easy to use. It is essential to avoid selecting techniques that create feelings of uneasiness or feeling stuck. The key to selecting intuitive tools is to be able to use them naturally without getting overly analytical or judgmental.

The training required for developing intuitive skills will vary depending on the type of mental health profession or healthcare practice. Many individuals working in the field of psychology or counseling do require proper training due to **professional mandates** and **ethical codes**. Reading books or trying to learn online intuitive techniques is not going to provide individuals with the legal and professional material required for specific areas of psychology or counseling. If an individual is starting their career in mental health, they will need the proper license or certification to meet the professional standards of their chosen field. Also, it would be beneficial when starting out, to review options regarding the appropriate application of intuitive techniques. However, if the person already has a license as a therapist, then what they will only require training in the intuitive department, to fine-tune their skills and knowledge for appropriate applications.

Targeted Clientele

Not all clients will benefit from the same techniques. Therefore, mental health professionals and healthcare practitioners will need to do a proper assessment to determine the client's needs. Regardless of how easy a technique might be for a therapist, they cannot use one method for everyone since every person has different coping skills and requirements for healing.

Timeframe

Healing takes time, though some methods work faster than others. The duration period for healing differs for each person and relies on a personal willingness to take direction and the ability to comply with treatment. Also, insurance coverage will factor into the timeframe of therapy, which means the professional needs to select techniques that are flexible and produce the fastest outcomes.

Complimentary Treatment Modality

Several intuitive techniques are naturally compatible with therapeutic modalities that professional can easily incorporate into their practice. However, there are some techniques reserved for particular situations and are not applicable at all times. For instance, offering chakra balancing during a period when a person wants to discuss how they feel about a recent occurrence is not appropriate. If an individual has a therapist who insists on having their client do a chakra balance when they feel a strong urge to discuss their feelings, then that therapist will be invalidating their client emotionally. It is essential for a therapist to listen to their client and take a cue from them on what is appropriate at the time of their session. Therapists cannot impose techniques without the client's consent or readiness.

Overview of Intuitive Techniques

Before moving forward, it is essential to review the selected intuitive techniques recommended for mental health professionals and alternative healthcare practitioners. There are many types of intuitive techniques; some require years of training and others can be inadequate for therapeutic work. The various intuitive techniques discussed in this book were selected based on the following criteria:

- Implementation flexibility
- Minimal invasiveness
- Ability to access unconscious
- Level of difficult to learn
- Potential efficacy

In exploring each category, the professional individual will develop some understanding of the benefits and potential applications of each technique. The areas selected will be in the following order:

1. Sensory System
2. Aromatherapy
3. Guided Meditation
4. Developing Intuition
5. Aura Scanning
6. Chakra Therapy
7. Healing Regressive Techniques
8. Intuitive Tarot Therapy
9. Reiki Healing

Each chapter will provide more details and enough material to guide both the mental health professional and alternative health care practitioner in selection techniques that enhance their therapeutic practice.

Sensory System

Before starting with any intuitive development training, it is vital to understand how individuals go through the process of gathering information. Understanding the biological and chemical aspects of how the sensory system impacts human development allows the reader to understand the normalcy of intuition. The sensory system is a precious resource for the therapist and practitioner to use since it covers a wide range of attributes. With the sensory system, a therapist or practitioner can pretty much incorporate several healing styles to provide a sense of harmony and calmness in their sessions with clients. One can use oils, incense, sounds, music, or colors to invoke different emotions and mental state. The sensory system can be paired off with a range of therapeutic modalities to create new associations that will develop positive anchors for clients working on changing behaviors. Therapeutic sessions can benefit from using the sensory system provided that the client has been appropriately informed and comfortable with the method used.

Aromatherapy

Essential oils have multiple benefits that can be useful in both mental health and healthcare. Scents can be utilized to activate memory recall, as well as help clients, relax during intense therapeutic sessions. Clinicians can create an ideal environment in which can promote a general sense of well-being and serenity for both themselves and their clients. The chapter on aromatherapy will review some benefits and practical applications. However, it is strongly recommended that clinicians seek further training in aromatherapy to enable them to understand the full range of fully applications.

Guided Meditation

Meditations do not require intensive learning or training to use.

Anyone can get a few good books on meditation or watch you-tube videos to learn how to meditate. Once the basics of meditation are learned a therapist will be able to guide their client through a series of meditative exercises that will help them relax, reduce stress and cope with situations that produce intense emotional states. There are also some useful visualization techniques that work well with Behavioral Therapy, (BT) Cognitive therapy, (CT) and Cognitive Behavioral therapy (CBT). Visualization can be used to help clients create a new mindset and envision new behaviors.

Developing Intuition

Natural intuitive skills vary from individual to individual. There is no definitive formulate that can create skills that an individual does not naturally possess. However, there are methods for improving what is dormant and naturally available for each. Intuition is a natural skill every individual has regardless of how logical and rational a person may be. The key to developing natural skills is to practice and fine-tune them through a series of exercises and meditations.

The role intuition plays in the development process of a human being is underestimated and minimized yet is valuable when it comes to retrieval of unconscious information. Before developing the ability to use logic, individuals rely on intelligence based on intuitive awareness which allowed them to learn and adapt to their world. (Wood, Smith, & Grossniklaus 2001).

The chapter devoted to the topic of **developing intuitive skills** will explore the process involved in enhancing and understanding the basics of how intuitive skills work.

Aura Scanning

This chapter covers the therapeutic value of reading auras and how to improve visual acuity. The chapter has several exercises that will enable individuals to improve the ability to visually scan auras and evaluate them for energy deficiencies and inconsistencies that impact overall well-being.

Chakra Therapy

The popular chakra system typically used was designed to cater to the Western mindset, so it works well with various life cycles and issues within the Western culture. It is an excellent tool for visualization, release work and balancing energy. The chakra system is also useful when working with Cognitive behavior, cognitive, psychoanalysis, and so forth. Therapists and practitioners can use the chakra system to review central issues, create new realities and mainly do release work, in general, Chakra therapy offers endless possibilities.

Healing Regressive Techniques

The techniques in regressive healing utilize methods from hypnosis to help individuals explore negative patterns and create new ways to change. Healing regression is useful in psychoanalysis, or therapies that are focused on dealing with childhood issues. Regressive healing is a valuable technique that is helpful in tracing back old patterns and emotional memories. This technique does require training and should be something a therapist has practiced doing before experimenting with clients.

Tarot Therapy

A tarot deck is a handy tool for inner work, but it does require some basic understanding of the tarot and its symbolism. The tarot can be a bit intimidating and a challenge for some individuals to learn, depending on who is their teacher and how they are taught to read them. The best-recommended method for understanding the deck is by using a technique referred to as **intuitive interpretive reading**, which means merely to let the cards trigger natural reactions and thoughts without worrying about their pre-assigned meanings. Tarot guidance techniques are useful in psychoanalysis, client-centered therapy and Gestalt. It can also be useful in coaching as a tool for guidance.

Reiki Healing

Working with Reiki can be an ideal therapeutic tool for clients who are struggling with emotional situations, restlessness or periods of stress. Reiki is also useful when combined with chakra healings and energy balancing. Reiki can be used both in individual and group sessions. Practitioners can facilitate healing circles that provide Reiki exchanges between practitioners or allow clients to experience Reiki treatments in a group setting with other participants.

Combining Intuition and Therapy

By now, any therapist or practitioner should have a basic understanding of the reasons why specific techniques will be paired off with some of the therapeutic systems. It is, of course, going to take practice to use the various methods with ease and confidence.

There is a quick reference chart available breaking down treatment modalities and corresponding intuitive techniques.

Brief Treatment Modalities Outline

Therapy Type	Treatment Focus	Objective	Intuitive tools
Addiction Counseling	techniques used: CBT, BT to help change negative behaviors	Clients address issues with cravings & drug-seeking behaviors	Visualization, meditation, chakra therapy, aromatherapy
Art Therapy	Creativity is useful for emotional issues.	Different forms of art used to express emotions & difficult thoughts.	Chakra therapy, visualization, tarot meditations
Behavior Therapy (BT)	Create new behaviors using conditioning, i.e., systematic desensitization techniques, & reinforcements.	Patients overcome issues with fear, phobias, & anxiety by using relaxation & exposure methods	Chakra therapy, visualization,
Bodywork Therapy	Designed to reduce stress and provide physical comfort	Clients benefit from the nurturing nature of massage therapy; useful with intimacy & physical issues.	Chakra therapy, visualization, Reiki treatment, aromatherapy
Cognitive Behavior Therapy	combines BT & CT techniques to address maladaptive thoughts & emotions to create	Client address negative thoughts and emotion to create new beliefs and	Chakra therapy, visualization.

	behaviors & thought patterns	behaviors	
Cognitive Therapy	The focus is on negative thoughts and how they contribute to emotional and mental distress	Clients learn to address negative thoughts such as overgeneralization, and negative beliefs	Chakra therapy, visualization
Group Therapy	Therapy through group support.	Group members help each other through supportive feedback and active listening	Chakra, tarot and guided meditations
Holistic Coaching	Clients work through obstacles to achieve goals in all life areas.	Aimed at developing strategies to overcome personal limits and obtain a quality lifestyle	Chakra therapy, visualization, tarot meditations and therapeutic spreads
Humanistic Therapy	Clients develop self-awareness by exploring their thoughts and feelings	Clients become empowered by developing insights into their issues	Chakra therapy, visualization, regressive therapy
Hypnotherapy	Hypnosis is used to cover emotional & unresolved issues	Exercises are used to help clients relax & tap into their unconscious	Chakra therapy, visualization, regressive therapy

Integrated Therapy or Eclectic Therapy	This style of therapy combines various therapeutic modalities	various forms of treatments provided by one therapist	Chakra therapy, visualization, tarot and regressive techniques
Music Therapy	Therapeutic use of music & musical instruments	Helpful for overcoming stress, anxiety and develop healthy social skills	Vibration sound therapy is useful, chanting, singing, 5th chakra work, aromatherapy
Psychoanalysis	explores unconscious conflicts related to past and present issues.	Therapist plays an active role in deciphering the issues faced by clients	Chakra explorations, regression, tarot meditations

The next few chapters will review each intuitive category to help the mental health professionals, and alternative health care practitioners understand how each system is potentially useful in the therapeutic practice. Keep in mind some intuitive techniques are easier to learn and utilize than others. The more natural methods not only require less time and training to learn but are useful in a broader range of therapeutic modalities.

Chapter Summary

The primary focus of this book is to supply the professional individual with a variety of material that can be adapted and incorporated into their therapeutic practice as needed. Of course, some techniques require modification due to the needs of the population served and the policies of the treatment facility where therapists work. Though many agencies rely on evidence-based practices, the fact is clinicians and practitioners often use therapeutic methods based on their experience and overall style of working. (Bartgis, & Bigfoot, 2010)

"When using intuition, the brain is back to the original state of function before rational thinking fully developed. As infants, we learned and adapted to the environment with the five senses and intuitive awareness." R. Castro

Chapter IV
Reviewing Treatment Modalities

"He who knows others is wise; he who knows himself is enlightened." – Lao Tzu

Exploring Treatment Modalities

To create a successful merging of traditional treatment modalities with intuitive techniques, mental health clinicians and healthcare practitioners need to know how each system works. In the last chapter, two charts highlighted vital components in treatment modalities and intuitive techniques to provide quick reference material.

In this chapter will we appraise in more detail some of the general types of therapeutic systems introduced in the last chapter that has evolved throughout the years. There are different treatment modalities, some are designed for long-term treatment and are focused on deep-rooted core issues, while others focus on current crisis and provide immediate results to help clients obtain stability, rather than provide a cure.

There is a range of therapeutic formats that are useful in treatment; the effectiveness of each treatment modality will vary depending on the presenting problem of each client. The selection of therapeutic styles will also vary depending on the professional training of each clinician and practitioner. Some professionals might prefer treatment modalities that produce quicker results, due to factors such as, program policies or the nature of the client's mental status and treatment compliance. (Knickman, et al. 2016) Not all clients will benefit from the same type of treatment or duration of care. (D'Angelo 2002) Clients dealing with addictions, temporary life crisis or personal obstacles will benefit from therapeutic styles that are concrete and present-oriented, while those with personality disorders or chronic personal crisis will require more in-depth and extended periods of treatment.

Many individuals will thrive on counseling or coaching techniques and do not necessarily require long-term care. However, clients with mental health disorders, history of trauma or abuse will require more extended periods of treatment and therefore need more in-depth mental health care. Also, insurance limitations can determine the duration of therapy; therefore, it is essential to find out how much insurance coverage is available to develop a proper treatment plan that facilitates maximum results for the duration of treatment. (Dermody, Martin, Reid, Corbett, Ward, & Dorter, 2017)

Evolution of Treatment Modalities

When individuals think of therapy, they often think of psychoanalysis and Freud. Though psychoanalysis paved the way for many psychological modalities, it is not as popular as it used to be as when initially introduced. Historically, Psychoanalysis did not produce viable statistical data to support many of its theoretical claims and as a result, failed to provide consistent outcomes. (Beystehner 2001) There are also other reasons psychoanalysis is no longer the dominant therapeutic strategy; it is expensive and time-consuming since psychoanalysis requires at least three visits per week for several years.

As the need for statistical evidence grew, the demand for psychological research expanded creating new forms of therapy based on evidence-based outcomes rather than theoretical claims. (Beystehner). In general, research is responsible for the expansion and efficacy of psychology. As psychology expanded, several therapeutic systems evolved producing various options for mental health treatment.

Navigating this Chapter

This chapter provides an outline of several treatment modalities to help clinicians and healthcare practitioners understand how different intuitive and therapeutic systems can be used together in a therapeutic session. The methods discussed within this book were selected based on how well they combine to provide therapeutic results. Each system is divided into two main categories; **Talk Therapy** and **Sensory-based techniques**.

Talk Therapy

This form of treatment consists of the client disclosing emotional issues to develop insight and gain an understanding that contributes to the development and improvement of personal coping skills. In talk therapy, clients talk about problems, feelings or ongoing struggles with various life issues. Clients can use talk therapy to help them find meaningful ways to cope with crisis-oriented situations.

Sensory-Based Techniques

This type of technique utilizes the five sensory systems to create a sense of well-being and mental balance. Sensory-based techniques are ideal for helping clients feel better by invoking physical calmness and reducing anxiety that can be triggered by talk therapy. A few samples of sensory-based techniques would be aromatherapy, Reiki healing, massage, art, music and even dance therapy. Sensory-based techniques are excellent tools for non-verbal or emotionally stifled clients; since they can induce relaxation which helps ease communication.

Talk Therapies

Psychoanalysis Theory

Psychoanalysis is a form of talk therapy developed by Sigmund Freud in 1890. Freud believed individuals suffered from mental disorders based on imbalances created by repressed impulses or childhood trauma during one of the psychosexual developmental stages of the person. According to psychoanalytical theory, individuals when confronted with trauma or intense emotions cope by using various **defense mechanisms**, which are balanced and regulated between the **ego**, **Id,** and **superego**. Individuals often deal with painful events by using defense mechanisms to change uncomfortable forms of reality into a format that allows them to function emotionally. Also, painful past events get minimized due to coping skills and the types of defense mechanism used during the time of the event. Though the actual memory is distorted and minimized, it is never entirely forgotten, which is why psychoanalysis works on recovering old memories through various retrieval techniques such as **hypnosis, word associations** and **Rorschach ink-blot** (Harrower-Erikson 1945). Psychoanalysts believe that the past holds the key to unconscious issues that impact how individuals react to current day situations.

Psychoanalysts are trained to work with the client's past and present life situations, even if the client's views are culturally in contrast to that of the therapist. (Tummala-Narra 2013) The psychoanalytical training provides a strong foundation for flexibility and adaptability to the nuances of non-traditional techniques. In other words, psychoanalysis, unlike cognitive behavioral therapies, does not adhere to strict evidence-base principals, which allows room for expansion. (Coleman 2014) The flexible nature of Psychoanalysis means that psychoanalysts are more willing to experiment with techniques that are not as mainstream or evidence-based, which allows them to be more at ease when using alternative treatment modalities, such as meditation, dream analysis, regression techniques, tarot and so forth.

Educational training: Advanced Degree in Psychology, Analytical training and Licensed in Clinical psychology

Treatment focus: Psychoanalytical Therapy utilizes diagnostic techniques that review repressed memories, emotions, and dream analysis. With the guidance of the psychoanalyst, clients learn to uncover the meaning behind their dreams and repressed feelings so that they can resolve internal conflicts. Clients spend a significant amount of time with their psychoanalyst, examining patterns and behaviors that have impacted them throughout their lives. Individuals typically see their psychoanalyst 3 to 4 times a week for months to years to help them work intensely on resolving inner conflicts. The critical focus in therapy is resolving **internal conflicts** that stem from unresolved childhood patterns.

Targeted Population: Psychoanalysis works well with individuals suffering from trauma, PTSD, depressive disorders, personality disorders, neurotic disorders, relationship problems and self-destructive behaviors.

Timeframe: long term, 2 to more times per week; results take a long time to manifest

Complimentary Intuitive Techniques

Psychoanalysis helps clients unveil hidden issues that are locked away in the unconscious mind. Many intuitive techniques will be useful in therapy since psychoanalysis often focuses on childhood trauma and repressed emotional occurrence using tools that are very similar to intuitive methods. The following would be ideal to incorporate into psychoanalytical therapy:

- **Tarot meditations** – A guided meditation is designed based on randomly selecting a tarot card to help clients tap into hidden feelings and memories. The tarot deck can be used in the same manner as the Rorschach ink-blot pictures to invoke feelings or thoughts. The Rorschach ink-blot have been used since 1921 on clients to reveal internal issues (Harrower-Erickson)
- **Chakra therapy** –A psychoanalyst can use the chakra system to trace old patterns and beliefs by tapping into the unconscious mind. (Judith, 1987)

- **Regressive therapy** – this method uses hypnotic techniques to trace events and their impact on the client's ability to cope with present-day life issues. Keep in mind, Freud often used hypnosis in his work with patients. (Bachner-Melman, 2001)
- **Reiki Energy** – helps reduce anxiety and create a calm and safe space
- **Journaling assignments** – this allows clients to keep track of emotional reactions outside therapy

Jungian Therapy

Jungian therapy also referred to as Analytical psychology, focuses on talk therapy just like Freud's system of Psychoanalysis. The focus on Analytical therapy is to help the client activate their true nature by exploring their dark side. Jungian trained analyst focused on the importance of symbolism and how useful it can be in detecting specific disorders (Roesler 2013). There is tremendous value in exploring shadow symbology in therapy since it helps unlock hidden elements and personal issues buried in the unconscious. (Krapp 1999)

Educational training: Advanced Degree in Psychology, Jungian Analytical training and Licensed in Clinical psychology

Treatment Focus: Jungian therapy can guide a person through the process of navigating intense feelings such as depression, anxiety, grief, as well as trauma, and phobias that developed from past experiences. It is similar on many levels to psychoanalysis, except that individuals focus on achieving balance and internal harmony, by embracing their dark sides rather than attempting to eliminate it entirely. In Jungian therapy, various techniques such as dream analysis, creative therapy like art, music or movement and even word association are used to uncovered repressed emotional memories. The client is encouraged to express themselves fully and freely. Sessions can range from one to a few times a week. The focus of therapy is to explore the roots of personal problems, blocked emotional memories as well as learn healthy ways to cope

Targeted Population: Clients who benefit from Jungian therapy are those suffering from trauma, PSTD, chronic depression, emotional issues that linked to low self-esteem issues, childhood trauma and phobias that developed from past experiences.

Timeframe: Medium to long-term; one to more times per week. Unlike other forms of psychoanalysis, Jung therapy is cost-effective, and the overall effects are long-lasting according to empirical studies. (Roesler)

Complimentary Intuitive Techniques

Jung believed that repressed experiences and memories resulted in imbalances. Jung also thought that some traits were globally common and it collectively impacted others as well. Keep in mind that many of the same techniques used in traditional Psychoanalysis are applicable in Jungian therapy. The following would be ideal techniques to incorporate into treatment, which are similar to the ones listed for psychoanalysis:

- **Tarot meditations** – meditations are designed using a random selection of a tarot card to help the client tap into unconscious feelings and personal archetypes and constructs.
- **Chakra therapy** – The chakra system is useful for exploring hidden issues and addressing personal shadows
- **Regressive therapy** – hypnotic techniques are valuable in tracing old patterns and hidden issues.
- **Reiki Energy** – useful in creating a safe space and reducing anxiety
- **Journaling assignments** – the client can track emotional reactions outside therapy

Cognitive Therapy

Cognitive therapy, (CT) is a form of psychotherapy, developed by Aaron Beck. CT was designed to help clients understand the relationship between negative thought patterns and maladaptive feelings. The focus of Cognitive therapy is to help clients consciously become aware of the connection between maladaptive emotional states and the negative thought patterns. (Beck, & Haigh, 2014).

Educational training: Advanced Degree in Psychology or Social Work, Cognitive training and Licensed in Clinical psychology or Social work

Treatment Focus: Cognitive Therapy is designed to help individuals develop insight into their cognitive distortions to reform their emotional states. Clients learn how to identify negative thinking patterns, such as **overgeneralizations**, **jumping to conclusions**, **catastrophizing** and **all-or-nothing**. By exploring their tendencies to have distorted beliefs or thinking patterns, clients can understand precisely how those thoughts contribute to their mental and emotional states. The primary focus is to eliminate or reduce harmful beliefs to minimize negative feelings.

Targetted Population: The type of client that benefit from Cognitive Therapy are those suffering from generalized anxiety, phobias, panic disorders, obsessive-compulsive disorders, depressive disorders, PSTD, and addiction disorders.

Timeframe: A period ranging from a few months to less than two years, 1-2 times week, includes individual and group therapy. Results occur fairly quickly

Complimentary Intuitive Techniques

- **Chakra Therapy** – The combination of chakra scanning and meditation is helpful in tracing negative emotions and thought patterns
- **Healing Visualization** – Visualizations are on useful in reconstructing old beliefs and visualizing new outcomes, combined with positive affirmations

- **Reiki Energy** – helps in creating a safe space and reducing anxiety
- **Journaling assignments** – this allows clients to track negative thought patterns, as well as emotional reactions outside therapy. If a person struggles to read, therapists can use collages made from magazine or newspaper clippings.

Cognitive Behavioral Therapy

Cognitive Behavioral Therapy (CBT) focuses on working through current maladaptive behavior patterns created by negative thoughts and beliefs. Clients are guided to review their maladaptive behavior patterns and learn new ways to replace old thinking by developing healthier coping skills and attitudes. While cognitive therapy focuses on the relationship between emotional states and cognitive distortions, CBT focuses on how both cognitive and emotional impairment influences behavior patterns. CBT encourages clients to focus on changing negative behaviors and replacing them with positive ones. (Martin 2018)

Educational training: Advanced Degree in Psychology or Social Work, Cognitive Behavioral training and Licensed in Clinical psychology or Social work

Treatment Focus: Cognitive behavioral therapy provides a client with tools for changing behavior patterns by engaging in new activities that shape new habits. In CBT, the actions and activities that a client engages in will facilitate healthy attitudes and benefit the emotional well-being of the individual. The focus of CBT is on creating new activities and assignments that reinforce new habits which shape how individuals think, feel and behave.

Targeted Population: The type of clients that benefit from CBT techniques are individuals suffering from anxiety, phobias, addiction, compulsive sexual behaviors, social phobias and adjustment disorders.

Timeframe: A period ranging from a few months to less than two years, 1-2 times week, includes individual and group therapy. Results occur fairly quickly

Complimentary Intuitive Techniques

- **Chakra therapy** – The combination of chakra scanning, and meditation is helpful in tracing negative behavior and thought patterns
- **Healing Visualization** – visualization focuses on creating new behaviors and new ways of thinking, combined with positive affirmations
- **Reiki Energy** – helps in creating a safe space and reducing anxiety
- **Journaling assignments** – this allows clients to track negative behavior patterns, as well as emotional reactions outside therapy. If a person struggles with reading, use collages made from magazine or newspaper clippings.

Humanistic Therapy

Humanistic therapy incorporates several branches of psychology: Client-Centered Therapy (Carl Rogers), Existential psychotherapy and Abraham Maslow's emphasis on Hierarchy of needs, as well as a Gestalt approach. (McLeod 2015)

Humanistic therapists help clients obtain insight regarding their inner conflicts as well as achieve a healthier lifestyle by gaining emotional balance. Individuals seek **self-actualization** and **self-fulfillment** through a series of non-directive, non-judgmental techniques that involve active listening and emotional support. The role of the Humanistic therapists is to be an emotional support system which allows the client to develop their insight at their own pace. The therapeutic relationship is one where the client experiences unconditional positive regard and is allowed to focus on their positive qualities rather than the deficits of their personality. (Reitan 2013)

Educational training: Advanced Degree in Psychology or Social Work, Humanistic or Gestalt training and Licensed in Clinical psychology or Social work

Treatment Focus: Therapists utilize active listening techniques, unconditional positive regard, and empathy that allow the clients to develop **self-efficacy, self-acceptance,** and **self-esteem**. Treatment helps the client overcome negative self-views by recognizing self-worth.

Targeted Population: Clients suffering from depression, panic disorders, anxiety, addiction, personality disorders, and schizophrenia are ideal candidates for Humanistic therapy since its client-centered. Also, clients struggling with addiction and relationship issues can benefit as well. Humanistic therapy is centered around improving the client's mental status by enhancing positive qualities and not focusing on their negative traits, which is a useful technique when working with psychotic clients. (Reitan)

Timeframe: The duration of therapy is a middle range, which can fluctuate from a few months to a couple of years, with a once a week individual session and group therapy.

Complimentary Intuitive Techniques

- **Chakra therapy** – Clients learn to meditate and balance their chakras
- **Healing Visualization** – visualization is used to focus on positive attributes and develop new ways of thinking, combined with positive affirmations
- **Reiki Energy** – helps in creating a safe space and reducing anxiety
- **Journaling Assignments** – this allows clients to track negative beliefs and thoughts outside therapy.

Client-Centered Therapy

This style of treatment is non-directive, which places the focus on the client and helping them develop insight. The therapeutic goal is to help clients identify conflicts and create an understanding of their emotional states without the therapists giving advice or interpretations. This style of therapy is designed to empower a patient by allowing them to grow and overcome issues through their efforts. In Client-centered therapy, a therapist applies active listening techniques and provides emotional support. (Green 2000)

Educational training: Advanced Degree in Psychology or Social Work, Client- Center training and Licensed in Clinical psychology or Social work

Treatment focus: In Client-Centered therapy, the needs of the individual client determine the treatment focus. The client might work on goals, focus on developing insight on personal issues or explore self-sabotaging behaviors. The role of a therapist is to facilitate the process of therapy and provide emotional support. The primary focus is to help the client develop self-esteem and a sense of empowerment by letting them do most of the work.

Targeted Population: The type of client who benefits from client-centered therapy is someone struggling emotionally but does not have severe mental health issues. This form of therapy is useful for individuals who have low self-esteem, a poor self-image or lacks confidence and who can benefit from gaining insight and being more active in therapy.

Timeframe: The duration of therapy is a middle range, which can fluctuate from a few months to a couple of years, with a once a week individual session.

Complimentary Intuitive Techniques

- **Chakra therapy** – Clients learn how to meditate and balance their chakras
- **Healing Visualization** – Visualization techniques are used for developing new ways of thinking and creating new realities.
- **Breathing Techniques** – to help the client relax and reduce anxiety
- **Journaling Assignments** – this allows clients to track negative patterns and thoughts outside therapy.

Integrated Therapy (Eclectic Therapy)

The goal of Integrated therapy is to incorporate a variety of modalities in therapy. This type of therapeutic style requires that the clinician be well-versed in the various methods of evidence-based practices and how to utilize them therapeutically. The individual should be adequately trained and equipped to handle the implementation of different techniques as required. The therapist will need certification in some of the methods they are implementing, assuring quality care. On many levels, Integrated therapy is ideal for intuitive techniques since it is flexible and not based on one rigid format. This style of treatment is useful both in individual and group therapy. (Hazelgrove 1998)

Educational training: Advanced Degree in Psychology or Social Work, License in Clinical Psychology or Social Work. Also, various techniques are combined therefore training will vary from individual to individual.

Treatment Focus: The client needs are the center of Integrated therapy, which means that treatment is designed depending on the individual needs of each person. No one fixed format or system is applied. With integrated therapy, the therapist might start treatment with a specific format and gradually adjust it depending on the needs of the client.

Targeted Population: Clients who have mild to medium range mental health and emotional issues will benefit from integrated therapy. Individuals with severe mental health issues or struggling with emotional distress will need more structure and uniformity in therapy.

Timeframe: The duration of therapy is a middle range, which can fluctuate from a few months to a couple of years, with a once a week individual session.

Complimentary Intuitive Techniques

- **Chakra therapy** – Clients are taught how to meditate and balance their chakras. Also, the therapist may scan and work on balancing the chakras for the client.
- **Healing Visualization** – Clients learn visualization techniques and new ways of thinking, combined with positive affirmations.
- **Breathing techniques** – to help the client relax as well as reduce anxiety
- **Journaling assignments** – this allows clients to track negative beliefs and thoughts outside therapy.

Integrated therapy has specific regulations and systems that are combined to provide balance and promote overall well-being. Sessions will vary from therapist to therapist since there is no one single standard for the type of Integrated therapies utilized in therapy.

Addiction Counseling

The role of an addiction counselor is to work with individuals who abuse drugs and struggle to remain sober. The addiction counselor can use various modalities to help an addict obtain sobriety and develop healthy coping skills to handle triggers and cravings. Keep in mind; addiction counseling is done **within a treatment facility** or by a therapist who has a professional license in addition to addiction training. (NIDA 2018) Private facilitators cannot do addiction counseling without mental health, social work or clinical psychology license. Therefore, this section is strictly for the therapist who is licensed and certified, and not a practicing Coach, Christian counselors or private non-licensed psychotherapist.

Educational training: Bachelor's Degree in Psychology or Social Work, Mental Health Counseling, and certification in substance abuse counseling.

Treatment Focus: Clients typically focus on learning ways to reduce cravings for drugs and maladaptive behaviors that prolong the effects of addiction. Clients explore ways to learn new coping skills, identify triggers and then develop sober plans for managing their potential cravings and behaviors that can lead back to relapse. Client engages in both individual and group therapy. Alternative methods are useful in helping clients reduce stress, anxiety and negative thought patterns. Intuitive techniques such as energy work and chakra techniques can help promote balance and calmness, as well as visualization and aromatherapy.

Targeted Population: The type of clientele that seeks addiction counseling only needs to meet criteria for addiction and a desire to get better. Different treatment facilities subscribe to different forms of treatment. However, the most common and useful forms of therapy include CBT, CT which focus on behavioral changes, identification of negatives beliefs, triggers and thoughts. There are also components of addiction therapy that focuses on emotional and mental health if a client is a Mentally Ill Chemical Abuser (MICA).

Timeframe: The duration period can vary depending on the client's drug history and struggles to remain sober. There is a tendency to enter numerous treatment facilities due to chronic relapses. Depending on the person's physical health and support system, the duration of treatment can range from 28 days inpatient to 2 years in a therapeutic community. The frequency of appointments per week will reflect the type of program they entered and the severity of their addiction. Insurance coverage can also determine the duration of treatment and will not cover private non-license therapy. (NIDA)

Complimentary Intuitive Techniques

- **Chakra Therapy** – Clients are taught how to meditate and balance their chakras.
- **Healing Visualization** – Clients learn can visualization techniques to explore triggers and develop new behavior patterns combined with positive affirmations,
- **Breathing Techniques** – to help the client relax and reduce anxiety
- **Journaling Assignments** – this allows clients to track negative beliefs and thoughts outside therapy.

Coaching Techniques

Coaching does not dive into the psychological aspects of problems faced by individuals but instead focuses on **finding solutions** and helping clients **regain balance** in various aspects of their lives. Coaching is designed to target specific problem areas and develop goals to help clients make concrete changes using multiple action plans.

A coach looks for ways to minimize self-sabotaging behaviors and enhance existing strengths, without focusing intensely on emotional or mental health issues. Of course, a coach is emotionally supportive, but their role is to help a client seek solutions rather than analyze the roots of their behavior patterns and emotional distress. A coach may offer energy healing sessions such as Reiki, chakra balancing, and guided meditations, but the main focus is on developing goals and eliminating self-sabotaging behaviors. (Castro 2017)

Educational training: Bachelor's Degree in Psychology or Social Work, Mental Health Counseling and certification in Coaching helpful but not required.

Treatment Focus: Coaching works by guiding individuals who are struggling with various life issues and overall goal stagnation. The primary focus of coaching is to improve performance, reduce self-defeating behaviors by identifying barriers and obtain life fulfillment through goal setting. Coaching is a style of therapy, but it is not based on in-depth psychological analysis, but rather on designing problem-solving systems that help clients overcome personal blocks and stagnation.

Coaching is supportive, focuses on motivating clients and enhancing their strengths. A critical factor in coaching is the application of self-actualizing methods that allow the client to have their emotional reactions, without being dismissive (Wilson, Havighurst and Harley 2012). Since coaching is emotionally permissive and works well with other alternative methods that require the ability to remain open and accepting of the client's natural reaction.

Targeted Population: Individuals struggling with career changes, unsatisfying relationships or poor body image can benefit from coaching. However, individuals that have mental health problems or deep emotional issues would benefit from a licensed mental health professional rather than a coach.

Timeframe: The duration can be middle to short-term, depending on the goals of the clients. The sessions typically focus on designing goals, identifying self-sabotaging behaviors and developing new strategies for coping with setbacks; therefore, the frequency of appointments per week will vary. Insurance does not cover coaching.

Complimentary Intuitive Techniques

Depending on the type of coaching style utilized, a coach can pretty much use any intuitive technique.

- **Chakra Therapy** – Clients are taught how to meditate and balance their chakras.
- **Healing Visualization** – visualization is used to explore barriers and develop new ways of thinking combined with positive affirmations
- **Tarot therapy** – Used as a guidance and clarification tool
- **Reiki Healing** – helps create a safe space and reduce anxiety
- **Journaling Assignments** – this allows clients to track progress and setbacks with goals.

Clients also learn several techniques so that they can practice meditation and chakra balancing on their own and for overall maintenance.

Summary of Talk Therapy

The role of talk therapy is significant in helping individuals obtain mental health and emotional balance. The styles of therapy vary from therapist to therapist, and no one type of therapy can ultimately address the individual issues faced by clients. Even the most brilliant therapist can face a snafu in their attempts to help clients overcome personal obstacles. In general, being professional and authentic when working with clients is the main component when doing therapy work.

Sensory-Based Techniques

Sensory-based techniques are mostly for the healthcare practitioners who do bodywork, creativity therapy or general healing. However, many mental health clinicians do incorporate some sensory-based methods into their sessions

The goal of Sensory-based techniques is to utilize the different senses as therapeutic tools rather than **directive talk therapy**. Of course, practitioners do use active listening skills in their session, but the primary focus is healing and energy work. The primary goal is to help individuals gain a sense of calmness, balance and mental clarity, which will facilitate their ability to handle any emotional revelation that may occur in therapy.

Sensory techniques can be an additional feature of the overall therapeutic program, or it can be used on its own for those just seeking to maintain overall balance. The sensory system is a vital part of human development since it is the initial stage of all developmental stages (Wood et al.). Our connection to the world begins with our senses and the initial impressions we collect, and though we develop the ability to analyze our surroundings, we always retain a sensory connection. Even when a person experiences a brain injury, the senses maintain a connection to its surroundings.

Sensory-based techniques discussed in this section consist of systems that incorporate some of the natural senses to help clients regain emotional balance and control. The types of sensory-based techniques covered briefly consist of the following:

- Art therapy
- Music therapy
- Bodywork
- Aromatherapy

Art Therapy

Art therapy consists of using creativity as a format for expressing internalized issues that may be difficult to express verbally. Art therapy uses creative symbolism to represent emotional realities. It allows an individual to safely express what they might struggle to verbalize due to the emotional overload created by traumatic or unpleasant events. Symbols tend to represent a hidden psychological truth for each person that can be beneficial to access and explore in therapy. (Jung 1967)

Educational training: Bachelor's Degree in Psychology or Social Work, Mental Health Counseling and concentration in Art

Treatment Focus: Art can be an excellent media for communication and expressing emotional issues when a client is struggling to put feelings into words. Art is useful for clients recovering from a brain tumor, a stroke or trying to cope with childhood trauma, emotional stagnation, and impaired communication skills. Art is also a great tool to use for free association and tapping into the unconscious realm.

Targeted Population: Individuals suffering from trauma and emotional crisis can benefit from art therapy. Many of the techniques in art therapy are **non-invasive** and permit clients to express themselves non-verbally in a safe manner. Victims of abuse and rape struggle to find the proper words to describe events since it can be painfully overwhelming. Art will allow individuals to disclose how they feel without the intensity invoked by verbal communication.

Timeframe: The duration of therapy varies since art therapy can turn into a creative hobby for individuals. However, treatment can range from medium to long-term therapy.

Complimentary Intuitive Techniques

- **Healing Visualization** – individuals can create pieces that they can use as visualization tools.
- **Tarot Therapy** – the tarot deck is used as an artistic tool for both visualization and inner journey work. Clients can also design their tarot deck for meditation

- **Journaling Assignments** – clients can create a scrapbook-style journal with pieces of artwork, a dream board to help them develop goals.

Music Therapy

Music therapists utilize musical instruments and all types of elements related to music, such as singing, and listening to music. The individual will engage in activities that allow them to express themselves musically, to communicate what might be difficult to express verbally.

Educational training: Bachelor's Degree in Psychology or Social Work, Mental Health Counseling and concentration in music

Treatment Focus: Music therapy is very similar to art therapy in the sense that it allows a client to express themselves creatively. Music is great for activating a wide range of emotions and will trigger memory recall. Music can be useful in retrieving hidden emotions and uncovering old memories associated with abuse, PSTD, trauma and old behavior patterns. (Music Therapy 2018)

Targeted Population: Individuals who are struggling with social phobias, inability to communicate or dealing with an emotional crisis. Music can allow individuals not only to express themselves but also find ways to get in touch with hidden emotional issues as well as old memories. Music tends to activate memories and produce emotional recall which can be useful for individuals suffering from a history of trauma, PSTD or have poor communication skills.

Timeframe: The duration of music therapy can vary just like art therapy since it can turn into a creative hobby for individuals. However, treatment can range from medium to long-term care.

Complimentary Intuitive Techniques:

- **Chakra therapy** – a combination of chakra notes and music can be useful in creating balance

- **Healing Visualization** – music can be paired off with guided visualization techniques
- **Reiki Healing** – Reiki treatments used in combination with soothing music
- **Guided Meditation** – general meditation techniques work well with the right type of music for inducing a relaxed state of mind

Bodywork Therapy

The area of bodywork therapy includes massage and reiki treatments. Both massage and reiki are excellent systems to combine when working with clients. However, the practitioner is required to have a license to practice massage work. The massage work can consist of a variety of bodywork techniques including some of the more popular ones such as Thai massage, Shiatsu, Acupressure, Acupuncture, Swedish massage, Deep tissue, Reflexology, stone massage and pregnancy massage. (Wong 2017). The type of massage a client will need always depends on their physical needs, as well as their ability to handle certain levels of physical touch. Bodywork is not just useful for relieving stress, but also for helping individuals overcome issues with intimacy and physical trauma.

Educational training: License in Massage therapy required

Treatment Focus: The focus is on releasing tension, helping clients reduce stress and obtain an overall sense of well-being. The treatment involves different ranges of physical touch from deep tissue manipulation to non-touching reiki treatments. The application of bodywork will vary depending on the training of the therapist and license. Be aware, that in some countries, it is illegal to practice direct bodywork without a license. One of the few techniques that do not require a license to practice is reiki; however, therapists do need to be adequately trained and attuned to the Reiki symbol to use Reiki energy in treatment.

Targeted Population: Individual who require physical treatment, especially for people with muscle tension, stress and anxiety can benefit from bodywork treatment.

Timeframe: The duration of treatment depends on how quickly a person can recover from physical issues, as well as their capacity to manage a stressful lifestyle. Also, treatment duration may be impacted by insurance coverage since most insurance companies do not cover alternative therapy. (Knickman et al.)

Complimentary Intuitive Techniques

Bodywork can work well with many alternative intuitive techniques.

- **Chakra therapy** – a combination of crystal layouts and balancing to assist the client in obtaining a state of calmness and balance.
- **Aura Scanning** – A good tool for healthcare practitioners who can use the information in developing a treatment plan for healthcare services.
- **Aromatherapy** - Various essential oils are used to induce a relax state and help calm down anxiety during bodywork
- **Reiki Energy** – helps create a safe space and reduce anxiety, as well as balance energy.

Aromatherapy

When it comes to the application of aromatherapy, it is essential to understand the therapeutic benefits of different oils. Both clinicians and practitioners can use aromatherapy in their practice. However, they need to know basic information about how aroma impacts moods and how to incorporate it into therapy appropriately. It is advisable that clinicians and practitioners take a few basic courses on aromatherapy to help them navigate the apothecary of fragrances with confidence.

Educational training: License in aromatherapy strongly recommended

Treatment Focus: The focus is on creating balance and helping clients reduce stress and feel generally harmonious. The application of aromatherapy will vary depending on the general knowledge of essential oils. Aromatherapy is easy to combine with other modalities and systems. The key to using oils is knowing which types will benefit the client and their current mental or physical status.

Targeted Population: Any individual who needs physical and mental treatment, especially for people with tension, stress, and anxiety can benefit from a nice combination of oils

Timeframe: The duration of aromatherapy can vary just like art therapy since it can turn into daily practice.

Complimentary Intuitive Techniques:

- **Chakra therapy** – a combination of the different chakras and essential oils can be useful in creating balance
- **Healing Visualization** – aromatherapy can be paired off with visualization techniques
- **Reiki Healing** – Reiki treatments used in combination with aromatherapy
- **Guided Meditation** – general meditation techniques work well with the right type of essential oils for inducing a relaxed state of mind

Summary of Sensory Systems

Sensory systems techniques are useful for both mental health clinicians and alternative health care practitioners since they are flexible and do not diminish the integrity of treatment modalities. The main issue with utilizing sensory systems is the policies and procedures of the different organizations and insurance coverage. (Knickman et al.) Otherwise, many of the techniques that involve the sensory system are adaptable and work within the field of mental health and healthcare.

Chapter Summary

The applications of therapeutic techniques will reflect the experience and skills of the mental health professional and healthcare practitioner, as well as the needs of the client. Therapeutic goals are developed and designed based on the needs of the client and their comfort levels. Forcing a client to participate in activities that are uncomfortable is counter-productive and can force a person into more profound repression. There is, of course, intentional use of discomfort to trigger specific emotional reactions. However, this must be part of a process and not performed mindlessly. In summary, therapists and practitioners have an ethical and professional responsibility to adhere to and are required know how to apply techniques efficiently and not at the risk of their clientele.

SECTION II

Intuitive Techniques

Chapter V
Exploring Intuitive Techniques

It is through science that we prove, but through intuition that we discover. - Henri Poincare

Exploring Intuitive Techniques

This chapter provides an outline of the different types of intuitive techniques that are useful in therapeutic practices. Keep in mind in the implementation of intuitive procedures we are not necessarily focusing on psychic work regarding predicting situations, but rather in developing an innate understanding of personal circumstances and events that impact the lives of individuals in treatment. A therapist can use intuitive techniques in therapy as well as teach their clients to use various methods for uncovering unconscious issues and attain self-empowerment.

Each method discussed in this chapter involves the use of at least one of the senses or at least a combination of them. Some techniques are easier to use than others and require less time to learn. For a clinician to integrate their intuitive skills into therapeutic work, it will be useful to explore a few methods and how to utilize them effectively. Keep in mind; we are not going to cover every single intuitive or divination technique since some are not as useful for therapeutic work.

The material in this book was organized to help mental health clinicians, and healthcare practitioners not only understand the benefits of intuitive techniques but learn how to incorporate them therapeutically. Most of the intuitive procedures are designed to let therapist and practitioners use their innate skills and do not require extensive psychic abilities to perform, which is why they were selected. Some methods do need some more advanced knowledge to incorporate them into therapeutic practice, and those types are discussed later in the book. Regardless of how well developed the innate skills of therapists or practitioner made be, professionals can still use many of the methods within this book.

Here is a list of the Intuitive Techniques chapters covered in this book:

1. Sensory Systems
2. The Benefits of Aromatherapy
3. Therapeutic Meditations
4. Developing Intuitive Skills
5. Aura Reading
6. Therapeutic Chakra Techniques
7. Healing Regressive Techniques
8. Hands-on Healing and Reiki in Therapy
9. Tarot and Psychotherapy

Each listed technique provides both the mental health clinician and healthcare practitioners with tools to amplify their therapeutic efforts. The techniques are not replacements for any professional training required for the field of work. The goal of this book is to provide information and guidance on how some systems work and how they can be incorporated into the mental health and healthcare fields.

Sensory Systems

The sensory system chapter will explore how information gathered through the different senses converts into emotional, mental and psychological experiences, as well as memories. Therapists and practitioners will understand how the sensory system contributes to the designing of reality and emotional well-being through color, scent, sound, taste, and touch. The sensory systems consist of the following:

- Auditory Sensory
- Gustatory Sensory
- Olfactory Sensory
- Tactile Sensory
- Visual Sensory

The chapter also reviews the different senses and how each one contributes to the overall well-being of the individual. The understanding of the sensory system will allow both clinicians and practitioners to develop treatment plans that incorporate the natural senses in addition to traditional therapeutic practices.

Benefits of Aromatherapy

The olfactory system activates memories regardless of conscious awareness. Through the sense of smell, there is an instant connection to the environment and often become emotionally triggered before verbal processing can occur. (NIDCD 2017) The moment the molecules of specific odors enter through the nasal membrane, the brain begins the process of activating neurons within the brain. As neurons become activated, they trigger the release of different mood neurotransmitters like serotonin, endorphins, and norepinephrine. The activation of neurotransmitters can help relax or excite an individual. (Yun & Yazdanifard 2013)

The chapter on aromatherapy reviews the different benefits and limitations associated with aromatherapy, as well as the different classifications of fragrances and their therapeutic value. The chapter is a brief review and does not provide intensive material since aromatherapy is a system with multiple layers of information. However, the chapter is useful for the professionals who want a basic knowledge of oils and could benefit from some ideas on therapeutic applications.

Therapeutic Meditation

In the therapeutic meditation chapter, we will focus on the practical use of meditation for enhancing insight and creating new realities. Meditation can be used not only to obtain clarity but reduce stress and create new ways of thinking. Meditation is the essential **foundation for building intuitive skills** since it will help the person calm their thoughts, learn to listen and focus, which are crucial elements in receiving any sensory input. Meditation is a tool that is essential for both clinicians and clients.

Meditation allows the mind to relax and calm itself enough to be able to listen and gather information. A relaxed mind can easily access unconscious information. Within the mind, there are treasures, or as Jung described collective unconscious. (Semetsky 2005) Through meditation, the internal information can easily surface and provide conscious assistance on various levels for both the client and the therapist.

Meditation offers various benefits for both clinicians and clients. The benefits provided by meditation are presented in two categories: **Personal benefits for clinicians** and **practitioners,** and **Personal benefits for the client**:

Benefits of Meditation for Clinicians and Practitioners:

- Prevents burnout
- Increases energy
- Improves listening skills
- Reduces work-related stress
- Help fine-tune intuitive skills
- Improves empathy
- Maintains focus and mental clarity
- Has a grounding effect
- Inspires creative thinking
- Provides emotional balance
- Enhances problem-solving skills
- Helps reinforce professional boundaries

Benefits of Meditation for Clients:

- Increases focus
- Clears the mind
- Reduces overthinking
- Provides clients with personal insight
- develops healthy coping skills
- Useful for exploring internal conflicts
- Improves patience

- Trains them to access personal power
- Stress reduction
- Helpful in reformatting negative thought patterns
- Reduces Anxiety
- Improves moods
- Helps clients identify negative patterns
- Helps clients visualize new possibilities

Meditation is a valuable tool in helping clients relax and be less tense during therapy. For the therapist, meditation is a useful tool in maintaining intuitive skills sharp, in reducing work-related stress as well as preventing burn-out. A regular practice of 5 to 10 minutes will help maintain balance and overall well-being for both the clinician and the client.

Developing Intuitive Skills

The chapter on developing intuitive skills offers some basic exercises that are specifically designed to improve focus and fine-tune the intuition. However, before practicing any of the exercises, it is essential to practice meditation. As previously discussed, meditation is an essential component in developing skills and building a solid foundation for practicing intuitive techniques. Obtaining information with intuition is often not a difficult task, once the person learns the basics involved in intuitive development. Of course, there are some challenging aspects when gathering any data, which involves being able to know precisely how to interpret and understand the material revealed.

The information received is often in the form of symbols, color flashes, thoughts or feelings. Since information can be cryptic, many folks often dismiss what they get as nonsense. (Franquemont 2006) One of the main reasons intuition is often not taken seriously is because the things we see are usually brief and occur as quick flashes or appear as vague images that initially do not resemble anything in our reality. To fully understand intuitive experiences, individuals will need to practice regularly and learn to decipher personal symbolism.

The information throughout one's life is retained in the form of abbreviated messages and images because it keeps us from becoming overwhelmed by sensory overload. One way of learning how to interpret abbreviated or symbolic messages is to learn to master a few essential retrieval techniques. There is no practical way to learn every single intuitive technique, however, whatever is learned will require some patience and practice, but the results are quite useful. The intuitive techniques in this book are arranged systematically since the ability to learn one method will facilitate the ability to learn the proceeding methods. Some of the best types of techniques that help in retrieving information are:

1. **Meditation** - helps develop focus and maintain concentration
2. **Visualization** – is useful in increasing imagination and the ability to develop insight
3. **Psychometry**-the ability to obtain information from objects or people through touch.
4. **Aura Reading** – trains the eyes to notice subtle images and colors visually
5. **Chakra Scanning** – allows individuals to tap into the energy field and obtain information
6. **Retrocognition** – retrieves information from the past using hypnosis techniques
7. **Tarot Meditation** – using the tarot deck for guidance and obtaining insight through meditation
8. **Journaling** – keeping track of the progress made is one way to develop skills and review critical factors that made impede successful results.

The techniques mentioned above will be explored a bit more detail in the upcoming chapters. However, the information will only provide instructions for a few areas, since some techniques are more involved than the scope of this book allows, therefore further studying is strongly recommended.

Aura Reading

The process of reading a person's aura is useful in determining issues with health and emotional status. The aura consists of heat emission being generated from the body, which can be visually detected in various shades of color. The aura provides a unique blueprint of how energy is being dispersed throughout the body and understanding it can provide insight into the person's emotional state that might not always reveal itself verbally.

The chapter on aura reading will provide more information on how to read the aura and understand how different colors influence the overall well-being.

Therapeutic Chakra Techniques

The chapter on the Chakra system covers basic principles and several ways that the system can be a useful tool in the therapeutic session. The chakra system is a particularly simple system to use and does not require psychic abilities to understand or utilized. However, there are at least two levels of chakra systems mental health clinicians and healthcare practitioners can use depending on the kind of work they are doing and treatment goals. Chakra work can be placed into the following categories:

- **Level I** - consist of basic guided meditations, with energy balancing and affirmations. Clinicians guide the client through a series of exercises. There is no interpretation involved, and the focus is on creating balance and a general sense of well-being.
- **Level II** – this level is useful when a therapist needs to help a client get grounded; create overall balance regarding energy, focus, and emotional well-being. This level is present-oriented and does not require intensive work or knowledge of the chakra system. This level is used whenever the client feels stressed, emotionally overwhelmed or feeling physically exhausted. Also, both clinicians and practitioners can use these techniques on themselves to obtain balance, prevent work burn-out and reenergize themselves after a tiresome

work week.

- **Level III** – This level involves scanning, interpreting and healing through visualization. This level requires some knowledge of how the chakra system works since it uses a variety of techniques based on the different chakras throughout the system. In Level III, both therapists and practitioners can use scanning, visualizations and healing work. Also, this level is useful in healing regressive work.

Healing Regressive Techniques

Regressive work involves hypnotic techniques that allow the mind to ease into a state of relaxation and awareness. Through regressive procedures, a therapist can obtain insight into the origins of some beliefs, as well as the hidden aspects of emotional roadblocks. The methods used in regression can consist of the following:

- **Chakra memory retrieval** – allows the client to identify the origins of core issues using the chakra system as a blueprint
- **Regressive forgiveness healing** – this technique involves learning to let go and use forgiveness to ignite the process of healing.
- **Regressive Reformatting**– this method is useful in helping individuals come to terms with painful memories by creating new ways to view the past.

Tarot and Psychotherapy

A tarot deck is an excellent tool for getting intuitive information. The cards can allow individuals to tap into a realm of symbolism-rich with personal meaning. An individual does not need to be a master psychic to use symbolism therapeutically since definitions can be deciphered based on personal views of symbols. Both the clinician and client can view symbols and interpret them the same way one would view art in an art gallery. However, the more a clinician understands the tarot, the easier it becomes to use it.

The tarot deck can open a portal of personal information through meditation or by focusing on randomly selected cards. Whichever way, the tarot gets utilized in therapy will depend on the therapeutic needs of the client and the skill set of the person handling the deck.

It is essential to remember, that the interpretation of the tarot cards comes secondary to the therapeutic process. The cards are used to open the unconscious channels and engage the client in an intuitive dialogue that reduces the censorship often created by the over-analytical mind. (Semetsky)

The uses for the tarot in therapy include:

- Identifying archetypes that influence personal constructs
- Exploring ways to resolve conflicts, by reviewing alternatives
- A useful tool for creative visualization

In the therapeutic session, a therapist can use the deck very specifically to address issues that impact the client. According to a study completed by Semetsky (2005), the tarot deck can be used in several ways in psychotherapy; it can provide a therapist with some direction and insight into the client's hidden issues. Some of the ways the tarot is useful in therapy consist of the following:

1. Developing insight into presenting problems
2. Reviews hidden fears
3. Identifies unconscious motivations
4. Explores negative patterns
5. Presents unresolved issues
6. Reviews personal options
7. Uncovers conscious motivation
8. Reveals self-sabotaging patterns
9. Explores current attitude
10. Review general expectations

11. Explores potential outcomes

Intuitive techniques can be useful tools for clarifying issues, obtaining insight into problems and finding concrete solutions for healing and changing behavior patterns. Regardless of training or professional background, any clinician or practitioner can incorporate intuitive tools into their practice.

Using Hands-on Healing or Reiki in Therapy

This chapter was written primarily for the mental health professional or healthcare practitioner who has been trained in Reiki healing or other similar laying-of-hands or healing techniques.

Reiki or laying-on-of hand methods are useful when clients are going through extreme emotional periods that make it difficult to disclose verbally. It is a soothing and nurturing technique that provides comfort and a sense of safety whenever a person is feeling overwhelmed and emotionally vulnerable.

According to a case study on Reiki treatment done in Air War College by Lanoy (2015), it concluded that patients who got Reiki treatments often had positive medical outcomes since they were often more relaxed and less stressful.

There are a variety of ways that Reiki can be used, for instance:

1. In meditation circles
2. Chakra balancing work
3. Regressive Healing techniques
4. Stress management
5. Emotional crisis

The combination of Reiki with other modalities is a natural union since it does not involve therapeutic analysis or intense clinical focus. It is useful in creating a comfortable and safe environment, primarily when working on emotionally charged topics. According to studies on the efficacy of hands-on -healing techniques, it revealed the techniques were effective in producing deep relaxation.

(MacIntyre, Hamilton, Fricke, Mehle & Michel 2008). The client's state of mind is an essential component in the process of healing. Therefore any technique that promotes calmness or stress-free mindset is valuable even if it is the result of a placebo effect. (De la Fuente-Fernandez, Lidstone & Stoessl 2006)

Chapter Summary

It is crucial that clinicians avoid worrying about having perfect intuitive skills; the fact is that intuition is only a part of the therapeutic package and is something used to enhance the quality of the sessions. Intuition is not a precise science, and neither is psychotherapy. However, the intentions of the clinician will carry them way beyond their professional tools, as well as how they "treat" their clients. Treating clients with respect, kindness, and compassion is half the battle, as well as maintaining healthy boundaries to retain professional integrity. When it comes to using intuitive techniques, professionals need to remember, clients, **are not in therapy for psychic readings**

Chapter VI
The Sensory System

We process our world through the senses. - Ro

The Sensory Connection

The senses connect us to the environment through various forms of stimulation, while our perception allows us to interpret the neurological responses as information. (Privitera 2018) To fully understand how the senses work imagine hearing a knock on the door and immediately the mind reacts conjuring up the thought of an unexpected visitor. Alternatively, imagine smelling something burning, and the brain will interpret the scent as danger or awareness that the food on the stove has burned.

Perception and the Senses

Once environmentally **triggered stimuli** gain entrance through the various portals of the **sensory system** it activates the **process of transduction**, which allows the brain to initiate the **communication between the neurons**. The **neurons trigger** chemically induced **reactions,** which in turn helps the proper mental or physical responses to occur. According to McLeod 2008, there are two ways information is processed, once it is received: which are known as **Bottom-up** and **Top-down**. Described as the following:

- **Bottom-up processing** refers to a **data-driven process**, where information is gathered through activation of five sensory systems.

- **Top-down processing** refers to information obtained by **pattern recognition**.

The two systems of processing information provide two types of experiences for individuals, one that **ignites instinctive responses** and the other **rational thoughts**.

The Science of the Sensory System

The human nervous system is a **receiving** and **processing** station of environmental signals or better yet information. Throughout the body, there are varies receiving nerve stations referred to as the **sensory organs** which become stimulated by the different vibrations created by elements like sound, weather, touch, light or smell. Each element creates patterns known as wavelengths that transmit signals to the brain. (The Visible Body 2017) The ability to react to external stimulation triggered by the environment is a term known as **sensation**. (Privitera)

Our body is continuously collecting data in the form of stimulation that converts into from one form of energy, into a form that the brain can translate, this process is known as **transduction**. (Privitera)

The five Sensory Systems

Before developing or enhancing intuitive abilities, it is vital to understand how the natural senses help connect individuals to their world. In examining the five-sensory system, which consists of, **sight, sound, scent, touch,** and **taste** one can learn how the senses influence perception and collect memory building data.

Keep in mind, that not all the senses are equally engaged in collecting information since not every sensory organ functions at full capacity. For instance, if a person has poor vision, the eyes can still gather visual data, but the information will be slightly impaired when compared to someone who has 20-20 vision.

Everyone has a different view of the world, which is influenced by the limits of his or her physical make-up. However, though there may be slight impairments, the sensory system collects data that influences the person's reality. The ability to gather data begins before the formation of logical thought or analytical awareness. Immediately upon entry into the world outside the warm and protective interior of the womb, the senses become overwhelmed with the task of gathering information.

At birth, the first breath tells the brain to respond to the change of environment. On the onset of birth, the body begins to gather information that prepares it to adjust, learn and grow; And all of this is possible because of the senses. The human developmental stages, specifically infancy begin not only with movement but with the innate ability to navigate the world through the sensory system. Pediatricians assess a child's developmental progress by testing how well the vision, hearing, reflexes and muscle movement is developing. Infants begin their developmental journey by exploring the surrounding environment through their senses and by touching everything. (Cherry 2017) The process of exploring the environment through the tactile system, explains why infants have to touch everything and how visually impaired individuals navigate their surroundings through touch.

Our understanding of concepts will vary, as well as the sensory develop and become neurologically more responsive to the environment. Individuals develop their senses differently due to variables, such as physical make-up, gender, age or even personal experiences. For instance, a young child will tend to be more sensitive to pungent tasting food; a blind person might have exceptional hearing or a woman with PMS might be more sensitive to intense odors.

We receive **sensory information** in many forms and degrees since the senses are environmental antennas continually gathering data. Unfortunately; we often overlook the variety of ways in which we collect information. There is a tendency to think that we only gather sensory information through the sense of sight or hearing, when in fact data is being continuously processed through taste, touch, and scents and transferred into our brain for processing.

For instance, the sense of taste is one of the less viewed as relating to intuitive or unconscious exploratory work. However, taste linked to the olfactory sense will trigger the memory of locked events; examples of intuitive work that involves the olfactory or gustation are the consumption of hallucinogens used in shamanic work to induce psychic experiences. Ingesting hallucinogenic substances have been used to trigger the unconscious mind in ways that go beyond the limitations of consciousness. (Metzner 1998)

The intuitive and rational mind work continually at retrieving and interpreting the data collected through the senses. (Dane et al.) The experiences encountered by each of the five senses transfers data that trigger chemical reactions within the brain. The chemical reactions in the brain create changes that either produces a state of calmness, excitement or the status quo. In addition to changes in the brain, the different reactions create **chemical anchors** that become associated with mental and emotional experiences that influence the formation of memories.

The senses are the windows to our inner and outer world that enable us to tune into the changes that surround us. There are endless combinations of information we can receive through our senses. Understanding how the sensory system works is vital in developing intuitive and awareness skills. Many individuals get stuck trying to develop skills through senses that are not in tune with their natural style of tapping into their surroundings; which is why reviewing how the senses function beyond their typical manner is valuable.

The senses provide the tools for gathering environmental information and as well as being a data bank of sensory induced memories. Through the sensory system, one can detect inconsistencies and access the databank of memories that help in the assimilation and adaptation to environmental changes. The senses are **quicker at detecting** environmental changes than the rational mind, especially when it comes to dangerous situations. For example, our sense of touch alerts the brain the second we encounter something dangerously hot or sharp; or when we see a fast-moving vehicle, our brain quickly knows we are in danger. The senses do more than gather information; they provide the brain with a processing system that relies on the quickness of intuitive understanding. (Dane et al.)

Sensory Access

The sensory system influences both the process of learning and the accumulation of experiences and memories, Through the "five senses," one can tap into the unconscious mind to retrieve emotional memories that may be difficult to access through talk therapy. Clinicians can develop ways to incorporate the sensory system in their work using a variety of techniques and tools such as guided meditations, intuitive methods, and sensory stimulation. Also, clinicians can teach clients how to tap into their sensory system to increase awareness and personal insight.

To help clinicians understand the benefits of using the sensory system the following areas have been highlighted:

Auditory – Through sounds and oral instructions: a clinician can help a client using **verbal cues** during talk therapy, vibrational sound treatments, and guided meditations

Visual – Tools such as art therapy, tarot decks, and guided visualization techniques help individuals access hidden emotions. Art is valuable in helping clients express themselves whenever they cannot emotionally disclose or verbalize feelings

Olfactory – Aromatherapy can be a useful tool that can induce a calmer state or help a client recall repressed memories. Through the use of scent, a therapist can help clients recreate old memories, as well as regain control when experiencing anxiety.

Touch – Physical touch is therapeutic for clients with a history of abuse or who have health issues. However, direct Touch techniques are for professionals who have a massage or medical licensed due to ethical and legal components.

Gustatory – Taste is a useful sense for the nutritional therapist who works with clients struggling with eating disorders. When activating the taste buds, a clinician can trace the link between comfort foods and eating habits. Also, taste can activate memories and help clients trace hidden patterns and emotions.

The material above has provided a brief outline of exactly how the senses are useful tools for therapy. This chapter will continue to explore how the sensory system helps shape patterns and behaviors, as well as how it can be used specifically in treatment.

The Role of the Senses

Problem-solving is a two-part process that includes thinking and knowing. The individual processes their environment both using two systems, systematic problem-solving through **rational thinking** and the quick processing system of **intuitive knowing**. (Dane et al.)

Physical vs. Intuitive experiences

The five senses provide individuals with direct experiences to the realities that help them grow and learn within the environment. The sensory system consists of a series of communication channels that deliver data to the brain, so individuals can learn how to adjust and thrive as humans. There are direct and indirect methods of obtaining environmental information.

The **direct signals** are processed physically through the various pathways of our five physical senses. Then there are the **indirect signals** that are also processed through our physical senses but tap into a deep level of our unconscious awareness. Within our unconscious realm, we are continuously dealing with a variety of collected memories, impressions, and emotional history. To access unconscious reality, a person requires tools that go beyond the conscious thinking process, which is where intuitive skills become valuable in retrieving hidden information and memories.

Sensory Systems and Intuitive Techniques

The five senses are great tools for working with clients in therapy. There are a variety of different sensory systems both clinicians and practitioners can incorporate into their therapeutic practice. In this section, various sensory systems are reviewed separately to help individuals understand how each category can be used and potentially combined with therapeutic work. Not all intuitive techniques are going to be mentioned, since not every method is appropriate for every type of practice.

There are five sensory systems listed according to categories, as well as the associated intuitive techniques and how to use them therapeutically.

I. The Auditory Sensory
The science of sound

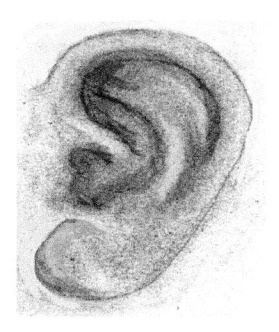

Sounds permit the brain to obtain information from the surrounding environment through a collection of vibrational sound waves produced by moving objects. (Hear it 2013) Each sound builds a bridge to the world, by triggering chemical reactions set off by the different vibrations generated by sound frequencies. Our brain receives and interprets the messages created by the various chemical reactions. Each chemical reaction produces a unique imprint into our memory bank and gets filed away by different **emotional associations** or anchors. Due to our emotional associations, whenever we hear certain songs or sounds, it can bring on a flood of emotions and reactions.

The sense of sound is always working, even when we do not recognize a sound or barely even hear it. The frequencies can be so low that an individual might not consciously detect any data transmitted through sound. The fact is if there is oxygen in a room, particles are moving and creating slight vibrations, with varying sound levels. The auditory system works 24/7, even while a person is sleeping there is continuous auditory stimulation. (Flexer 2017)

In therapy, sound can produce different mental states, from calmness to anxiety. The right sounds in a therapeutic room can invoke a sense of peace and a willingness to participate in therapy. A therapist or practitioner can use a variety of auditory tools in their therapy sessions to help their clients relax and get in touch with repressed memories.

Auditory Senses: Intuitive and Healing Systems

Sounds can have a calming and relaxing impact on therapy and can be used to induce a calm state of mind. Different types of sounds or music are useful in creating an ideal setting for meditation, using relaxation techniques or doing regressive work.

The following utilizes a range of verbal instructions and sounds that engage the auditory senses.

- **Guided Meditations** – there are a variety of meditations that can help both clinicians and clients. Meditation is useful in developing better concentration, mental clarity and enhance intuitive abilities. Meditation is an adaptable tool that can combine well with a full range of healing systems.
- **Healing Regressions** – this involves hypnotic suggestions that can help clients trace old patterns, uncover emotional issues and recall memories from past events.
- **Chanting** – is useful in creating a trance-like state and helping individuals deepen their focus and ability to relax.
- **Drumming** – steady drumbeats are used to produce a hypnotic state for shamanic work and soul retrieval.
- **Vibrational Sound** – works very much like drumming in the sense that it will induce a relaxed state and can be used to get a client into a hypnotic trance.

Sounds or music can be combined with therapy to help individuals who struggle with verbalizing feelings or general communication. (MacWilliam n.d.) In general, the auditory system can be useful in creating a relaxing environment which can help individuals participate with more ease in therapy.

II. The Gustatory Sensory
The Science of Taste

The chemicals in food stimulate the gustatory cells on the tongue, allowing the receptors to activate reactions in the brain. The brain then sorts through its collection of interrelated gestation archives and proceeds to alert the memory department to react according to its taste history. (The Visible Body) In essence, the ability to distinguish different flavors depending on the brain's ability to sort through a collection of taste samples gathered throughout the years. The brain attempts to match a particular flavor from memory, which allows the individual to respond favorably or not based on a recorded taste history.

The sense of taste is not always utilized in therapy unless the therapist is dealing with a client who has an eating disorder. The connection most folks have to the sense of "taste" is very similar to that of the olfactory senses since, without the sense of smell, it is difficult to have distinctive taste buds.

Through our sense of taste, we do create food associations. Taste consists of more than just taste buds; it is connected ability to smell odors and retain memories of scent. Through the taste buds, people recall events that provide both nurturing and emotional feelings. (Hatfield 2005)

Many memories get created through events that include the consumptions of food or beverages. Events such as a child's first birthday, first school lunch, and even funerals can create associations with food. Even individuals that play significant roles in our lives can leave behind a memory linked to food; for instance, a person can recall the scent of their grandmother's fresh apple pie or the first time they tasted airplane food, and so forth. Also, there are negative memories associated with food, which contribute to eating disorders, food addictions, and poor diets that impact many individuals.

The gustatory system can be used by clinicians who work with individuals struggling with food addictions or eating disorders. Using a combination of memory retrieval and reviewing food associations a clinician can uncover the client's food issues and negative associations.

Taste Sense: Intuitive and Healing Systems

The gustatory system is useful when working with individuals with eating disorders or food addiction. Therapists working with clients who have food or body issues can benefit from techniques that allow them to achieve some control. The following are some examples of useful techniques:

- ❖ **Guided Meditations** – Meditation can be used to help individuals relaxed when it comes to food and their relationship to it.
- ❖ **Hypnotherapy** – through trance work, a therapist can access the core of issues related to food and body image
- ❖ **Visualizations** – images can be used to help a client visualize a new and healthy relationship with food, as well as their body image.

The Gustatory sense is useful in helping individuals with food-related issues since it helps uncover food associations and the emotional connections. In general, the sense of taste can also be used intentionally to invoke specific memories.

III. The Olfactory Sensor
The Science of Scent

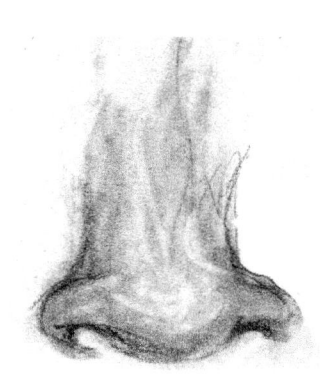

The ability to detect odor allows the body to determine changes when there are no visual or auditory cues to alert us. Odors will enable the olfactory senses to know where there is a fire or if the food a person is about to eat is edible. Our sense of smell activates memories cues in addition to visual cues. The olfactory system allows the brain to recreate emotional states associated with past events, which means individuals can revive old feelings by merely being exposed to a scent. Molecules of odors and fragrances travel through our nasal passages, activating the olfactory sensory neurons. As the molecules enter the nasal pathway, the receptors are activated releasing chemicals that signal the brain for it to respond with proper identification of the scent. (NIH 2017)

The sense of smell not only detects different odors, but it can awaken our healing abilities, trigger emotional responses, as well as the recollection of past events. Through the olfactory sense, one can heal physically, emotionally and spiritually. Aromatherapy is an example of how fragrances work to relax, soothe and even energizes our bodies and improve emotions. (Harding 2008)

Smelling Sense: Intuitive and Healing Systems

The healing qualities of the olfactory senses can be activated and used to create a different emotional state of mind. There are a few healing tools that can be used with the olfactory system that includes the following:

- ❖ **Aromatherapy** – there are many excellent oils available for aromatherapy. However, some oils require diluting before using. Oils are used in various ways, such as in baths, applied to the skin, burned in diffusers to scent rooms, or used in making candles or incense.
- ❖ **Chakra therapy** - chakra work can be combined with aromatherapy to improve energy and balance the system.
- ❖ **Regressive Therapy** –aromatherapy can be combined with regressive techniques induce a trance and relaxation.

Though aromatherapy is pleasant and comfortable to use, clinicians need to have some basic knowledge about the healing properties of oil and how to use them since some oils can be harsh on the skin. (Harding) Essential oils can be used in many ways and definitely, can change the energy of a room making it comfortable and peaceful, however, always check with the clients since some individuals may have allergic and emotional reactions.

IV. The Tactile Sensory
The Science of Touch

The tactile sensory pertains to the ability to gather information through touching surfaces, detecting environmental changes like temperature, pressure, vibrations and reacting to chemicals that enter through the skin surface. Also, the tactile senses allow individuals to pick up data on a person's physical well-being through the energy centers known as the chakra system. Through touch not only can one detect health problems, emotional issues, but also tap into traumas that trap themselves within the body. (Miller)

Tactile Senses: Intuitive and Healing Systems

Though many techniques related to the tactile system are physical, direct touching is not always necessary. Several techniques can be used with the tactile system, which includes **both direct** and **indirect touch.** The direct touching methods are for individuals licensed in the medical or physical professions, such as medical practitioners, physical therapist or massage therapists. The indirect touching methods can be used by clinicians who provide mental health services or provide alternative healing treatments. The healing systems consist of the following:

Direct Touch

- ❖ Deep tissue massage – this type of massage not only works the muscles, but it also helps unblock energy.
- ❖ Acupressure – this technique works like acupuncture since it focuses on various pressure points, but it does not require needles.

Indirect Touch

- ❖ Psychometry- This technique allows a therapist to pick up energy imprints left on items owned by the client without the need to touch directly.
- ❖ Chakra Scanning – This method combines Psychometry with aura reading, which provides information in the form of images, emotional impressions or intuitive understanding.
- ❖ Reiki Treatment – This treatment uses the body as a source of healing that can be used for balancing the energy centers and promoting overall balance.

Most of the above techniques do require further exploration and may not be appropriate for every client. Before using any of the mentioned techniques, a therapist or practitioner should get additional training aside from reading books.

V. The Visual Sensory
The Science of Sight

Varying degrees of light are detected by retina in the eye, stimulating the central receptors known as rods or cones, creating electrical signals. The eyes transmit the electrical waves through the optic nerve, sending messages to the brain, which then translates the signals into visual imagery. (Than 2016)

The sense of vision is one of the most acknowledge of the senses, next to auditory senses since it is accessed the most for gathering information. It connects us to shapes, colors, symbols, and general information. It helps us categorize and define our world into fragments that are easier to interpret and remember by the brain. Each color or shape stimulates the brain in varies ways that can invoke a variety of sensations and experiences. Visual images are collected that contribute to memories and emotional anchors that create both positive and negative associations. When using the visual senses, what an individual is doing is allowing their mind to look for patterns that produce intuitive impressions.

Visual Sense: Intuitive and Healing Systems

The visual senses provide various opportunities to explore different intuitive realms, both with the physical sight and the inner vision. With the physical sight, a therapist can use techniques that help develop concentration, and useful in tarot and aura readings. The inner vision is useful for visualizations and meditation techniques. The following are examples of methods that require the use of visual senses for accessing information:

- ❖ **Visualizations** – the techniques for visualization are like meditation; the main difference is that in meditation, information is obtained by listening. while in visualization, the reality is designed using visual cues that represent the things that require modification
- ❖ **Tarot Meditations –** A therapist can use the tarot deck to help guide themselves or their client through a vision quest for inner discoveries
- ❖ **Aura Readings** – A therapist train their eyes to look for energy discrepancies, to help them review the body for energy drains.
- ❖ **Chakra Scanning** – a therapist or client can scan the chakra system for visual impressions. The images revealed during scanning can consist of details or symbolic colors or shapes

The visual sense can be a powerful tool in visually reviewing the chakra system, creating new realities through visualization, gather information through aura readings and chakra scanning. However, it is essential to learn about the different associations linked to varying types of visual cues. Every individual has their connection to different symbols, colors, and objects in everyday life

Working with Sensory Systems

The five sensory system will allow a person to gain access to a realm that logic and rational thinking can sometimes overlook or overanalyze. In combining natural talents with therapeutic training, the clinician will develop a holistic practice that helps enhance the lives of their clients. The senses not only work with the brain to gather information they also contribute to the interpreting process and work in combination with other senses as well.

According to Munger (2007), objects that create motion impact not only the auditory system but also the visual senses. Also the olfactory works with the gustatory system in other to provide humans with functional taste buds. Without a scent, food would be tasteless, which means, a person would not be able to detect when food is spoiled.

Clinicians have the option of being able to use a combination of techniques that include the different senses during sessions. For instance, a therapist can do a therapeutic session using regressive techniques on the chakra system, while using music and aromatherapy at the same time. The regressive techniques will help trace old patterns within specific chakras, while the aromatherapy can create a sense of safety and trust during the session. The music can also create a relaxed atmosphere conducive to any type of trance, meditative or visualization work. Also, scents can induce calmness, combined with relaxing music, which will help a client feel less vulnerable while doing emotional healing through the chakra system.

Personalized Sensory Systems

Understanding the sensory system will open the doors to improving intuition. Before moving forward with the sensory system, it would be useful to find out which one of the senses is the most developed and which ones are the least dominant. There is an exercise to help sort out which of the five senses are the most active. The task is not designed to determine if an individual is psychic or not, but merely to help evaluate which of their five senses is the most developed and dominant in their daily function. The following exercise is useful for both the therapist and client to use.

Personal Sensory Exercise

Let us begin. Turn off all electrical equipment and phone. Find a quiet place, with minimal distraction. Get a comfortable chair to sit on and allow the body to unwind.

Take the time to relax and breathe in slowly. Focus on relaxing the body, beginning with the face. Imagine the breath as a light breeze that calms and soothes, as it enters the body.

Feel a gentle breeze touch the forehead lightly**, relaxing all the tissues** in that area. Breathe in, and let the breath move slowly down into the chest, stomach, and legs, making everything feel light and comfortable. Slowly allow the breath to work its way down into the shoulders and then travel all the way down, making the entire body feel relaxed and calm.

Take another deep breath, again feel the breath traveling down the back of the spine. Breathe deeply. **Feel the breath** in the spine spreading out throughout the body. Allow the spine to stretch, downward towards the ground. Let the breath travel down the spine and into the ground. Slowly the breath works its way down the spine into the center of the earth and becomes connected to the core.

Now **imagine the body** standing outside in an open field. Notice the vivid colors in the surrounding area. Become aware of the **color** of the sky, then the ground, and the river. Next, notice some birds flying around. **See** them flying above.

As the birds fly, listen closely and **hear them.** Imagine different birds are around. Sparrows are flying and chirping, hear the pigeons and the seagulls all engaged in their choirs of sound. Then, everything becomes quiet, and each bird vanishes out of view and into the distance. Enjoy the silence for a moment.

Then notice and **listen** to the breeze moving through the trees that surround the area. Listen to the noise the wind makes as it runs through the trees and leaves. Focus on the sound of the wind moving the leaves on the branches. Take a moment and enjoy the sensation of listening.

Next look at the river nearby and **listen to** the water racing downstream. **Notice the** water splashing against the rocks. While focusing on the water, in the distance, a small boat is approaching packed with people dancing to music. As the boat gets closer, **the sound** of music and **people laughing increases,** allowing the sound to be clear. For a moment, enjoy the music and witnessing people enjoying themselves. Watch the boat slowly move away. Witness the sound of people laughing and music gently fading away.

Next, walk close to the water. Put one foot in the river and **feel the water** wetting the toes. Slowly slip into the shallow end of the river. Let the refreshing water hit the warm skin. Enjoy the sensation of invigorating water cooling the pores for a few moments. Step out of the water **and allow the warm sun to dry the wet skin.**

As the skin dries, stand quietly, and notice the vivid green grass. **Feel** the ground underneath the bare feet and notice **how the** grass feels. The grass is soft and also smells fresh. Once again touch the grass, this time use the hands to feel the grass. Enjoy the sensation.

Notice a bunch of bright flowers on the ground. There are some lavender flowers, roses, and hyacinth. **Smell the** flowers. Pay attention to the different fragrances, some scents are mild, and some are strong. Enjoy the different fragrances for a few minutes, then let the scent fade away as the focus turns to the different plants

Look around and notice the various plants around. There are small plants with berries; some are red and some blue. The colors are bright, and the sizes vary. Some plants are larger and more colorful than others and contain different fruits. Grab some fruit and take a few bites. Some fruits are sweeter than others, but they are all tasty. Now enjoy the taste of each fruit for a few moments.

Quietly stop and stand for a moment. Observe the surroundings one more time. Go back to the spot where the journey started. Look around once more. Think about the entire experienced and try to recall as much as possible. Take a few moments to think and then begin to end the journey.

Let the body return to the room. Grab a seat and imagine the ground beneath the feet once more. Focus on the core of the Earth, and the connection that was established earlier with the energy from the body. Imagine the connection from the body being disconnected and returning to its original state. Slowly become aware of the physical body, beginning with the feet and gradually working up the legs, pelvic area, tummy, and chest. Slowly move the focus towards the chin, neck, and face area. Prepare to awaken slowly. Allow the muscles to wake up on the count of three: One. Two. Three.

Once done, answer the following questions briefly. Avoid censorship, since the exercise is designed to measure the strengths and weak areas, and not performance.

> 1. Write down the experienced, making sure to Include all details regardless of how insignificant it may seem.
>
> 2. What type of colors appeared? Was there more than one color?
>
> 3. What type of objects appeared? Describe the different items as best as possible.
>
> 4. What kind of textures were detected? Is it possible to describe the different sensations?
>
> 5. What kind of fragrances were detected? Were they sweet or strong?
>
> 6. What were the different sounds heard? Were the sounds very low or loud? Briefly describe the types of sounds heard.

Review the notes. What seems to be the most significant points in the sensory exercise? What were some of the most comfortable things to recall? Was the experience more than expected? In which areas where there struggles? Keep in mind; it does not matter how much or how little was obtained from the task since the exercise was designed to determine which one of the senses was the easiest to use.

Chapter Summary

The main reason this chapter was included, is to help individuals understand that a lot of the intuitive impressions obtain are not necessarily a mystical and mysterious occurrence, but rather a natural component of being human. Before the ability to analyze and thinking logically developed, the senses were gathering data and storing memories in the brain.

The sensory system allows the body and mind to adapt and learn how to make sense of its surrounding with the information it gathers. For instance, the olfactory and gustatory system allows for the detection of rotten food, and the auditory system contributes to the ability to learn language through sound distinction. While the visual sensory allows the eyes to store visual files of familiar faces, places, and things that contribute to a personalized memory bank. Moreover, the sense of touch provides a sense of reality and formed bonds with others by activating the neurotransmitter oxytocin.

The senses fed the intuitive channels with information that allowed the individual to understand their world before learning any language and rational problem-solving skills. According to an article on childhood development, Piaget described the **pre-operational cognitive stage** as **the intuitive stage**, since young children appeared to be confident of their knowledge and understanding of their environment. (Oswalt).

It is vital to remember, that regardless of how rational a person may be, the intuition is the foundation of human development, therefore never disregard its value. Studies have indicated that both intuition and analytical thinking systems play a vital role in how individuals learn and understand their reality. Intuitive thinking is regarded as fast, automatic and based on the unconscious holistic processing of the environment; while rational thinking is slow and deliberate, using verbal and conscious processing of the environment. (Witteman, Bercken, Claes, & Godoy 2009)

Chapter VII
The Benefits of Aromatherapy

I always remember my childhood house with happy memories. There was a beautiful garden, and outside my bedroom window was a jasmine vine which would open in the evenings, giving off a divine scent. - Carolina Herrera

Aromatherapy

This chapter is devoted to the benefits of aromatherapy as an adjunct to mental health and healthcare modalities. Essential oils serve as a valuable component in enhancing moods from uplifting to relaxing. (Fonareva 2013). Essential oils have been used in a variety of ways from medicinal to aromatic room fresheners, as well as worn as fragrance and even used in cooking. Though oils can be relatively simple to use and fairly safe, it is advisable to learn the fundamentals since the right oil can make a huge difference in the health of an individual.

Aromatherapy Background

Aromatherapy has a long history of being used by a variety of individuals from laymen to medical practitioners. According to studies (Fonareva) aromatherapy has been used throughout history to treat a variety of conditions in diverse populations, from infant care to adult health care. Various types of fragrances have been part of many cultures throughout history beginning as far back as Ancient Egypt, India, Pre-Empire China, and the Middle East. Fragrances such as patchouli, musk, and myrrh were valuable commodities, especially since decent hygiene was a problem. Scents were not only used to conceal odors but to enchant potential lovers, reduce headaches, calm anxiety and even induce sleep and relaxation.

Studies have demonstrated the benefits of aromatherapy in the management of different types of moods. For instance, symptoms of agitation can be reduced with the application of lavender on the skin according to medical studies. (Snow, Hovanec, & Brandt 2004) Aromatherapy is an excellent adjunct to therapeutic modalities since it is cost-effective, has a low incidence of side-effects and fairly easy to use.

Fragrances and the Olfactory system

Different senses create different experiences that are stored in the memory system and are retrieved whenever the memory is triggered. The olfactory system has its separate memory system that can be activated by fragrances. (Yun & Yazdanifard)

The olfactory system works in conjunction with the gustatory system, which allows most scents to convert into flavors, as well as retain imprints within the memory system. During the process of smelling any odor, neurotransmitters are activated creating different emotional responses. The neurotransmitters such as serotonin, endorphins, and norepinephrine assist in the activation of different emotional responses, which is how certain scents can be relaxing while others can be energizing. (NIH)

The different odors create a link between the environment and the person's neurons, creating potential lifetime imprints. Odors can trigger memories that can reactivate a variety of emotions and moods that can be stimulating, irritating as well as soothing. (Jackson 2011)

Therapeutic Benefits of Fragrances

According to studies, fragrances have the potential to enhance the quality of health. (Jo, Rodiek, Fujii, Miyazaki, Park, Ann, 2013). Fragrances can improve moods which allow individuals to develop the proper attitude required for healing both mentally and physically. Individuals who have a positive outlook can maintain the motivation required for any health regimen. Meanwhile, individuals who become depressed or anxious due to illness do not recover as quickly as individuals who maintain a positive attitude and adhere to recommendations. (Jo et al.)

The research proposes that scents have a way of invoking feelings based on associations to specific events that trigger strong emotional responses. (Yun & Yazdanifard) Whenever a particular scent is used, it can invoke intense feelings of pleasure or pain, depending on the initial experience associated with the scent. For instance, the fresh scent of honeysuckle flowers can activate a sense of well-being that automatically helps an individual recall a specific event that took place during the blooming of those flowers. Meantime, the same scent can create an adverse reaction to someone who has allergies or a negative association with the scent

When it comes to scent, many folks are familiar with the cosmetic value of oils in the form of perfume or scented candles. However, oils have a wide range of useful applications that are worth noting; some benefits include the following:

1. Meditation enhancer – creates the ideal mood for meditation
2. Reduce Anxiety – helps clients become calmer and less anxious
3. Sleep enhancer – quiets the overactive mind and stabilizes erratic energy
4. Natural energy stimulator – provides a natural energy booster
5. Enhances Libido – improves mood
6. Great for calming nerves – relaxes and calms erratic energy
7. Mental clarifier – helps calm the mind and clear mind fog
8. Stress reducer – calms the nerves, reduces stress-related tension
9. Improves Focus – clears the mind enough to improve focus
10. Mood enhancer – helps in uplifting the mood
11. For balancing the Chakra system – great for balancing general energy
12. Useful in reducing side-effects – some drugs can make clients anxious, some oils are very calming

The different ways to use fragrance will vary depending on the needs of the client and the therapeutic goals. (D'Angelo) Not every client will benefit from the same type of fragrance since everyone has a different association with scents. Before selecting fragrances, it is essential to determine if the client is comfortable with the idea of using aromatherapy and if they have any allergies or negative associations to certain scents.

Limitations

Though many individuals enjoy different types of fragrances, enjoying them is not enough to use them in therapy. The wrong oil selection can induce relaxation during a period when more energy is needed or increase energy during a time when the individual needs sleep. For instance, an oil scent like lavender is very pleasing, but its calming effect is not very useful for someone with a low sex drive or who needs to stay awake to write a term paper. However, lavender is a great choice for helping individuals relax who are too anxious to sleep or focus. (Lillehei 2014).

Aromatherapy is not a panacea that cures all ailments. Like every form of therapy, aromatherapy does have its list of limits that both clinicians and practitioners should be aware of before implementing any regimen that includes essential oils, which consists of the following:

1. Strong fragrances are **not often allowed** in professional settings.
2. Incense or candles may not be allowed in some agencies due to **potential fires**.
3. Some clients are extremely **allergic to certain scents.**
4. Certain scents can **trigger unwanted memories.**
5. Fragrances have different **effects on brain chemistry**, which can trigger excitement or melancholy in some individuals.
6. Some oils **can irritate** the skin when used directly. (irritation is different from allergies)
7. Certain oils **can cause photosensitivity** when used in direct sunlight.
8. Some oils can **activate emotional triggers** clients might not be ready to handle.

9. Some individuals have a **limited understanding** of aromatherapy.

10. There are oil brands that **can be too expensive** to use.

11. Some individuals **dislike strong scents.**

12. Many oils work due to the **placebo effect**. (Snow, Hovanec, & Brandt)

Though it is prudent to have a working knowledge of aromatherapy before integrating it into any form of therapy, some basic guidelines can still allow even the novice to take advantage of the benefits of scents. The key to using aromatherapy or alternative techniques, in general, is to understand the underlying needs and respect the limitations of the client. (D'Angelo, 2002).

Therapeutic Application of Aromatherapy

The natural tendency of aromatherapy to improve and enhance moods makes it an ideal tool for therapeutic work. Both mental health clinicians and healthcare practitioners can take advantage of the therapeutic benefits of aromatherapy. The different applications of aromatherapy will vary depending on the nature of the session and the treatment goals. Specific ways of using aromatherapy consist of the following:

1. **Visualization** – fragrance is ideal for creating the mindset and the proper mood required for visualization. The professional can select oils that help activate desired thoughts and moods that enhance visualization exercises.

2. **Meditation** – scents are great for creating calmness and relaxation. Some oils reduce anxiety and promote a calm state of mind which enhances the meditation experience. (Redstone 2015)

3. **Regressive healing** – oils can be used to invoke memories and unlock repressed emotions. The olfactory system has an independent memory system, which can become activated by the right scent. (Sapp 2016)

4. **Chakra Balance** – The right oils can stimulate, balance and restore the energy levels within the chakra system. (Judith)

5. **Creating Safe space** – many oils have a calming effect that helps clients relax and feel less vulnerable during sessions.

6. **Mood stabilizer** – for clients who are experiencing specific moods due to a crisis or emotional event, certain oils will assist in helping them calm down and feel less anxious or emotional. (Yun & Yazdanifard)

The different methods of utilizing fragrance will depend on what is appropriate within the working environment since some places forbid the use of incense or candles and diffusers.

Ways to Use Aromatherapy

There are many ways to use fragrances in therapy, and it is useful to review the options available before investing money in expensive oils. The number of oils and oil blends available for therapeutic use is practically endless, which is why it is vital to review the various methods and healing categories to ensure optimal usage. According to studies, oils can help calm, energize or balance emotional states. (Butje, Repede, & Shattell, 2008). Oils can be in the following way:

1. Incense – Available in stick, cone or powder form
2. Diffuser – oils are dispersed into the environment using an oil diffuser
3. Candles – scented candles can be burned during meditation, bodywork or in an office
4. Fragrance – oils can be used as a perfume
5. Sprays – used as an air freshener whenever candles or incense are not allowed
6. Bath salts – used in baths
7. Sachets – can be carried in a pouched

8. Potpourri – ideal for rooms when candles or incense are not allowed

During therapy sessions, some of the best ways to use oils would be in the form of incense, oil diffuser, candle or potpourri. In the event candles or incense are not allowed, merely smelling the oils can do the trick. A few drops of oil on the wrist or sniffing it directly from the bottle will enable a person to enjoy the therapeutic benefits. However, when allowed, it is ideal to use candles, incense, or a diffuser, since they produce the most delightful lingering aroma which both the client and the professional can enjoy.

Categories of Fragrances

Different types of odors can trigger a range of moods by activating the neurons that trigger the production of neurotransmitters such as serotonin, endorphins, and norepinephrine. (NIH) Depending on the type of fragrance selected, scents can enhance, energize or induce relaxation. Most fragrances fall into different categories depending on their chemical make-up. The mood classifies the oil categories they invoke, such as calming, energizing, or harmonizing. Before selecting an oil, it helps to know which type of mood the client is in or which mood they wish to enhance.

The key to using fragrances is to select scents that stimulate the appropriate neurons to trigger desired moods. To induce the proper mood, the clinician or practitioner needs to know about the different oil classifications and their therapeutic values. There is a myriad of oils and brands to select from which can be confusing. Some oils have multiple functions and are useful for a variety of moods. For instance, bergamot is an oil that is useful for both calming and motivating an individual. However, to keep things simple, this book will only cover some common essential oils that are easy to find and not extremely expensive. Examples of groups of oils that impact specific attributes are the following:

Aromatherapy Oils

Attributes	Oil Selection
Awareness:	Basil, Bergamot, Grapefruit, Peppermint, Rosemary
Calming:	Lavender, Bergamot, Orange, Sandalwood, Ylang-Ylang, Melissa
Focus:	Lemon, Basil, Lemongrass, Rosemary, Frankincense, Chamomile
Confidence:	Cypress, Fennel, Ginger, Grapefruit, Jasmine, Orange., Pine
Decisiveness:	Basil, Cedarwood, Frankincense, Ylang-Ylang, Lime
Energy:	Bergamot, Lemon, Frankincense, Rose, Jasmine, Cloves
Harmony:	Orange, Rose, Jasmine, Ginger, Cloves, Geranium
Peace:	Chamomile, Neroli, Juniper, Frankincense, Yarrow
Insight:	Cypress, Clary Sage, Jasmine, Cloves, Sandalwood
Joyfulness:	Sandalwood, Frankincense, Lemon, Orange, Bergamot
Motivation	Bay, Bergamot, Frankincense, Lemon, Grapefruit, Jasmine
Relaxing:	Lavender, Geranium, Clary Sage, Sandalwood
Self-Esteem:	Jasmine, Geranium, Cedarwood, Sandalwood

The oils selected are merely samples of what is available and were chosen due to their interchangeable uses. For instance, an oil like bergamot can be used in meditation to increase energy, or in visualization to improve focus. The idea when selecting oils is to pick ones that can have multiple benefits as well as pleasing to the senses. Most oils can be used daily, therefore, select one that reflects the individual personality and has a pleasant effect on the individual.

Chapter Summary

The primary goal of this chapter was to provide a general overview of aromatherapy and its therapeutic benefits for mental health and healthcare treatment. This chapter was not designed to provide a substitute for proper training or give any individual the impression that they can randomly select oils without some comprehensive knowledge. In reviewing the information, the professional can learn to develop some understanding of the various practical applications of aromatherapy in treatment; however, individuals interested in implementing aromatherapy in their practice need to seek further training.

Chapter VIII
Utilizing Meditation in Therapy

To accomplish great things we must first dream, then visualize, then plan... believe... act! -
Alfred A. Montapert

Why Meditation?

Meditation is excellent for silencing the mind, reducing excess chatter and regular worries. (Cahn & Polich) As the mind is silenced, one can listen to the inner voice of reason and find the tools for resolving many personal conflicts. However, to obtain ongoing benefits, it is helpful to practice meditation as regular as possible and to maintain a comfortable and relaxing approach.

In this chapter, various meditation methods are presented to assist mental health clinicians and healthcare practitioners in the process of selecting the most useful techniques for their therapeutic practice. This chapter will not only provide information on how to use meditation but also includes a sample meditation that can be used or modified for both the professionals treating clients or the client in therapeutic care.

Meditation and Western Culture

Meditation gained mainstream acceptance in the Western world because of Transcendental Meditation ™ being introduced by Guru Maharishi Mahesh in the 60's. Transcendental Meditation initially was a widespread practice that promised enormous benefits. (Dienstmann 2015) Initially, to learn TM, it required being taught by a trained TM teacher, which meant that the independent learner and financially disadvantaged individual were excluded from learning meditation. The fact that TM required an instructor to teach it kept it from spreading even further.

According to Boals, (1978), the role of meditation in Western culture became normalized due to having the reputation of being a useful relaxation tool that reduces tension and stress. Studies have demonstrated that meditation helps patients suffering from anxiety and panic disorders by reducing symptoms and providing long-term self-regulation without medical intervention. (Miller, Fletcher & Kabat-Zinn 1995)

Meditation has a valuable role in therapy since it provides more than just methods for relaxing and reducing stress, it creates an opportunity for developing insight and more profound understanding of oneself (Kutz, Borysenko, and Benson 1985)

The Value of Meditation in Therapy.

Meditation is an excellent tool for mental health clinicians and health-care practitioners to use as a complementary technique with conventional therapy. Though meditation has become a personal tool for many individuals, its many benefits are overlooked and under-utilized. Meditation can be the key to altering negative thought patterns and helping individuals develop valuable insight. (Rea 2016)

Meditation has a lot of potential benefits that both the therapist and the client can use in therapy that go beyond relaxation. Meditation is fairly easy to use, cost-effective and time efficient. Meditation can be used both in individual and group therapy. However, it is essential to recognize that meditative, intuitive or alternative techniques are beneficial adjuncts to therapy, but they are not recommended as replacements for therapy. Conventional mental health therapy is designed to treat specific symptoms and problems that meditation does not. (Goleman 1976) Though meditation has therapeutic limits, the benefits it provides goes beyond reducing stress-related symptoms and creating calmness.

The different styles in which meditation can become useful will vary and often rely on the personal needs and diagnosis of the client. Before embarking on the task of using meditation techniques, clinicians need to be aware of the client's limitations since some techniques can create more confusion than relief. (Corton 1985) For instance, clients with trust issues, or attention deficit disorders might struggle initially with meditation and become more emotionally unstable. (NCCIH 2016) Therefore, before introducing meditation or any intuitive technique into therapy, the clinician needs to have established a solid and trusting therapeutic alliance with the client.

How Meditation Works

According to research, meditation activates specific areas of the brain that impact reactions to stress and adverse events in our lives. (Cahn & Polich, 2006; Davidson et al., 2003). Studies in Neuroplasticity indicate that regular meditation practice can contribute to reparative changes in the brain's structure and its function. (Davidson et al.) Different regions of the brain are engaged and activated depending on the type of physical activity, such as exercising, working or resting. The brain also reacts to activities design to help recharge, recuperate during rest and replenish nutrients.

Meditation is an activity the brain recognizes as one that will relax and de-stress it due to mechanics involved. When it comes to relaxing, one region of the brain that impacts that ability is the amygdala, located in the limbic system. The amygdala is responsible for controlling our ability to handle fear, and emotional reactions, as well as memory recall. Studies have indicated that individuals who practiced meditation regularly showed changes in amygdala activity, which impacted stress levels and overall emotional well-being. (Leung, Lau, Chan, Wong, Fung, & Lee 2017). According to another study, the amygdala also helps overall moods, in addition to reducing the impact of stress. (Way, Creswell, Eisenberger & Lieberman 2010) (See chart one below)

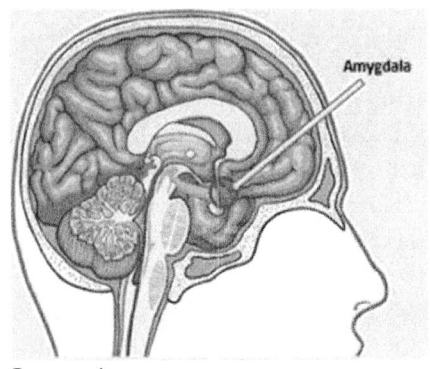

Image 1

    In short, meditation works by stabilizing the activities within the amygdala region of the brain that control emotional reactions and memory recall. Specifically, how meditation works in stabilizing the amygdala is by using breathing exercises and creating mental emotions that creates new emotional imprints through synaptic engagement. In other words, both the breath and the mental imagery activate the release of neurotransmitters within the brain, unlocking potential reactions within the amygdala. (Taren et al. 2015).

    According to research techniques like mindfulness meditation reduce stress-induced cortisol levels, which contribute to overall relaxation and calmness. (Tang, Hölzel & Posner 2015) Meditation in many ways can imitate psychotropic medications, without the permanent side-effects. However, the efficacy of meditation is just like medications which can be impacted by low compliance, attitudes and it **does not cure all** problems.

Limits of Meditation Techniques

    Meditation is a useful adjunct to therapy, but it is not a panacea that fixes every problem. Though most reports are positive concerning the benefits of meditation, there have been some reports indicating meditation could worsen some psychiatric symptoms. (NCCIH) In general, most studies have indicated no adverse effects resulting from meditation; however, it does have some limits which strongly indicate that it cannot replace conventional therapy. (Goyal et al.) Before using meditation in therapy, clinicians need to be aware of the limitations as well as the benefits. The following are some questions to consider before using meditation with clients:

1. Is the client comfortable and willing to meditate?
2. Does the client have any physical or developmental limitations that can impede meditation?
3. What is the reason for using meditation?
4. How will it enhance therapy?
5. What type of meditation methods can the therapist utilize?
6. What does the therapist hope to achieve by using specific meditative techniques?
7. Does the client have the proper skill set to maintain focus?
8. Will the client be willing to continue to use meditation at home?
9. What are some of the potential struggles a client can face during meditation?
10. Is there a quiet place for group meditation?
11. Does the treatment facility approve of the use of meditation?

There are some definite limits associated with meditation that a therapist should be aware of before using meditation. (NCCIH) Keep in mind that in utilizing any technique in therapy, whether it is evidence-based or intuitive based, clinicians should be well-informed of the limits associated with selected methods. In the case of meditation, the limits are the following:

1. Introspective styles of meditation can trigger emotions that the client may not be able to cope with (NCCIH)
2. Client's ability to focus and concentrate can impede their performance
3. Their ability to trust meditation should not be disregarded or overlooked

4. The clinician's limited knowledge of technique can impair outcome. (NCCIH)
5. The duration of the method can be stressful
6. Distractions such as noise levels or lack of privacy can interfere with meditation
7. The vocal tempo of the person providing instructions can be distracting.
8. Physical health and being uncomfortable can be a distraction and unpleasant during meditations

The limitations listed do not necessarily mean that meditation should be avoided. The idea in exposing limitations is to make professionals aware that one technique does not fit every single situation, and due to the different needs of each client, meditations just like any other technique should be modified and adjusted accordingly. (D'Angelo)

Practical Uses of Meditation

Many individuals are aware that meditation is useful in reducing stress and a key component in spiritual practices, specifically in the Eastern cultures. However, there are many ways to use meditation which consist of the following area:

- **Anxiety** – a useful tool for **calming anxiety**
- **Depression** – helpful at obtaining **insight into depressive states** and triggers
- **Inner exploration** – an excellent **tool for introspective work**
- **Insight Enhancer** – **Develops insight** and increases awareness
- **Visualization** – helps clients visualize **new realities** and goals
- **Emotional balance** – helping in creating emotional balance by creating a **calming state**
- **Behavior modification** – a great way to teach clients how to visualize new **behavior patterns**

- **Mental training** – helps the individual develop **mindful thought patterns**
- **Chakra scanning** – an excellent **tool for exploring** the chakra system
- **Creating balance** – helpful in reducing stress and creating **overall harmony**
- **Developing concentration** – **improves focus** and concentration
- **Sobriety** – helpful in **exploring triggers** and using healthy coping tools
- **Stress management** -**reduces overthinking** and worries that contribute to stress
- **Relaxation tool-** valuable at helping the individual to **relax and get comfortable** in therapy

Clinicians and practitioners need to select meditation technique by the needs of each client and potential benefits (D'Angelo). Some clients will thrive and practice meditation at home, while some will become inpatient and prefer using other methods.

Meditation Guidelines

Learning to use different types of meditations will provide individuals with many tools for personal development in addition to relaxation (Cahn & Polich) According to research, meditation techniques can help clients gain control and be less reactive to stressful situations. (Tang et al.). Though meditation has concrete benefits, using it effectively in treatment can be tricky and unproductive, especially if a clinician lacks the complete understanding of the various meditation techniques and awareness that not all clients thrive equally. The **following guidelines** are recommended to help clinicians:

1. A therapist needs to **learn to meditate**. Knowing firsthand how meditation works will enable the therapist to assess the effectiveness of a technique

2. **Avoid unnecessary distractions**. Make sure all phones are off and that no one will interrupt.
3. A therapist needs to **establish a trusting relationship** before using meditation to uncover trauma or deep emotional issues.
4. When using meditation for introspective work, make sure the client has the **proper coping skills.**
5. When using introspective styles of meditation, make sure to provide some **closure at the end** of the session to ensure comfort and prevent the client from leaving feeling vulnerable.
6. **Less is more** with meditation. Keep the instructions simple and allow the client to get into the process gradually.
7. Use **simple language** when providing meditation instructions. Specific keywords and imagery can be distracting during meditation.
8. **Speak clearly and slowly** when guiding anyone through the process of meditation.
9. **Take time when** guiding anyone, but keep the **meditation brief**, since time is needed to process outcomes.
10. Make sure the **client is comfortable** with the idea of using meditation.

Meditation should be a pleasant experience and not one which produces stress due to performance anxiety. There is no need to meditate like Tibetan monks for hours to obtain any benefits. A person can meditate 5 to 10 minutes every other day and achieve excellent results. Individuals should allow themselves to enjoy the process and not worry about "getting" results since meditation is about relaxing the mind and letting it ease into a natural state.

Preparing for Meditation

Getting ready for meditation can be a simple or an elaborate process depending on the individual needs and personal preferences. To maximize the benefits of meditation, the individual should consider the following suggestions:

1. **Create a safe space** – when working with individuals in therapy, the clinician and practitioner should create an environment that helps the **client feel safe** and **comfortable** with the process of meditation. It is essential to be mindful that many clients have trust issues and might struggle to relax initially.
2. **Phones off** – Make sure that all phones are off and that **space is a quiet** as possible
3. **Do not disturb** – Keep a sign on the door to **avoid individuals from coming in** and disturbing the meditation. Make sure that another staff is aware that there is a meditative session and that they should avoid knocking on the door.
4. **Have a box of tissue** – On occasions meditation **exercises can trigger emotional responses.** Therefore it is helpful to have tissues available.
5. **Be mindful** – Clinicians and practitioners should be **aware of any physical signs** that indicate discomfort or emotional distress. However, it does not mean that the meditation should be interrupted, but it does mean that the client might need to process the experience.
6. **Reduce excess noise** – make sure that any equipment used during meditation is tested and works correctly beforehand, to avoid any unnecessary technical snafus during the session.
7. **Music selection** – the music or sound selection should compliment the meditation both in duration and style. Avoid using meditation sounds or music that end before the meditation is complete since it can be distracting. Also, avoid music tempos that are faster

than the verbal instructions since it can impede one's focus and the ability to relax.
8. **Technique selection** – make sure to select a meditation that is comfortable and easy for the client to follow. Avoid techniques that create emotional discomfort too early in therapy since clients need time to establish a trusting bond.
9. **Be patient** – Initially, meditation may seem to produce minimal results. Keep in mind if an individual has never meditated or has trust issues, they will struggle to meditate. Do not force the practice if it becomes a struggle and stress inducing. Proper preparation helps enhance the quality and benefits of meditation. The practice of meditation offers more than just relaxation and reducing stress levels. In creating the right mindset before meditating, individuals can maximize their experience. Things such as noise, distractions or being uncomfortable can influence the process of meditation. Therefore, it is ideal to take time to create the right environment. (Creath 2004)

Different Types of Meditation Techniques

If one looks online for a listing of the different types of meditations, one can become more confused than enlightening by the variety of choices. As mentioned before, not every client will use meditation, and not every meditation is useful for therapy. (Dienstmann) A few things both clinicians and practitioners need to review before selecting any meditation technique when working with clients or personal self-care will consist of the following:

1. **Meditation skills**: Has the individual ever meditated?
2. **Available time:** How much time is available for meditation.
3. **Purpose of use**: What will the meditate accomplish in therapy

Knowing the different functions of the available types of meditations will enable clinicians and practitioners to incorporate meditation into their work with clients. In addition to learning about the different functions of meditation, both clinicians and practitioners should try a few meditation techniques so they can understand what a client might experience. Keep in mind not all types of meditations are for every kind of client. Some clients will have a difficult time relaxing and listening to the clinician's voice, while others might not maintain focus.

This section will review different styles of meditations as well as discuss compatible systems of therapy. Do keep in mind, once a person is entirely comfortable with the idea of using meditation in therapy, the therapist can modify the techniques accordingly. The information is mutable and adaptable to the individual style of each therapist or practitioner working with patients.

Meditations on Traditions

This section on meditation is divided into two main categories, to simplify the process of exploring the different meditative techniques. The different meditation sections consist of two primary philosophical systems, selected due to their cultural values; The sections consist of Eastern and Western spiritual traditions

In each category contain subgroups that highlight essential information on the different meditative styles. Each meditation is discussed briefly to provide enough information so individuals can make informed choices. (Dienstmann)

Eastern Spiritual Meditations Traditions

- ➢ Buddhist Meditations traditions
- ➢ Hindu Meditations
- ➢ Yoga Meditations
- ➢ Chinese meditations

Buddhist Meditation Traditions

Buddhism is a spiritual practice that does not include the worshipping of a God, but a path of personal development. The path of Buddhism allows an individual to evolve through personal insight and awareness. The tools for achieving awareness and insight consist of a series of practices that include mindfulness breathing, meditation, and contemplation. (Dienstmann) Under Buddhist traditions we have the following types of meditations:

Zazen (Zen meditation): Rooted in Chinese Buddhism (Ch'an) and consist of straightforward practices. The Zazen practices consist of the following two methods:

- ❖ Focus on the breath gently moving in and out the nose, while counting from 1 to 10 and then backward. One should repeat this process several times

- ❖ **Shikantaze** – this practice involves merely sitting in silence without thoughts. Practicing what is known as **Effortless Presence**.

Vipassana: Is a term in Pali, which means insight. This meditation focuses on mindfulness breathing and developing clear insight. The meditation consists of the following:

- **Posture**: Sit in a position that allows the spine to be upright but relaxed. Sitting with the legs crossed is preferred, but one can sit on a chair provided the back be kept straight. Prepare to close the eyes and begin the meditation.

- **Breath**: Focus on the breathing and notice the stomach rising and falling. Notice the circular motion of the breath, as it naturally occurs.

- **Attention**: Continue focusing on the breath. Any thought that arrives let it go. Let the breath travel from the belly and upwards towards the nose. Moreover, release. Repeat this process several times.

Vipassana meditation allows a person to learn how to control random thoughts by focusing on their breathing. As thoughts arrive, they are released immediately.

Mindfulness Meditation: This type of meditation is also based on the Buddhist practice known as Vipassana. Mindfulness practice involves focusing on the moment, acceptance and paying attention to the different feelings, thoughts, and emotions that occur without judgment. The key is to witness the experience without adding any additional judgment or critical thoughts. This meditation is the type that helps in developing concentration and focus.

Metta Meditation - Loving Kindness: Metta is a Pali term that refers to the **four sublime states**, benevolence, loving-kindness, goodwill, and peace, which are generated through meditation. In Metta meditation, the focus is on directing the energy of the four sublime states to the following:

- Oneself
- A Good friend
- A Neutral person
- A Difficult individual.

Send the energy to all four mentioned above and then devote energy it to the universe.

Metta meditation is designed to help individuals struggling with **self-love**, **forgiveness** and **connecting** with others. The goal of the meditation is about developing compassion, joy and overall well-being.

Hindu Meditation Traditions

The meditations mentioned under the heading of Hindu, have philosophies and principles that are based on Hindu ideologies but can also be found in other traditions like Buddhism, Taoism, among several. (Dienstmann) The meditations focus on vibrational energy created through sounds, energy enhancing, and mindfulness exercises. There is a combination of vibrational chanting, gongs, and yoga breathing techniques.

Mantra Meditation – Sacred words of power are used to increase vibrations related to the sound and significance of specific words. The use of mantras requires precise pronunciations to activate their vibrations. Since proper pronunciation is essential in the use of mantras, spiritual teachers are responsible for assigning mantras to their students. However, one can use the Sanskrit word "OM" as a general mantra, during meditation. Mantras are ideal for creating a sense of calmness and a peaceful mindset by reducing fluctuating thoughts and erratic emotional states.

Atma Vichara "I Am" – Meditation

The "I am, "meditation is also known as Self-Inquiry, which is a translation of the Sanskrit word, **Atma Vichara**. This type of meditation seeks to attain awareness of one's true nature. It is designed to help us find ourselves. The meditation focuses on a **personal self-inquiry**, by simply asking, "Who am I"? Using the question of "who am I," it is essential to feel feelings without judgment or associating it with anything specific. The meditation is designed to allow a person to witness without trying to adjust the thoughts or emotions. The "I" is the focus and the subject of meditation.

TM (Transcendental Meditation): This form of meditation was introduced to Westerners in the late 60's and early 70's by Guru Maharishi Mahesh Yogi. TM meditation consists of practicing mantras for 15 to 20 minutes per day. This meditation is typically taught only by trained TM practitioner and not often available for free.

Yoga Meditation Traditions

Several types of meditations fall under the Yoga Meditation traditions, which are part of a variety of practices performed under the yoga principles. The goal of Yoga Meditation is aimed at achieving spiritual purification and inner wisdom. Classical yoga follows several rules of conduct that include different physical postures, breathing exercises and contemplative forms of meditation. (Dienstmann) For simplicity in therapeutic work, clinicians should focus one following the meditative practices since they are easier to incorporate into therapy.

Third Eye – The third eye meditation focuses on the center of the forehead, known as Ajna in the Chakra system. The general goal is to **internally focus** using the 3rd eye as a guide while keeping the physical eyes closed. The 3rd eye is used as an internal guide to help the individual during visualizations and guided meditations.

Chakra Meditation – There are various meditation styles which can be used to create balance and healing using the seven-chakra system. Clinicians can focus on specific chakras to work through some issues that a client may be facing. Also, there are a variety of visualization techniques used on the individual chakras, as well as the whole system to release blockages, improve balance and overall well-being. (Sherwood 1988)

Gazing Meditation - (Trataka) this is a simple process which involves focusing one's attention on a flame or symbol (yantras) while the eyes are open. This meditation is helpful for individuals struggling with focus and concentration. It is an effortless technique that does not require much training to do. (Goel N.d.)

Sound Meditation – (Nada **Yoga**) A soothing and straightforward process which involves the use of calming music to induce a relaxed state of mind. According to studies, sound creates vibrations that help individuals enter a trance-like state. (Wong, Chang, Chee & Dayou) Sound, whether chanting, music or nature sounds are known to have a therapeutic impact on individuals. When it comes to sound meditation, the person is encouraged to sit in silence and focus only on the music with as little thoughts as possible. The music plays while the individual listens, quietly breathing as they focus on the vibrations of the music and nothing else. The goal is for the person to develop the ability to focus on their internal sounds and let go of all noises and thoughts that linger in the background. Eventually, the person can concentrate on **para nada**, which is sound without vibration, thus allowing for the manifestation of "OM."

Chinese Meditation Traditions

The meditations listed under Chinese traditions focus on systems influenced by the philosophy of Taoism also known as Daoism. (Dienstmann) The philosophy behind Tao is about living in harmony with nature. Meditation is used to transform the body and mind to achieve unity and balance with the inner and outer surrounding energies. In Chinese Meditations, the focus is on creating a harmonious balance between the spirit, body, and mind.

Taoist Meditations 道

The following five Taoist meditations focus on helping individuals direct their attention to specific goals. (Dienstmann) Each meditation has its purpose and function designed to improve the state of being by invoking internal harmony.

坐忘 Zuo Wang – Emptiness Meditation: This meditation is designed to help one **forget** and **let go** of harmful thoughts or feelings. The experience of letting go helps a person find inner quietness and peace by obtaining emptiness. The emptiness meditation is a useful technique for **reducing excessive thoughts or feelings** that are unproductive by training the mind to let go.

存想 Cun Xiang – Visualization: This type of meditation uses a visualization method designed to focus on spiritual entities, heavenly spirits and other celestial energies outside and inside the body. This technique is suitable for individuals seeking **to improve their spiritual connections**

庄子 Zhuangzi – Breathing Meditation: Breathing allows energy to circulate throughout the body, producing unity of mind and energy. This breathing meditation focuses on the breath and becoming aware of its rhythm as it moves gradually throughout the body. Let the breath soften until it becomes a gentle force. The breathing method is useful in calming down an anxious and excited mind, by breathing deeply and slowly the breath, until one achieves a sense of calmness.

內觀 Neiguan- Inner Vision: During this meditation, one is taking an internal view of one's inner world, body, mind, and soul.

Through the internal world, one obtains knowledge of how to create balance and harmony. The inner vision meditation is useful in maintaining the proper focus and insight as well as acquiring general balance.

內丹 Neidan – Internal Alchemy: In this meditation, energy is cultivated to generate maximum health and overall vitality. The energy is used to sharpen the mind, improve the movement of chi throughout the body as well as energize the spirit.

The concept of the Internal Alchemical consist of the **philosophy of the Three Treasures**: 精 Jing for the body, 氣 Qi the energy force, and 神 Shen the spirit; The three treasures are used as a focal point for creating balance and harmony. The internal alchemy is a transformative meditation that utilizes the breath, visualization and movement exercises like Qi Qong. The alchemy meditation is used to create a sense of peace and harmony.

Western Spiritual Meditations

✝ ☪ ✡

The Western types of meditations are suited for individuals who follow Western Spiritual traditions. (Dienstmann) The Western spirituality serves Individuals inclined towards a belief system that embraces spiritual practices outlined by the Abrahamic religious branches of Judaism, Islam or Christianity. Unlike Eastern traditions, the Western system has fewer variations in their meditative practices. Naturally, every religion expresses their contemplative techniques slightly different. For many, the contemplative work creates merely a mindset that allows the individual to feel spiritually connected, which can be useful for individuals who may feel alone in the world.

Contemplative Reading: This type of practice involves reading selected text from sacred scriptures such as the Torah, the Koran or the Bible and contemplating on their spiritual messages.

Contemplative Prayer: sacred words or passages are said in silent prayer

The Western Spiritual traditions of meditating are ideal for individuals looking to reconnect with their spirituality and develop a spiritual practice. Clinicians who use Western spiritual traditions do not need to be practicing religiously, but they do need to know some basics to accommodate clients **who need to explore their spirituality.** When it comes to spirituality, the role of the therapist would merely be one of support and active listening.

General Guided Meditations

We have explored briefly some of the more popular meditative techniques that are available from both the Eastern and Western perspective. In this section, the focus is on practicing meditative techniques and seeing how they work based on the first-hand experience. In practicing meditation, a clinician can determine which meditation to use during sessions with clients.

The selected meditation groups are simple and basic in their format, and they also do not require any commitments to spiritual practices to obtain concrete benefits. When it comes to using meditation in therapeutic work, simplicity and adaptability is often the key

Guided Meditations: These types of meditations allow participants to obtain guidance through instructions provided by a teacher or therapist. The advantage of using guided meditations in therapy is that a clinician can design the meditation according to the specific needs of the client. A tailored made meditation means that a person will engage in an introspective and contemplative exercise that targets personal goals. The benefits are limitless since a therapist can target emotional as well as behavior issues depending on the details included in the meditation. Guided meditations can be designed to match the client's ability to focus and modified with each stage of improvement. (Dienstmann) Guided meditations can be enjoyed with or without music, eyes open or closed, laying down or sitting. The formats used will depend on the goal of each meditation.

Visualizations: A clinician can use visualization to help clients reconstruct their thinking patterns and belief system, by using visual cues that trigger new thoughts and feelings. Visualization techniques engage **all the senses** in the creation of new realities. According to studies, visualization provides clients with an opportunity to create the proper mindset needed to achieve healthy results. (Rennie, Uskul, Adams, & Appleton 2012)   Meditation provides an opportunity to observe, while visualization offers an opportunity to create changes by designing new realities. The key focus of meditation is **contemplation** and for visualization is **envisioned.** Clinicians can use both meditation and visualization to help clients observe their reality and then envision new possibilities with new outcomes.

Affirmations: The goals of affirmations are to help reinforce new beliefs by creating new scripts. A person can use affirmations to create new thoughts that encourage new behaviors. According to studies, affirmations can help alter personal scripts that influence an individual's ability to recover from illness. (Falk et al. 2014) Affirmations can be included in visualization work, to reinforce intentions.

Practical Meditation Application

Several forms of meditation techniques have been reviewed to provide general information on what is available. However, many techniques have limitations due to the amount of time required for practice and the training involved in learning. When it comes to selecting meditative tools, the clinicians should select techniques that are simple for their clients to follow and learn, as well as use at home.

Meditations are designed to develop the ability to think, maintain focus, as well as improve intuitive skills, which in turn benefits most individuals. However, not all meditations are appropriate for all individuals or conditions, which can make it difficult at times to select the most efficient meditative technique. There are **two quick reference charts** available to help facilitate the selection of meditations. One chart consists of **practical applications** which include the following:

- ❖ Presenting Problems
- ❖ Meditative techniques
- ❖ Complementary treatment modalities

❖ Treatment goal

The second chart consists of meditative themes, designed to help the individual clinician or practitioner select appropriate imagery and techniques that provide desired outcomes. The **meditative theme chart** consist of the following areas:

❖ Meditation theme
❖ Purpose
❖ Targeted issue

Each chart provides materials that can be used by both mental health professionals and alternative healthcare practitioners. The charts allow professionals of different backgrounds to easily review at a glance which meditative technique is the most appropriate for the needs of their clients.

The **Practical Application Chart** is useful in selecting the most appropriate meditative technique for the presenting issues in therapy. The type of meditation use will depend a great deal on the treatment modalities practiced by the individual clinician, as well as the treatment goals. Practice each meditation as often as needed.

Practical Applications Chart

Presenting Problems	Meditation Techniques	Complementary Treatment Modalities	Treatment Goals
Anger	Metta Meditation; 4th chakra visualization	Cognitive Therapy; CBT, Holistic coaching	Letting go, & forgiveness
Anxiety	Mindfulness meditation, breathing (**Zhuangzi**), Gazing meditation (Trataka)	Cognitive therapy; CBT, Client-centered;	Relaxation techniques, reducing negative thoughts
Addiction	Mindfulness meditation, Sound meditation, 2nd chakra visualization	CBT, Cognitive therapy (treatment program recommended	Identify triggers & develop sober coping skills
Career frustration	Guided meditation, 3rd & 5th Chakra visualization,	Holistic coaching; client-centered	Explore options & creative goal setting
Communication problems	3rd, 4th & 5th Chakra visualization,	Client-centered therapy; Holistic coaching	improves communication skills & boundary setting
Creative blocks	3rd & 5th chakra visualization, guided meditations	Client-centered therapy; Holistic Coaching	Unblock chakras & unlock the creative flow
Coping issues	visualization, 1st chakra, Grounding	Client-centered therapy; Holistic	Develop creative problem-solving

		meditation	Coaching	skills
Depression		Metta meditation, 2nd & 3rd Chakra, Emptiness meditation **(Zuowang),**	Psychoanalysis; Cognitive therapy; Client-centered therapy; Holistic Coaching	Improve energy flow, find the joy in life
Frustration		Guided meditation, mindfulness meditation. Vipassana	Client-centered therapy; Holistic Coaching	Explore healthy ways to cope, learn to let go
Family conflicts		Metta meditation; mindfulness meditation, fourth & 5th chakra	Psychoanalysis; Cognitive therapy; Client-centered therapy; Holistic coaching	Communication, boundary setting, & forgiveness
General fear		3rd chakra visualization, Zazen Meditation, guided meditation, visualization	Psychoanalysis; CBT, CT Client-centered, Holistic Coaching	Explore core issues, develop healthy coping
Grief		Metta meditation, mindfulness meditation, Guided Meditation. Prayer contemplation	Cognitive therapy, Client-centered, Holistic Coaching Spiritual counseling	The goal is to provide sacred space
Health issues		Inner Vision **(Neiguan),** Vipassana meditation, chakra balance, Grounding meditation	Client-centered therapy, Holistic Coaching	Improve attitude about health, follow-up on care

Identity issues	**Atma Vichara** meditation, **Vipassana** meditation,	Psychoanalysis, Humanity counseling, Client-centered, Gestalt therapy	Self-acceptance, self-love
Loneliness	guided meditation, 4th & 5th chakra meditation **Atma Vichara** meditation	Client-centered therapy, Holistic Coaching	Learn to trust, to accept & give love
Mood Swings	Emptiness meditation, mindfulness meditation,	CBT, Cognitive therapy (treatment recommended if severe)	Assist in maintaining stability
Marital Conflicts	2nd, fourth & 5th chakra, Metta meditation, Mindfulness meditation	Client-centered therapy; Holistic coaching	Improve communication, let go of anger and develop trust
Poor Concentration	1st & 6th chakra, Vipassana meditation, Trataka meditation,	Client-centered therapy; Holistic coaching	Improve focus and concentration
Relationship Problems	Metta meditation, Mindfulness meditation, 4th & 5th Chakra	Client-centered therapy; Holistic coaching	Learn to accept & give love, improve communication
Self-doubt	Guided meditation **Atma Vichara** meditation, Vipassana meditation,	Client-centered therapy; Holistic coaching	Increase confidence and self-esteem

	mindfulness meditation,		
Sexual issues	2nd & 4th Chakra, Metta meditation, Guided meditation, **Atma Vichara** meditation,	Psychoanalysis; cognitive therapy; Client-centered therapy; Holistic coaching	explore sexual issues, & develop healthy attitudes regarding sex
Stress-related issues	Chakra balance, Vipassana meditation, Trataka meditation, grounding meditation	Cognitive therapy; CBT, Client-centered; holistic coaching	Develop healthy coping skills and promote energy balance
Work issues	3rd & 5th Chakra meditations, visualization	client-centered therapy; holistic coaching	Develop coping and communication skills
Unhealthy Coping Skills	**Atma Vichara** meditation, Vipassana meditation, Mindfulness meditation,	Psychoanalysis; cognitive therapy; client-centered therapy; holistic coaching	Learn healthy ways to cope and let go of old patterns

The practical application chart provided suggestions to help the clinician or practitioner in developing a game plan based on the presenting issues of their clients. However, each meditation is flexible and can be personalized with specific themes that are tailored to the issues faced by the clients. The following **Meditation Theme Chart** provides a few sample ideas for the types of themes that can be used during meditation.

Meditation Themes Chart

Theme	Purpose	Targeted Issues
General Meditation	This meditation is basic & with no frills.	Suitable for beginners, ongoing practice
Grounding Meditation	To increase focus, stabilize erratic energy, & reduce stress symptoms	Anxiety, stress and poor concentration
Energy Balance	To improve balance, & stabilize energy	Fatigue. Low-energy, as well as stress and anxiety
Flower Bud Opening	To open the 3rd eye	problem-solving, clear thinking
Candle focus (use an actual candle)	enhances focus, a substitute for vocal instructions	Poor concentration, focus, & mental fatigue
Butterfly meditation	for improving visualization skills	creative blocks & emotional stagnation
Picture Meditation (use favorite images)	Enhances focus, concentration, & creativity	When struggling with creativity
Water meditation (use water images or a glass of water)	Improves awareness; for letting go of old memories	For resentment, anger, & frustration
Tunnel	Excellent for	To reduce

Meditation	visualizing goals	stagnation & improve problem-solving skills
Camp Fire (sit in front of a campfire or candle)	Useful for emotional and transformative exercise.	For anger and obsessive thoughts

Meditation Recommendations

Anyone using meditation should practice as much as needed since it will help improve confidence and develop the required skills. The key to practicing is to allow oneself to fine-tune the skills and enable the opportunity to obtain concrete results and productive outcomes. Once the therapist or the client finishes the meditation practice, they should write down whatever thoughts or feelings they experienced.

Hands-on Practice

The following meditation designed to help the clinician or practitioner practice meditation themselves before trying it on the clients. The meditation includes a combination of a natural breathing and visualization techniques. Individuals should allow plenty of time to do the exercise and practice as often as needed. Before providing meditative guidance to any client, the clinician or practitioner should practice the meditation a few times until they are adequately proficient and comfortable in using the technique. The meditative experience will allow the clinicians to understand the underlying benefits and limits involved in meditation, as well as ensure that the exercise is simple to follow and produces beneficial results. Remember, with the following exercise; the primary focus is to follow the breath and allow oneself to relax as much as possible.

Practice Exercise - General Grounding Meditation

Find a comfortable place to sit. Breathe in slowly. Relax the body, beginning with the face, imagine the breath representing a light calming breeze. Let the breeze slowly cover the body, and gently creating a feeling of calmness and ease. Slowly allow the gentle breeze to work its way down the body and gently begin to relax every muscle and tissue. Allow the breeze gradually to turn into oxygen. Let the oxygen gently move down through the tiny muscles of the **forehead,** making it feel light and calm. Continue to slowly let the oxygen travel down the **entire head, face, chin,** and **neck,** releasing all tension and tightness. Become aware of **the shoulders** and slowly allow them to become very calm and comfortable.

Once more breathe in deeply and let the breath travel downwards into the chest area. Feel **the lungs** become full with each deep breath. Relax. Continue to allow the air to go down, again relaxing all the tiny tissues in the lung area. Feel the lungs become light and free of tension. Let the oxygen move down **the arms,** relaxing every muscle and nerve-ending. Feel, the oxygen moving through the **finger**tips and relaxing them. Once more breathe in deeply, let the air travel into the **belly**, filling it gently. As the stomach takes in the oxygen, feel all the stress and tension push out upon exhaling.

Again, continue to breathe slowly and gently. Let the breath work its way down from the belly to the **pelvic** area. As the breath fills the pelvic area, feel all the tightness pushing away. Slowly breathe out, allowing all tension to be released. Continue breathing and let the oxygen travel down into the thighs allowing them to become very light and very relaxed. Once more, allow the breath to work its way down to the calves and feet. Feel all the tightness in the legs vanish as the breath fills every tiny muscle.

Now, notice how relaxed and calm the entire body feels. The whole body is feeling comfortable and very peaceful. Allow the mind to focus on the spine. Imagine the oxygen traveling smoothly and gently down the spine and moving down the legs and feet. Envision the oxygen branching out from under the feet. Breathe deeply and visualize the breath working its way down and out of the feet and into the floor beneath. See the roots grow deeper and deeper into the ground. The roots are now deep inside the earth and inside the core. As the roots connect to the center of the earth's core, let energy from the earth's core work its way upward. Bring the energy up the roots. Move the earth's energy upward until it comes up from the ground and up through the feet.

As the energy from the earth travels up the feet, feel the power working its way upwards. Feel the immense energy surging up the legs, thighs and pelvic area. Feel the lower body slowly become recharged and revived with every bit of power moving throughout both legs. Once more, continue to let the energy travel upward into the belly area and slowly into the chest. Feel the surge of power energizing the entire body. Let the power spread from the chest to the hands and fingertips. Feel the body become strong and filled with energy.

Continue to let the energy travel through the arms and up to the shoulders and neck area. Feel the intense surge filling the body. Allow the energy to work its way up the neck and face, making it feel alive and alert. Let the energy cover the head. Take a few moments and enjoy the energy. Feel the entire body become alive and alert. Feel the body become stronger and filled with tons of fantastic energy. Enjoy the power vibrating throughout the entire body, reviving and charging it.

Sit for a moment and enjoy the sensation of being filled with the earth's vibrating energy. The energy is calm. Then become aware of the head and slowly let the energy descent down the face. Let the energy work its way down slowly and gently. As it works its way down, continue to feel the presence of the earth's power. Continue to let the energy move slowly downward, towards the chest and stomach. Steadily, the energy moves down, pass down the pelvic area, thighs, and calves.

Feel the energy gradually travel down the entire body until it goes out from the feet. Let the power go back down through the roots until it returns to the core. Allow the energy to return to the center of the earth, and slowly disconnect from it. Bring the focus back up the roots and the feet. Become aware of how the feet and calves feel. Allow them to awaken gradually. Continue to focus on the legs and thighs, again allowing them to wake up slowly.

Breathe nice and slowly, pay attention to the belly and chest area as they gradually energize. Once more focus on the neck and face muscles as they become alert and refreshed. Feel the entire body become awake and filled with energy. On the count of three, begin to open both eyes slowly. One. Two. Three.

Meditation Tips

The meditation should be repeated a few times and documented on each occasion. The written information should be used to see if there were any changes, struggles or improvements.

The meditation should be repeated a few times until it feels natural and comfortable. Many techniques do improve with practice. However, do keep in mind the anxiety of performing can block one's ability to get results.

Chapter Summary

This chapter intended to introduce a wide range of meditation options. Effective outcomes mediation is based on consistency and not necessarily on the duration. Many meditative practices are specifically designed for the busy lifestyle and doable almost anywhere. Overall, only the individual can decide what routine works best for their needs and personal preferences. When it comes to meditation, the idea is to find a safe way to relax, while learning to be mindful. (Sayers, Creswell, & Taren, 2015)

Meditation is to dive all the way within, beyond thought, to the source of thought and pure consciousness. It enlarges the container, every time you transcend. When you come out, you come out refreshed, filled with energy and enthusiasm for life. - David Lynch

Chapter IX
Developing Intuitive Skills

Look deep into nature, and then you will understand everything better. – Albert Einstein.

The Process of Developing Intuitive Skills

This chapter is designed to help the **individual learn how to improve** their natural intuitive talents, but it will not provide intense training, and the individual will not turn into a mind reader nor predict the next set of lottery numbers. However, this chapter will provide mental health clinicians and healthcare practitioners with information on how to improve focus and learn to listen to their intuition with better results.

The exercises in this chapter are not going to give the individual skills they do not naturally have per say, but what the exercises will do is train the person to pay attention and learn to fine-tune their listening skills when it comes to their inner voice. Keep in mind **practice is essential** for developing any skill in life. (Neal, Vujcic, Hernandez, & Wood 2015) In the case of developing intuitive skills, results will occur provided there is **consistency** and **commitment** to improving.

Many of the exercises are similar in their format, with slight variations depending on the intended goals. The repetitive nature of the exercises will allow the brain to adjust and develop the habit of paying attention to specific tasks.

The human brain learns **new habits** and behaviors **based on repetition**; therefore, repeat the exercises as often as possible. Habits develop because of ongoing routine and repetitive behaviors. (Neal et al.) In the case of intuitive abilities, practicing meditation and visualization techniques will reinforce the necessary behaviors to enhance skills. In many ways practicing techniques similar weight training, the more individual exercises, the stronger the muscles become. Therefore, consider meditation and visualization practice as an exercise for the intuitive mind.

Psychic Abilities vs. Intuitive skills

Most individuals know about psychic abilities and what it entails. However, not everyone knows how to differentiate between intuitive skills and psychic abilities. For many, psychic abilities and intuitive skills are the same.

Though psychic abilities and intuitive skills share similar traits, they are not the same thing. (King) Psychic abilities are used to obtain guidance and information through a variety of divination tools through a technique known as a psychic reading. Psychic readings provide clients with **valuable insight** into personal issues by **accessing available information**. However psychic readings do not provide the same type of guidance as intuitive techniques.

Intuitive skills are valuable in **obtaining awareness** through intuitive techniques that also can include divination tools. The goal of using intuitive techniques is to help clients **learn new ways** of coping and **develop insight** into negative patterns. In addition to providing information, intuitive skills can serve as a diagnostic tool that provides a deeper **understanding of the individual's reality** which helps clinicians develop relevant treatment plans.

To fully understand the difference between psychic readings and intuitive skills, think of readings as providing a forecast through the access of information, which can be useful in **avoiding conflict**; While, Intuitive skills provide information that allows a person to **gain insight**, so they can actively learn how to change or **minimize conflict**. (Newell 2013).

Activating the Intuitive Arsenal

Every individual has the potential of having intuitive abilities. (King) However, not everyone knows how to access their natural talents. The key to developing dormant intuitive abilities depends significantly on personal needs and how one typically perceives the world through the natural senses.

Some methods do require natural talents while some can be

developed and fine-tuned with different types of meditations and exercise drills. Both mental health clinicians and healthcare practitioners can decide which method will work best in their professional practice by exploring a few techniques and their practical applications. The intuitive techniques were selected based on their potential compatibility with therapeutic work. Not every single type of intuitive technique is appropriate for therapy since some are more inclined towards psychic readings rather than therapy.

In this section of the book, each intuitive techniques systematically presented in a progressive order, so each instruction prepares a person for the next exercise. Below is a brief list of the techniques covered in this chapter:

- **Visualization** – helpful in exploring issues as well as creating new realities and improving overall mental health. (Rennie et al.) For the clinician, visualization techniques help to develop creative problem-solving skills as well as serve as a tool for reducing potential burn-out
- **Psychometry** – Involves acquiring information by touching a person or that object. However, unless a person has a license as a massage therapist, nurse or doctor, touching is not advised. An individual can practice psychometry using an object touched by the individual. "divination of facts concerning an object or its owner through contact with or proximity to the object" – Merriam-Webster
- **Chakra Scanning** – Is a beneficial practice for gathering information about the client's current and past status. Chakra scanning combines the skills used for aura reading and Psychometry and Retrocognition. Chakra scanning is achieved by holding one's hands a few inches over each chakra.
- **Aura Scanning** - with this skill a therapist can review the conditions of a client's aura to help determine their emotional states. Aura reading is an excellent tool for assisting clients who struggle with verbalizing their feelings.
- **Documentation-** maintaining written records on dreams, meditations, a personal glossary of symbols and random thoughts is helpful for future references

Intuitive techniques are useful for **clarifying issues**, reviewing **personal life scripts** and **finding concrete solutions** for healing. The exercises within this book are designed to help the individual understand how to use the different types of intuitive techniques within this chapter. Once again, the exercises are designed to provide a person with the experience of knowing how to go about developing skills, but they will not turn that person into a psychic.

Mental health professionals and healthcare practitioners can use this chapter to review the areas that require fine-tuning and further training, as well as for practicing a few exercises. Also, before getting into any of the exercises, it is useful to have a notebook and pen or pencil to document the experienced. Other than writing material, a person does not need any fancy equipment. Before moving to the next section, take a few minutes and write out the thoughts in the following area:

1. How well did meditation work?
2. What was the most comfortable exercise to do and why?
3. What was the most challenging exercise?
4. How often was the meditation practiced?
5. Is every exercise completed? Why or why not?
6. Make sure to practice more than once.

It is important to realize that both meditation and visualization techniques are tools to assist in the enhancement of natural skills and not a task to measure performance or how well an individual is doing in therapy. The purpose of implementing the assigned techniques is to enhance and facilitate the development of individual intuitive skills. This chapter has two sections, and each with subcategories classified as follows:

Section I - Visualization Sensory Perception

- **Inner Visions**
- **Hand Scanning**

Section II - Hand Scanned Visions

- **Psychometry**
- **Chakra Scanning**

Also, for each subcategory, there are a series of assigned exercises each designed to provide the experience of how each category works. It is recommended that the Mental health clinicians and healthcare practitioners explore some of the exercises and document their experiences. In doing the exercises, each clinician will be able to assess the practicality and benefit of each exercise before implementing them into treatment.

Visual Sensory Perception

The visual sensory system can provide a wealth of insight because of information gathered through visual impressions. The primary goal of the visual system is to assemble an internal model of our external reality. (Milner & Goodale 1998) Within the internal realm, lies vital information which contains the tools needed to assist individuals in the process of creating changes and improving their lifestyles.

Visual impressions occur through two **Visual Sensory Systems** referred to as **Inner Vision,** and **Hand Scanning**. In this section, there will be a review of each system, followed by a few exercises designed to develop and strengthen visual acuity. It is suggested that clinicians take the time to practice each technique before using them with clients. It is essential and ethical that clinicians comprehend how different systems fully work because clients should not be experimental lab rats.

Section I - Inner Vision
Inner Vision System

The inner vision system utilizes visual techniques to access the internal world known as the unconscious. According to Milner and Goodale (2008), individuals can process visual information in a variety of ways. The inner visions provide the opportunity to look internally and explore a world created through our intentions, thoughts and many times desires. The internal world is explored using guided visualization exercises. The inner vision is strengthened using meditation exercises, improving focus, and concentration. The following topics will be explored to provide the necessary tools for developing efficient visualization skills:

- **Working with Visualization**
- **Improving Visualization Skills**
- **Visualization Meditation Exercises**

The internal world consists of unconscious realities and memories that influence each day. Exploring the internal world provides both clinicians and practitioners with information that can facilitate change as well as improve emotional and physical function. According to research, the internal world strongly impacts a person's mental and physical abilities which is why athletes use visualization techniques to improve their performance in sports. (Warner, & McNell 1988)

Working with Visualizations

Visualization techniques are useful tools in helping individual redirect the traffic in their inner world. It does not provide magical solutions, but it can spark creative problem solving and inspire ways of creating new realities. Visualization works by intentionally directing the mind to think and feel in specific ways, which also influences behavior patterns. (Hagger 2017) Visualization is a proactive activity, in which the individual is the director, actor, and creator of new realities.

Visualization is **not a passive activity** like meditation, in which one listens and receives inspiration. Visualization uses symbolism to facilitate cognitive processes that activate potential behaviors. (Chen, Floridi, Borgo 2013). In simple terms, visualization is about using the imagination to create new thinking patterns that contribute to new behaviors.

Though visualization has many benefits, it is not easy to implement. Many individuals have difficulty visualizing in their meditation because they struggle with the idea of internally "seeing" images. The reason visualization can be difficult to practice has a lot to do with one's **internal belief system**.

The critical problem with visualization stems when a person compares themselves to individuals who get immediate and detailed results. It is important to realize that in real life, everyone has a slightly different view of the world. When it comes to visualization, a person needs to allow themselves to see what appears naturally, rather than to force themselves to see something that is not occurring for them.

Individuals do not perceive their surroundings in complete mindfulness due to a natural tendency to get distracted or overly analytical. It is normal for an individual to second guess or dismisses both external and internal experience. However, the lack of focus and second-guessing will impact the visualization experience.

The visualization experience is a personal one. Initially, visualization can be strange and difficult for individuals who struggle to "see" things during meditation. There are several different exercises a person can do to improve their ability to visualize. Working with meditation can be tricky for some individuals, therefore to assure productive outcomes use the following suggestions:

Preparing for visualization

- **Get comfortable** – being comfortable is essential since it reduces distractions created by cramping or stiffness
- **Be patient** – allow the experience to unfold naturally and without rushing it
- **Be flexible** – each exercise should follow a fluid format to help the intuitive process
- **Keep things simple** – direct and simple guidance minimizes distractions often created by too many details.
- **Minimize noise** – Reduce noise levels to prevent disturbances.
- **Practice** – It is helpful to repeat visualizations a few times since it increases confidence and performance levels
- **document**- this will help to track improvements and identify areas that need addressing

Preparation for any technique will vary depending on the needs of the individual, goal of the session and amount of time available for the exercise. Through practice, the individual can gain better results, but whatever a person does, they should enjoy themselves and relax during the process of doing visualizations.

Improving Visualization Skills

Improving visualization skills is a possible and doable task, but it does take practice and patience. According to studies, visualization techniques can improve what is known as the **convolutional neural network**, (convnets) which allows for the recognition of images. (Yosinski, Nguyen, Fuchs, & Lipson 2015) Through repetitive practice, the individual can improve visual acuity by training convnets to response more proficiently. Research at Carleton College demonstrated that visualization skills could improve through a series of exercises. (Titus, & Horsman 2009). Keep in mind the entire physical structure of the human body improves through consistent usage, which is why athletes constantly train.

There are a few exercises available in this section to help individuals improve their ability to concentrate and maintain a visual image. The exercises consist of different images, designed to develop focus and concentration. Each exercise is brief and takes a few moments to do. Also, the person has the option of selecting any symbol or picture of their choosing. The general idea of each exercise is to for the person to attempt to recall what they see, so in time they will be able to see images with ease. The exercises take a few minutes, so make sure to set a timer. After completing the exercise, take a few minutes to document their experience.

Exercise # 1

picture 1

    The following exercise is designed **to improve the recollection of details** and **focus**. The goal of the exercise is to **measure one's ability to recall details.** You will attempt to recall as many details as possible within the photo while keeping your eyes closed. Turn your timer on to three minutes. You begin by focusing on **picture #1** for one minute and then **closing your eyes.**

    While your eyes are closed**,** try to **recall as many** details as possible. Then, slowly **open your eyes** and allow the image to come into focus so that you can examine it for about one minute. Imagine the image changing in size and shapes. First, the image is small; then it becomes large. Next, the **image changes from light to dark** and then grey shades of color in between the dark and light hues. Then close your eyes and try to see the images again with your eyes closed for one minute. Open your eyes and write down whatever you experienced.

Exercise #2

The following exercise is very much like exercise **number one**, which is also designed to **improve** the recollection of details. The main difference in this exercise is **the use of color**. You will attempt to recall different colors, rather than focusing only on black and white images. The object is to focus **on picture #2** for one minute, and then **close your eyes**.

Set the timer for one minute. Again, attempt to recall as many details as possible within the photo while keeping your eyes closed for one minute. Then slowly **open your eyes** and allow the image to come into focus and begin to review each detail. Imagine the image is **changing in size and shapes**. First, the image appears small; then it slowly becomes larger. Take a few seconds to allow your eyes to adjust to the changes in size.

Now, focus your attention on the separate objects and their corresponding colors. Keep **alternating between red, white, green, brown and beige colors**. Do this a few times until it becomes easy to do. Then once more, **close your eyes** and try to recall the colors and images you just looked at for another minute. It is a good idea to take the time to do this exercise and not rush through the process. After the exercise is complete, write down your experience and be aware that there are no incorrect answers, just personal interpretations.

Exercise #3

This exercise follows the format of the previous two exercises, which is also designed **to improve focus** and **visual memory of objects**. The exercise includes a photo that contains both colors and shapes to use as a focal point. Again, set the timer for 3 minutes. Focus on **picture #3** for a few moments and then close your eyes. Immediately after closing your eyes, try to recall as many details as possible from the photo. Then, once more **open your eyes** and examine the details in the photo for about one minute. Make sure to take a mental note of the different colors, as well as the plants and flowers within the picture. Notice how each flower is aligned and placed inside the photo.

Once more, **close your eyes** and attempt to recall as many details as possible for one minute. Try to envision each color, alternating between green, yellow, purple and brown. Though this exercise uses a flower, you can use any picture that provides similar elements to help you develop focus and visual recollection. This exercise should be repeated a few times until you obtain satisfactory results. The purpose of this exercise is to enhance recollection skills, increase concentration and focus. And again, make sure to write down your experience with the exercise.

Visualization Meditations

Many individuals struggle to visualize, and recall details experienced during visualization. The main problem individuals have with recalling visualization experiences are similar to those experienced in dream recall; which is forgetting details seconds right after opening one's eyes. The assignments provided in this section are designed to improve focus and recollection of the visualization experience. Remember that though a person might not recall every detail, practice will facilitate the progress. The following tips are designed to produce concrete results with visualization techniques:

1. Practice as often as possible to **improve skills**
2. Practice **drills at intervals** of two minutes to ten minutes
3. **Avoid comparison** to others
4. Start with **simple techniques**
5. Every detail is **part of the experience**, including random thoughts
6. **All senses are involved** in visualization experience
7. **Being relaxed is** an **essential** component in improving focus
8. **Less is more**. Sometimes a few details are enough to reveal hidden issues.

For a person to obtain results in recalling visualization details, they should practice often. Keep in mind that idea with each exercise is to improve the attention span, as well as the ability to see with the eyes closed.

Visualization Meditation Drills

The meditation exercises in this section of the book contain only a few items, which will produce quicker results. The exercises should be repeated several times until you feel confident with your skills.

The idea is to help you develop the ability to focus as well as visualize with ease and productive outcomes. Document the results of exercise immediately after completion. The next series of exercises are designed for clinicians, so they experience the meditations on a personal level before using them with their clients.

Tri-Color Focus Meditation Exercise # 4

picture 4

Find a quiet place and a comfortable chair to sit on. Get a timer and set it for 5 minutes. Begin by looking at **picture #4** for about 30 seconds and then close your eyes and relax. Imagine a white light above your head. Allow the glow of the light to spread throughout your body making it feel relaxed and light. Now allow yourself to visualize picture #4. In your mind, see the squares with three different colors. The box begins to open gradually. As the box opens, the vision becomes sharp and clear. See the colors coming up, one at a time. First notice the red, then the yellow and finally the blue. Allow each color to expand, slowly filling the room. The room filled with colors.

Now, allow the colors to get back to standard size. Hold each color mentally. Now see the colors change. First, envision the red, then slowly let it change to bright yellow, next change the color to blue. See all three colors, the blue, the yellow and the red and notice how bright they are.

Watch the colors become dim and begin to shrink to a small size until they disappear. Imagine the light moving back from your eyes to the feet and then back up to the head. Release the light back. Feel your body waking up gently. At the count of 3 open your eyes, 1, 2, 3.

The meditations in this book are designed to help individuals develop better focus and awareness by directing the attention to specific images. The exercises do not have many variables that create distractions and are designed to help retain concentration. Keep in mind the more you practice, the easier each technique will become.

Shape Focus Meditation Exercise # 5

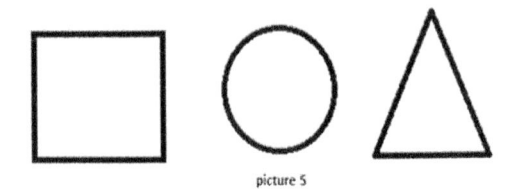

picture 5

Find a quiet place. Get a comfortable spot to sit on. Turn on your 5-minute timer. Now, at a look at **picture # 5** with the three different shapes. Notice each different shape begin to open gradually. While keeping your eyes opened envision the box opening slowly, as the box opens, the image becomes sharp and clear. Next see the other shapes take turns appearing and coming into focus, one at a time. Allow yourself to see the details so you can remember them. Begin to close your eyes. Visualize a white light above your head. Feel your entire body begin to relax and become very light

Now, imagine seeing the square, then the circle and finally the triangle. Allow each shape to grow and fill up the room. Once the oversized images fill the room, begin to touch the outline of each one and notice their smooth texture. Feel the coolness with your hands. Now, allow each shape to become small in size and hold them in your hand. As you hold the three shapes, examine their colors. At first, you only see the black outlines. Starting with the square, see it change from black to different colors. First, you see the color red, then slowly it turns into a deep wine shade, then purple and back to black. Next, watch the circle turn from violet to hot pink, then light pink and then black. Slowly watch the triangle turn from peach to yellow, gold and then white and back to black.

Take a moment and once more look at all three shapes which are now black. Slowly watch the symbols become small until they disappear. Imagine the light moving back from the eyes to the feet and then back up to the head. Slowly, release the light back. Feel the body waking up gently. At the count of 3 open your eyes, 1, 2, 3.

Document whatever experience occurred during the exercise, making sure to include any difficulties encountered. Regardless of how you did, remember that practice will always produce stronger results.

Flower Focus Meditation Exercise # 6

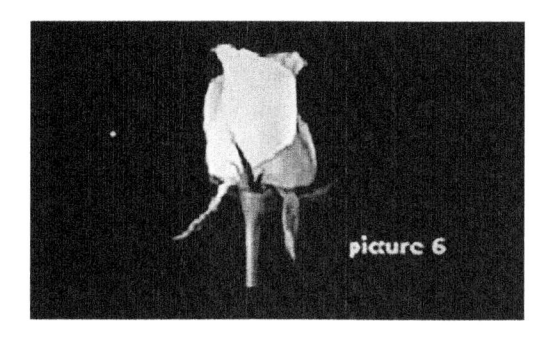

picture 6

The flower focus meditation is another exercise that will you help in viewing colors and objects. Remember to take your time and be patient. Being critical or impatient will stifle the ability to relax and go with the intuitive flow.

Find a quiet place to meditate without distractions. Begin to breathe nice and easy, making sure to relax your mind and let go of all expectations. Keep your eyes open and continue to relax. Image a white light above your head and feel the warmth of the light traveling down your entire body, making it relax even more. Before closing your eyes, examine **picture # 6**. Notice the details of the picture and try to remember as much as possible.

Closing your eyes and envision your surroundings. Now imagine the small rosebud from the picture placed in a vase in the middle of a table. The rosebud begins to open gradually. As the rose blooms, your vision becomes sharper and clear. See the rose opening from a small bud into a huge flower with a sweet, relaxing fragrance. Pick up the rose your hand and watch it changes colors. First, the rose is red, then slowly it turns a deep wine color, and then it begins to get lighter until it becomes pink. Finally, the rose goes back to being white.

Focus on the rose and watch it slowly become small until it disappears. Imagine the light moving back from your eyes to your feet and then back out through your head and then disconnect. Feel your body waking up. At the count of 3 open your eyes, 1, 2, 3,

At the end of the exercise, write down your experience. Describe what happened, even if seems odd or not related to the exercise. During the documenting, take note of random thoughts or emotions that might have been triggered by the exercise.

The Impact of Expectations

When it comes to meditation or visualization techniques, it is natural to have some expectations. For individuals who have never meditated or practice visualizations, their expectations may reflect what others have experienced. Moreover, for individuals who have some experience meditating, their views are often based on previous outcomes which may have not always been ideal.

Expectations can influence the outcome of any activity as well as influence the emotional state of an individual. Expectations can create barriers and apprehension when it comes to experiencing new activities. (Woojan, & Pachmayer 2016)

It is useful to acknowledge our natural biases or expectations, so they do not influence the natural process of any meditation or visualization exercise. Our views may impede both visualization or meditation techniques based on the following:

1. fear of performance failure

2. To experience nothing

3. To be emotionally triggered

4. To get bored

5. Relive scary episodes

6. Lose control

7. Not sense anything

Both the professionals and clients have their expectations when it comes to therapy sessions, and at times those expectations can clash. It is essential that when it comes to using any technique that the clinician or practitioner is fully aware of the client's limitations and personal expectations. If any exercise feels uncomfortable or produces any distress, it is a professional responsibility to cease the activity. No clinician or practitioner should push any client into a position against their will since to do so it is both unethical and counterproductive.

Benefits of Visualization

There are many benefits associated with learning basic visualization techniques. It is not just useful for improving intuition and manifesting new realities. It is a tool that both the therapist and the client can learn to master. The client can benefit from learning visualization techniques that allow them to scan their chakra system, as well as develop the skills to create new realities.

There some benefits associated with learning visualization techniques, which include but are not limited to the following:

- Facilitates **behavior changes**
- Valuable **mood enhancer**
- Improves athletic **performance**
- Enhances **creativity**
- Expands **thinking abilities**
- Allows a person to **process emotions**
- Helpful in developing **consequential thinking**
- Useful **problem-solving** technique
- Increases **concentration** and focus
- A valuable tool for **learning**
- Improves **memory**
- Great for **brainstorming**

- Enhances **imagination**

The many uses of visualization will vary depending on the type of professional services and the needs of the individual client. It is essential that both the mental health clinician and healthcare practitioner avoid using the same techniques on all their clients. For optimum benefits and outcomes, each visualization should be explicitly designed and implemented with the clinical treatment plan as a guideline.

Enhancing Visualization experience

Initially, most individuals struggle to achieve results in both meditation and visualization because of personal expectations. The key to productive results with visualization or meditation techniques has a lot to do with attitude and practice. However, to ensure therapeutic results with both visualization or meditation the following tips should be considered:

- Practice
- Keep a journal
- Keep techniques simple
- Focus on breathing to relax the mind
- Avoid being interrupted
- Repeat exercises
- Keep the practice brief
- Avoid self-criticism
- Recognize not all visualizations are perfectly detailed

Meditation and visualization techniques can yield productive results when used accordingly, but it takes time to become comfortable. Overall, the key is to practice and not expect perfection.

Summary of Section I

In section I, information on visualization techniques and

exercises were supplied to assist both the professional clinician and practitioners in learning the various practical uses of visualization. Each exercise was deliberately designed to assist the person in developing their ability to focus and retain visual details to help them achieve productive outcomes with visualization.

Many individuals tend to struggle when it comes to visualization because they cannot recall or envision details. Each exercise should be done separately and often until the individual feels confident with their skills. (Valvano 2017)) It is suggested that individuals practice even after obtaining results, to maintain their skills intact.

Section II - Hand Scanned Visions

Hand Scanning Techniques

The hands serve us in many ways; they allow us to know when something is extremely hot or cold, sharp or wet. The hands are part of the tactile sensory system that delivers different types of messages to the brain. Without the receptors in the hands, we would be unable to avoid situations that are dangerous, such as getting 3rd-degree burns from touching fire or getting cuts from touching sharp edges. It is safe to say that the tactile system delivers relatively accurate messages to the brain on a consistent level.

Through the tactile sensory system, we can do more than detect temperature changes or feel texture; we can detect changes in energy levels. The hands can detect subtle energy shifts that deliver information to the brain. In this section known as the **Hand Scanned visions**, we will review the different methods used to obtain information through the tactile system. The topics consist of the following:

- **Psychometry**
- **Chakra Scanning**

Psychometry and Chakra scanning are two methods that allow sensory impressions to transmit through the hands. As the energy transmits via the palms, it projects internal visuals that can be seen by the individual scanning. The energy transmitted ignites information that can be symbolically seen, sensed or visualized in varying details.

The technique of retrieving information with the hands may seem daunting. However, the key to hand scanning is to learn how to pay attention. In general, many techniques that involve intuition are about "paying" attention and not dismissing the impressions presented.

Psychometry

The scanning technique of psychometry utilizes the hands for retrieving visual impressions. Psychometry. Is valuable for assessing the emotional state of individuals in distress or struggling to disclose painful experiences. It creates an empathetic connection with the client and their emotional states. Psychometry will not provide elaborate details, but it will help convey the general view on how the individual is coping.

The technique of Psychometry can be done in two ways; **scanning an object** that belongs to an individual or **scanning their hand**. To practice scanning, it works best when done with others. Therefore, for the sake of this exercise, ask a co-worker or friend to help you practice by providing you with an object. When doing the exercise, see yourself as a witness viewing someone else's experience. To get started, do the following exercise:

Psychometry Exercise # 7

Select the object for scanning. Take a deep breath and relax. Slowly, allow all thoughts and mental noise to quiet down. Imagine a light above your head, coming down your entire body and allowing you to feel completely relaxed and at ease. As you breathe, the light moves through your body and your hands. Feel the energy flow between your hand and the object being scanned. As the energy flows, it creates a connection. Visualize the energy from the object working its way up your hands and the arms all the way to the brain.

Then take note of the immediate reactions as the energy surges through the hands. What are the thoughts or words that come to mind or visual impressions? Witness the events that take place. Take a mental note, without judging or wondering if it makes sense.

Breathe nice and easy. Once more review what you saw and then let go. Visualize the energy going back to its source and slowly disconnecting from your hand. Make sure that the energy disconnects both from the hand and the object. Slowly feel the body recharging and becoming alert.

Open your eyes and write down whatever came up, without censoring or worrying if it makes sense or not.

Chakra Scanning

The techniques of chakra scanning allow both clinicians and clients to review the chakras for hidden information that provide useful tools for release work and creating concrete changes. The methods for scanning the chakras are similar to the methods used with psychometry, except instead of an object, one is using the chakra centers as a source of information retrieval. There are two ways to do scanning techniques; **self-scanning** and **scanning the others**.

The technique for scanning chakras is simple but does require letting go of self-judgment and performance expectations. Always remember, intuition does not rely on critical thinking, but rather free-flowing associations. To practice chakra scanning, find a co-worker or friend who is willing to help. The following exercise will focus on the crown chakra, located on the top of the head.

Chakra Exercise # 8

Get a candle and light it. Turn off most of the lights. Let the friend sit in a chair and stand behind them. Take a few seconds to relax your thoughts and make sure to let go of expectations. Slowly, take a deep breath, close your eyes and relax. Imagine a bright light above your head. Allow this light to relax the muscles on the head, shoulders, arms, and hands. Continue to let the light move down the entire body making it feel completely relaxed and comfortable. Slowly, move your hands up to the top of the person's head.

Imagine the energy from your hand entering the person's crown chakra and creating a connection. Let the energy create a connection that travels up your arms activating the neurons in your brain. As the neurons are activated, the brain begins to translate the signals into images, symbols or messages. What are the immediate thoughts or reaction as the energy surges through the hands? What are the feelings or visuals experienced? Pay close attention to any sensation, regardless of how strange it may seem. Observe whatever occurs without judgment or critical thinking.

Take a few minutes to witness the experience, then begin to let go. Imagine the energy connections separating. Separate slowly and gently. Feel your energy levels returning to normal.
Focus on your breathing. Take a deep breath and feel your body recharge. Allow yourself to feel energized and alert. Once the exercise is complete, write down what occurred. Writing immediately after the exercises helps you retain the memory.

Summary for Section II

Psychometry and chakra scanning methods are useful tools that can enable both clinicians and practitioners to tap into hidden energy blockages that impact the overall well-being of their clients. The methods are valuable in allowing clinicians to gain insight and obtain information that is pertinent to the specific client.

Chapter Summary

This chapter focused on two types of **visual systems** that involve **internal methods** of obtaining information through visual imprints. Each system provides unique tools that will allow both mental health clinicians and healthcare practitioners to gather personal information on each client that will serve well when creating treatment plans. The exercises also offered opportunities for clinicians to develop intuitive skills and understanding on how to fine-tune their visual acuity.

Chapter X - Aura Scanning

The aura given out by a person or object is as much a part of them as their flesh. - Lucian Freud

Scanning the Human Aura

The human aura holds the key to overall well-being and hidden aspects that influence the lives of individuals. (Srikanth 2017). Studies have indicated that viewing the human aura provides clinicians with a wealth of information into hidden emotional and physical realities. Mental health clinicians and healthcare practitioners can obtain information by engaging the physical sight as a tool for scanning. Through aura scanning, clinicians can assess for mental distress, unresolved emotional issues and facilitate engagement with clients who struggle to communicate.

External Visual Scanning

This chapter focuses on visual scanning with the eyes open, referred to as "external visual scanning." The techniques in this section will allow the clinician to learn basic information on the human aura and provide instructions to facilitate aura scanning. It will take practice and time to get used to the technique of scanning as a beginner.

This chapter provides general information on the human aura and how to use the physical sight to gather information. The topics covered include some of the following:

- **Exploring the Aura**
- **Scientific Explanation**

- Esoteric Explanation
- Developing Visual Acuity
- Understanding the role of color
- Scanning Auras

The process of scanning with the physical eye requires learning how to see beyond the obvious, as well as constant practice and patience.

Exploring the Human Aura

The human body retains valuable information both physically and energetically which contributes to the body's aura. The physical body influences memory on numerous levels. Jurik (2015) The body retains physical memories that are the byproduct of both chemical and mental imprints, which become triggered by emotional reactions due to environmental events

For the clinicians to understand how the aura system functions, the topic needs to be reviewed from two different levels; **scientifically** and **esoterically.** By reviewing the aura scientifically, it will allow the clinician to understand how the body's functions emit surges of energy that could be useful for retrieving information. In exploring the esoteric aspects of the aura, one will be able to comprehend how it is possible to obtain intuitive information.

Scientific Explanation

When individuals think about the aura, they often think it is merely some strange feel-good term for energy. Science refers to the human aura as a magnetic field that surrounds the body. (Sahoo 2014) The aura is the outer layer that forms as the result of vibrational energy produced by the body's constant use of energy. The body is in constant flux since life depends on the movement of blood, which uses tons of energy, which is why we require fuel in the form of food. The fuel we consume converts into chemicals that travel throughout the body to deliver neurochemicals to the brain, which sends back more chemicals that keeps the life force going.

The aura is created by heat emissions produced by the body's energy system since it engages in varies activities that utilize different levels of energy. The emissions vary depending on the different degrees of temperature changes that result from energy distributed throughout the body. The body's distribution of heat can be measured using Magnetic Resonance Imaging, (MRI). An MRI works by measuring the energy released within various sections of the body and creating a scanned image. Areas that have less energy due to blockages often emit less energy, producing different gradient images detected through an MRI scan (NIBIB).

In summary, the aura is merely an energy sphere or halo created by the build-up of heat emitting from the body. The human eye has been detecting energy longer than technology; however, as demonstrated through technology, the body releases different amounts of energy levels measured through scanning devices. When an individual is scanning the aura, what they are mostly doing is looking for varying heat emissions throughout the body.

Esoteric Explanation

Even though this section explores the Esoteric concepts of the aura, it is essential to remember; energy creates heat when its active. According to EIA (2018), there are two types of energy which consist of potential and kinetic energy. Potential energy is stored and waiting to be activated, while kinetic energy is energy in action.

What is the aura? Every living individual and object has an aura. It is the energy field that surrounds the body. This energy field vibrates with vitality and life force. It is a combination of energy that's projected from the physical, mental and emotional aspects of each. The aura contains a record of experiences stored in the form of colors, energy pockets or blockages. As a person or object experiences changes, so does the aura.

There are both **permanent** and **temporary imprints** on the aura. Permanent imprints tend to result from changes created by trauma or extreme discomfort and tend to affect the natural shape, density or color of the aura. Temporary imprints tend to occur due to changes in health or lifestyle and do not remain for long but can linger for extensive periods. Temporary imprints can heal quicker than permanent imprints and respond well to color, crystal, and energy healing. Permanent imprints take long to heal and require persistent work with karmic patterns and unresolved issues.

Learning to read the aura gives a person the advantage of being able to tap into data on oneself or others. The aura contains a variety of information on issues ranging from health, emotional well-being to spiritual dilemmas. It is useful to read the aura not only for understanding personal issues but also for obtaining tools to help to release harmful patterns and obstacles.

The Aura and Colors

The aura made of vibrating energy can take on various shapes and colors that indicate its condition. The different degrees of energy produce different heat emissions that when viewed in an MRI machine can be seen in varying colors. Depending on the colors and shape, the aura can reflect a state of balance or imbalance.

Colors represent specific heat signatures which can indicate physical as well as emotional conditions affecting the individual, making them a great diagnostic tool. There are **scientific explanations, psychological associations** and **esoteric meaning** attached to different colors and how they impact on individuals.

Scientific Explanation

Colors are wavelengths that stimulate the three cone photoreceptors found within the eye, allowing the stimulation to create a visual perception. (Conway et al. 2010) Each human eye has its unique way of perceiving color. Though several individuals may experience the same color, they will each have their unique reaction. (University of Rochester 2005). According to research, the brain will detect colors but will prescribe its own and unique experience depending on the individual. As colors are detected through the cones in the eyes, different neurotransmitters become activated which in turn send signals to the brain's response system. The neurotransmitters that are stimulated consist of serotonin, endorphins, and norepinephrine which induce a variety of mood changes.

Psychological Associations

Understanding color goes beyond aesthetics and personal preferences. According to studies colors impact individuals on a variety of levels, from behavior patterns to mood swings (Jalil, Yunus, & Said 2012). Colors can enhance focus, produce calmness and excitement. Also, colors can be used to invoke desires and even influence how individuals spend money on products. (Singh 2006)

Esoteric Meaning

The esoteric meaning behind colors is the result of cultural associations which differ from group to group. Colors have come to represent values, beliefs, and attitudes. According to an article in the journal "Scientific America," colors can resemble attitudes and meanings that range from being considered socially acceptable to inappropriateness. (Martinez-Conde, & Macknik 2014) An example of a color that has strong cultural meaning is red. For instance, in China red is used in wedding ceremonies to bring the new couple luck in their marriage. Meanwhile in Spain red resembles passion and is used during bull-fighting by the matador to provoke the bull into fighting. (Martinez-Conde, & Macknik)

The Colors of the Aura

There may be various colors in a person's aura or just a few. The location of the colors throughout the body offers information on what's going on, as well as the intensity and clarity of the color. Each color offers information on what's affecting the person and how they are coping with their environment. Of course, colors change due to changing conditions. However, there are also consistent colors that appear, reflecting a general view of the person being scanned. Below is a brief listing of colors and their general meaning. Keep in mind that the color meanings will differ depending on cultural background and personal symbolism. The meanings are based on general associations but can be modified according to individual needs.

White - It is the most natural color to detect when starting out. It contains all the colors of the spectrum combined. The different shades of white will indicate how the aura is doing. The clearer and brighter shade indicate a healthy flow of energy.

Yellow - Just like white, it is easy to detect when a person first begins to scan auras. There is a tendency to respond to surroundings situations logically rather than react emotionally. The person tends to be interested in things that develop the intellect, provide mental stimulation and a learning experience, rather than emotional stimulation. Of course, this does not mean lack of emotion, but rather a preference for conditions that stir the intellect rather than feelings.

Blue - It is a very soothing which tends to indicate calm and quiet energy. Blue is connected to the 5th chakra, the center for communication and creative expressions. It may also indicate low heat in the body and heavy focus on mental activities instead of physical. Extreme amounts of blue may indicate higher levels of stress and depression in some individuals due to improper balance. The person may find themselves disconnecting to their emotions and placing more focus on coping mentally with situations.

Violet – Associated with spiritual matters and ideals. Whenever a person is focused intensely on their spiritual path, there is a lot of upper chakra activity going on. The individual connects to energy that stimulates the intuition, spiritual enhancement and awakens consciousness. There made be a tendency to get spacey and be more involved with spiritual matters than physical. The person may not be very grounded or physically connected due to lack of balance.

Orange – Orange is associated with the 2nd chakra, which influences sexual energy and physical vitality. Of course, in many cultures, red is connected to passion; however, orange is also another color associated with passion. It projects a glow of warmth, pleasure and sensual energy. An imbalance may reflect tendencies to overindulge in pleasure seeking activities that can lead to addictive behavior, i.e., sex, food, alcohol, drugs, gambling, shopping, to name a few. The person tends to overindulge in pleasure seeking activities and does whatever to avoid pain and discomfort.

Red -Red associated with first charka activities, such as survival, physical energy, vitality and overall well-being. Whenever there is excess red energy, there tends to be extra focus on physical issues. Red may turn into aggressive behavior when not focused in a balanced matter, such as physical activity or in areas that require endurance. Many people tend to associate red with anger and aggression, while some may connect it with passion and physical vitality. Any association made to red often depends on a person's connection to the color (Martinez-Conde, & Macknik)

Pink - Pink is associated with a loving, gentle, and compassionate energy. Though pink may not be everyone's favorite color, it tends to signify a friendly and kind nature. Whenever someone is beginning a new relationship, the heart chakra is very receptive and tends to project a powerful vibration that gives off a pink tone. Of course, an excessive amount of pink may reflect a certain amount of vulnerability and lack of healthy boundaries.

Black – There are a lot of associations for black. For some people, black may be disturbing, perhaps due to social conditioning or lack of understanding. However, black may indicate a well-grounded person, who's confident and secure in who they are and has healthy boundaries. Black is also a color used for grounding the energy whenever a person is spacey and flighty. It may also indicate low energy due to illness or poor circulation.

Brown- There are various shades of brown that may appear on the aura. The more intense the shade of brown is, the higher the chances of there being a problem. Brown may indicate a health problem beginning to develop or currently existing. Of course, those who love brown might disagree, so if a person has a connection to it, use their interpretation. Brown may reflect a well-grounded and balance individual.

Gray - It has similar qualities to brown. Gray can indicate problems with emotional or physical health. Grayish colors are often present when the energy is low or stagnated either due to poor physical or emotional states.

Green - It represents the 4th chakra, the heart area. Green is associated with balance, harmony, and compassionate energy. The aura reflects a state of growth and change, often for the best. It reveals emotional and physical strength. It also appears with individuals who are into healing work since healing requires some compassion, as well as the ability to be giving and caring. It is a favorite color for many; however, if a person does not like green, then another preferable color should be used.

Gold - It is associated with awareness, spiritual goals, and personal power. Of course, a dark type of gold versus a bright shade will reflect how the person is coming to terms with their power.

There are many ranges of colors and associations which vary depending on personal preferences and cultural influences. How colors are used will depend on the reasons for integrating colors into therapeutic goals. For instance, if a practitioner is assessing for health reasons, the colors can indicate the physical conditions of the individual. If the clinician is assessing for emotional states, the colors will indicate mood ranges and provide clues on how to create a beneficial treatment plan.

Developing Visual Acuity

Though we depend a great deal on our eyes, we tend to neglect them. The eyes have muscles that weaken with time, just like our body. (Srikanth). However, strengthening the eye muscles can be far more challenging than working out the body.

To psychically use the eyes, one needs to maintain their focus in specific ways, which require physical endurance. The ability to fixate on an object requires physical eye strength which a person may lack due to weak eye muscles. (Taylor n.d.) Focusing for extended periods enables the eye to see images long enough to develop a conscious awareness, rather than a flash of insight.

The visual perception changes by the variations of light that enter through the retina. (Milner & Goodale) As light enters, the rods and cones activate receptors that trigger chemical reactions which signal the brain. These chemical reactions stimulate responses in the brain which in turn create a recording of visual experiences. Our eyes are doing more than just observing images; they provide information that is stored and reserved in symbolic coding. Maintaining the strength of the eye's ciliary muscles allows a smoother transmission of data between the optic nerve and the brain, which in turn results in more precise visual experiences both physically and intuitively. (Srikanth) See Image # 2 below:

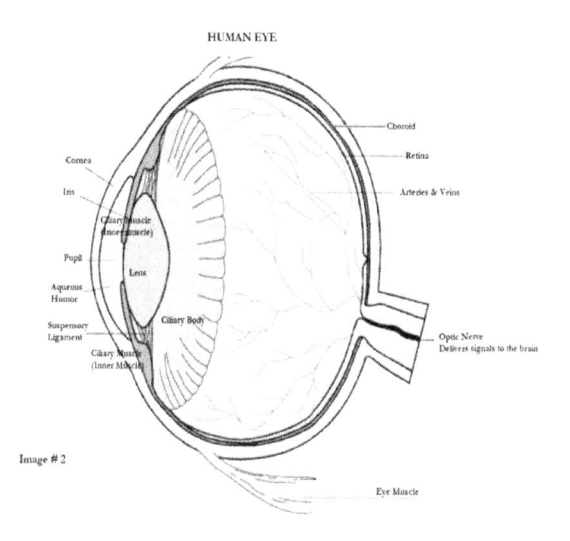

HUMAN EYE

Image # 2

Regular training of the physical eyes will enable a person to see intuitively with proficiency. The individual can improve visual acuity by learning to minimize the interference they get from the constant visual stimulation in the surrounding environment, as well as, develop visual endurance. Techniques are available which allow the eyes to work more efficiently and maximize the to respond to color and visual stimuli.

The exercises that proceed may feel strange and unnatural when first attempted since the eyes are not often required to focus intentionally. The change of focus will force the eyes muscles to work differently in the attempts to adjust to the new eye movement.

Do each exercise a few times a week, but do not overdo it. Take your time and let your eyes adjust. When it comes to the eyes a little will go a long way. To help you increase your ability to focus visually, do the exercises that follow:

Exercise # 9

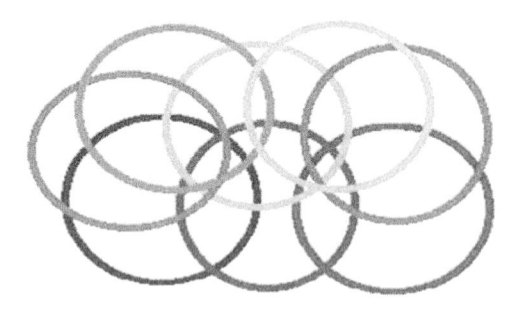

picture 7

    Begin by taking a deep and steady breath. As you calm your mind, begin to feel comfortable. And start to focus on picture **number # 7**. Allow your eyes to view the complete picture. Then slowly begin to focus only on the different colors for a few seconds. Notice the different shapes and zero in on the points that connect the shapes. Now alternate between the circles and the different colors. Is it possible to see where circles overlap?

    Is it possible to visually trace the different colors? Place the attention on the inner circles, and then the outer ones. Practice the exercise at least 3 to 5 times in a row or more. Now close the right eye and focus with the left eye on the image. Hold the focus for a count of 4, and then repeat the exercise with the right eye. Try to visualize the image with the eyes closed a few times. Then when ready, feel free to stop.

Exercise # 10

picture 8

Begin by relaxing. Take a deep breath and allow the mind to relax. Concentrate on picture # 8. Allow your eyes to notice the entire picture. Slowly move your attention to the center square and zero in on the grey outlines of the white spaces. Focus on each colored square using both eyes, then alternate between the left and right eye. It is ok if the mind wonders a bit, but make sure to bring the focus back. Then alternate between the upper and lower lines that outline the inside of the square. Then go back to looking at the entire picture. Do this at least 3-5 times in a row or more. When ready, open your eyes.

Exercise # 11

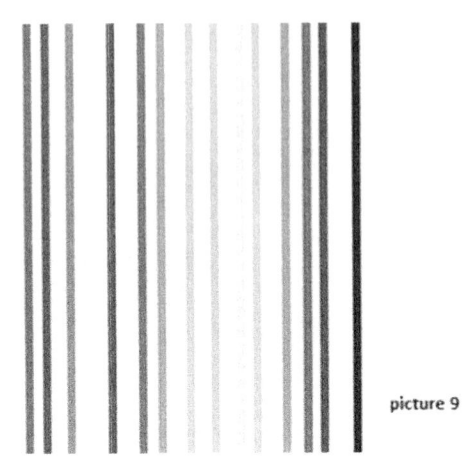

picture 9

Once, again begin by relaxing. Breathe slowly and deeply, allowing the mind to let go of all expectations and critical thoughts. Breathe deeply and relax the mind. Now focus the attention on **picture # 9.** Notice the entire picture. See the lines and try to look at the different colors. Some colors appear to be similar, and some are not. There are small differences between the space and the grades of colors. Be aware that the shape is not imperfect; it is an intentional design. Witness the reactions to the colors and space. Now select a color that is soothing and let the color create a relaxing state of mind. As the mind is relaxed, take note of the colors that are less relaxing. Which colors feel less relaxing? Once more focus on the entire picture. Close the eyes briefly and try to recall the colors and spaces. Then open the eyes again. Alternate your focus between the different colors and spaces. Repeat the process a few times and then stop. Write down your experience.

Exercise #12

picture 10

Again, relax. Breathe slowly and allow the mind to become still. Focus on **picture #10.** Allow your eyes to notice the circular motion of the spiral. See the two colors forming the spiral image. Let the mind go and focus on the colors and shape. What thoughts come to mind? What feelings does the shape invoke? Once more focus the attention on the center, let it guide the eye through the circular motion. **Close the right eye** and with the **left eye follow** the pattern of the spiral. Then **close the left eye** and let the **right eye follow** the pattern. Close the eyes and think of the image and try to recall as many details as possible. Repeat the exercise a few times. Upon completing the exercise, take some time to write down the experience.

Scanning Auras

It is possible to read the energy field around the body with or without the eyes open. When a person learns to read the aura, what they are doing is tapping into the energy field and reading the patterns created by energy. (Srikanth) Each pattern indicates a specific issue connected to the aura which tends to change with physical or emotional transformations. As an individual scans the aura, they are assessing how the energy is currently impacting the person. (Srikanth)

It is not very difficult to tap into the auric field, however, understanding the information within may present a challenge. The information presented by the aura comes in the form of symbolic communication; through colors, symbols or images that represent fragments of a larger picture. To understand these fragmented bits of messages, it helps to keep a regular record of what occurs and write down personal insights related to the symbolism. With time and practice, the individual will be able to decipher the different meanings behind their internal symbolic system.

There are methods for tapping into the auric field which allow individuals to use either their hands or visual sight. It is recommended to experiment with a different technique until one feels comfortable. In the beginning, the individual will probably get warm sensations or see the color white surrounding the body.

In this section, there are two sample exercises to help **train your eyes** to scan the aura: 1. Learning to scan oneself. 2. Learning to scan others. The person will practice scanning their aura first before trying to scan anyone else. The individual will try one exercise with their eyes open and the other with them closed. The plan is to give the person a chance to experience two different ways of getting information.

Exercise # 13 (Reading One's Aura)

Get a candle and light it. Turn a few lights off and sit quietly in a comfortable chair in front of a mirror. Now close your eyes and relax. Imagine a bright light above your head. Allow this light to slowly relax the muscles on the head, shoulders, arms, and hands. Continue to let the light move down the body, relaxing the chest, stomach, thighs, and feet. Imagine the entire body completely relaxed.

Make sure to keep your eyes closed. Focus your attention on your 3rd eye located on the middle of your forehead and imagine it opening up slowly. With your 3rd eye look in the mirror and see yourself. Review the outline of your body and notice the glow around the body. As you review your body with the 3rd eye what kind of images, colors, or symbols appear?

Next, open your eyes, and again look at your body in the mirror. Focus on the outer edges of the body and let the eyes see whatever comes up naturally. What do the eyes see? Do the eyes see any colors? Are the images or colors bright or dull? Write down whatever is visible, even if it seems minor. Repeat this exercise a few times to help develop the skills to see auras. It does take practice, so be patient.

To help facilitate the process of documenting the experience, answer some of the following questions and write down answers to whatever applies personally:

- **What was the experience like**
- **What type of images became visible?**
- **Where in the body were the images?**
- **How many colors were there?**
- **What kind of thoughts came to mind?**
- **What were the feelings experienced?**

Also practice as often as possible to improve the skills.

Exercise #14 - Reading a Client's Aura

Always make sure you relax before engaging in any intuitive practice. Breathe nice and slow and let go of all expectations. Turn off most of the lights and sit in front of the person before beginning the session.

Now close the eyes and relax. Imagine a bright light above the head. Allow this light to slowly relax the muscles in the head, shoulders, arms, and hands. Continue to let the light move down the body, relaxing the chest, stomach, thighs, and feet. Imagine the entire body completely relaxed and comfortable.

Slowly, open your eyes and focus on the outline of the client's body. Keep the eyes on the center of the image and allow the eyes to pick up the glow around their body. As you focus on the glow around the body, what are some of the feelings you experienced? What images or thoughts do you notice? Allow your eyes to move down their shoulders, back, legs, and feet. Do this very slowly; allowing the eyes to see whatever comes up. When the exercise is complete, take note of whatever occurred. Make sure to write things down before discussing them with the client. To make the most of the exercise, it helps to answer some of the following questions:

- **What type of images were revealed?**
- **Where in the body were the images located?**
- **Are there any visible colors?**
- **What thoughts come up?**
- **Are there any symbols?**

Remember to document results.

Chapter Summary

This chapter had a variety of information and exercise techniques designed to enhance visual perception and develop the ability to retain focus during visualization. The goal of this chapter was to allow each reader the opportunity to learn about a few methods and a chance to practice scanning.

The idea of reading auras might seem complicated and pointless to some individuals. However, any intuitive technique learned provides the clinician and practitioner with an additional tool they can use in therapy. There are times when a client is unable to disclose or verbally express themselves in a session emotionally. Every tool a professional can use becomes valuable in developing a connection with their client and helping them through difficult periods.

Chapter XI
Therapeutic Chakra Techniques

I do believe that there are creative chakras or different sorts of energy centers. -
Mahershala Ali

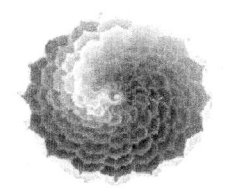

The Energy Life Force

Individuals in every culture have always been fascinated by life; from developmental stages, personal transformation, and death. In trying to control life for immortality as well as improving the quality of life, many individuals have embarked on the quest to find the secret behind the energy source that controls and influences the life cycle of all creatures and elements on earth and beyond.

Several types of philosophies evolved out of the desire to control the energy life force in attempts to improve the quality and duration of life. The philosophical systems of energy can be grouped into two systems which consist of **external** and **internal locus of control.** Each philosophical system provides **the individual with tools for** personal development and control. For some individuals, the life force involves seeking **spiritual guidance** in the form of religious instructions. While for other individuals the life force involves more **scientifically influenced guidelines** and improving living conditions through physical and emotional care.

Internal vs. External Control

In the process of developing systems to navigate the energies of the life force, some cultures created systems that were more internally involved, while others focused on systems that involved external goals. The cultures that believed that individuals were **responsible for personal opportunities** and survival, often focused on developing systems that helped the individual cope with their environment. Meantime, in cultures where individuals believed in an **outside force controlling** the events in their lives, they focused on developing spirituality systems and social structures that provided tools for personal development.

The ability to handle and manage life changes based on a sense of personal accountability is referred to as an **internal locus of control**. (Joelson 2017) The internally driven systems focused on self-improvement techniques that include meditation, energy work, and internal awareness to achieve bliss and enlightenment. Cultural examples of internal locus control systems in Eastern Spiritual Traditions focus less on dogma and more on proactive spiritual engagement for example practices like Buddhism, yoga and amplifying the body's chi.

The task of trying to understand and control one's actions can be tricky and difficult for some, especially individuals with mental imbalances. Reliance on external forces to provide guidance became essential for individuals who lacked personal direction, the clarity and confidence to rely on themselves. The **externally focused system** caters to the mindset of developing behaviors and overcoming challenges to help the individual achieve personal fulfillment. Individuals who have an **external locus control** mindset relied on the guidance of individuals who provided spiritual wisdom or social structure. (Joelson) Cultural examples of **external lotus control systems** in many Western religious traditions provide spiritual direction through guidelines in the form of dogma, prayer, and contemplation on spiritual scriptures.

Cultural Evolution of Energy Systems

In pursuit of understanding the mysteries of life, energy systems evolved through the centuries and in almost every culture. Various energy systems developed that were motivated by both internal and external needs for personal control. Regardless of the internal or external motivation; every energy system provides individuals with ways to maximize their existence and develop a fulfilling life.

The fascination with mortality and lifestyle enhancement created a need to understand and control energy. Cultures throughout the world created systems that represented their understanding of how energy works, which resulted in the development of systems ranging from spiritual beliefs to scientific philosophies. Energy, whether it is scientific or spiritually based, it has been a core element in many traditions and cultures throughout the ages.

Various cultures not only have different philosophies regarding how the energy life force impacts individuals, but they also have different terms when referring to energy. The names for energy life force range from Lifeforce, Chi, Qi, Prana, and so on; and how individuals access the essence of those centers vary from culture to culture. The following chart contains a list of the different names along with brief descriptions.

Energy Systems

Energy Systems	Culture	Description
\multicolumn{3}{c}{Native America Systems}		
Orenda	Iroquois	The name of spiritual powers associated with the community creates a stable connection with the natural environment. The concept of spiritual connections to the environment is widely shared throughout the Native American tribes but are referred to by various names.
Manitowi	Algonquian	A Native American tribe which share similar spiritual belief system as the Iroquois tribe, except for some variations in ritual practices
Dige	Apache	similar to the Iroquois tribe, except for some ritual variations
Wakonda	Omaha	similar to the Iroquois tribe, except for some ritual variations
Waken Tanka	Sioux	similar to the Iroquois tribe, except for some ritual variations
Digin	Navaho	similar to the Iroquois tribe, except for some ritual variations
\multicolumn{3}{c}{North, South Asia, and Oceanic Cultures}		
Prana	Hindi	Lifeforce that comprises all cosmic energy, consisting of

		5 types of pranas known as the 5 Vāyus: prāṇa, apāna, uḍāna, samāna, and vyāna
Ananda Marga (Path of Bliss)	Hindi	A spiritual path revised by Prabhat Ranjan Sarkar. It includes biophysical aspects of the seven chakras and the mental aspects of the 5 Kosas
Shaktism	Hindi	Focuses on the energy center within, which is accessible through meditation and Kundalini yoga
Qi or Chi	Chinese	Referred to the vital force in every living thing
Ki	Japanese	Similar to the Chinese energy system
Chi	Indonesian	Similar to the Chinese energy system
Tondi	North Sumatra	The system of energy based on a spiritual system of the Tondi "Life-soul" (Karo) received from Mula Jadi Na Bolon (deity)
Mana	Polynesians	Known as spiritual energy that can impact everything from people to objects
	African and Middle Eastern Cultures	
Ase	Yoruba of Nigeria	A spiritual system in Yoruba Religion based on an essential life force that impacts a variety of aspects in one's life
Ka	Egyptians	Based on the concept that the human soul consists of five sections: Ren (Name),

		Ba (Personality), Ka (Vital spark), Sheut (Shadow) and JB (Heart)
Barakah	Sufi	Islamic mysticism that consists of blessings from the divine and the worldly
Lataif-e-sitta	Sufi	Based on six subtleties known as Nafs, Qalb, Sirr, Ruh, Khafi, And Akhfa which are psycho-spiritual centers that impact the sensory centers
Kabbalah	Hebrew	A spiritual practice that unlocks the divine mysteries of the sephirot
Ancient and Medieval European Systems		
Odic Force	Baron Carl Von Reichenbach	Forces from the electromagnetic fields of positive and negative flow through individuals, according to Reichenbach he believed that the flow impacted hypnosis.
Vital Fluid	Medieval Alchemists	Also referred to as vitalism which is rooted in the idea that imbalances in vital forces contribute to disease
Vis Medicatrix Nature	Ancient Greeks	Hippocrates developed a medical system using the concept of vital force related to temperaments and personal attributes

Though the names may differ, the ideas behind energy systems are similar throughout the different cultures, which is about connecting to the energy source.

The Western Chakra System

The focus of this section is on the Western Chakra system and the value of integrating it into therapeutic care. The word Chakra in Sanskrit refers to circle or vortex of energy. In simple terms, a chakra is a circle of energy. The chakra system is a term that comprises the various focal points of energy located throughout the body. Each energy center contains a cellular imprint of our emotional, physical and mental interactions with our surroundings.

The current philosophies related to the chakra system was made accessible in Western culture by several English-speaking authors, one of them being Anodea Judith, who wrote the book "Wheels of Life." The material presented to Westerners is an interpretation of one of many traditional energy systems that exist in the Hindu culture. (White 2012)

The work done with the Chakra system in Western culture is not one based on an ancient tradition, but rather an adaptation. The information used in the chakra system adopted by Westerners was written in 1577 by Pūrṇānanda Yati. (Wallis n.d.). The Chakra system modified and tailored made according to the cultural and psychological needs of Western society. The psychological attributes and healing recommendations are modifications made to meet the needs of clients and patients treated with Eurocentric therapeutic and medical philosophies. (White)

The Value of the Chakra System

The chakras system is a storage house of patterns that contribute to the shaping of our constructs. Every pleasurable or traumatic event we experience creates a mental and emotional imprint within the body, cells, and chakra (energy) centers. These imprints result from our psycho-bio-social responses, as well as from the collective memories of events that have occurred.

The body retains a record of events, specifically traumatic events because trauma activates the adrenal glands in efforts to prepare it for flight or fight (Cherry 2017). The spontaneous release of neurochemicals during trauma, produce an accumulation of chemicals within the brain's neurological system, preparing it for action and mental processing. Regardless of our ability to recall devastating events, our body never forgets trauma. (Miller)

Taping into the chakra system can provide a therapist with a variety of ways to help clients cope with trauma and emotional barriers. It is not just a system that works well for creating balance and overall energy; it can be useful in helping clients explore and heal memories often trapped in the body. The body, which includes our cells and energy points, will retain information since it is a warehouse not only of data for functioning but also a memory bank. (Miller)

Physiologically, the body undergoes chemical changes whenever emotional or traumatic events occur. The adrenal cortex releases glucocorticoid, known as cortisol which gets released whenever a person encounters situations perceived as dangerous. (Helsel 2014) The body prepares itself by producing chemicals that increase alertness and awareness during distressful and perilous situations. During traumatic and stressful events, the production of cortisol leaves behind chemical imprints in the brain and energy points throughout the body. (Helsel)

The topic of energy is discussed to help individuals understand the role it plays. Typically, many view energy as an abstract concept, difficult to understand and even imagine (O'Connell 2016). Many individuals struggle with the idea of energy since there is a tendency to believe mostly on evidence-based data and tangible concepts. The energy is the force behind actions and activities.

What is Energy?

"Energy is defined in physics as the capacity to do work," change or grow. (Solar Energy n.d.) It is the potential ability for an object, person or mineral to move, grow or change through the process of undertaking action. Energy can be considered the activating force behind living matter, or the vibrating force of power that propels living matter to move forward or transform itself.

(O'Connell 2016)

Every item in and outside the planet is affected by energy. Whether it is a mineral, animal or plant, energy has a tremendous effect. Energy affects particles of atoms, allowing them to work together to create any form of reaction. Each reaction will vary, according to the different combinations of atoms.

Energy creates cycles of changes or transformation in all living matter. Within each transforming cycle, there is a beginning, middle and an end. Each cycle will be different for each living source and generate a certain amount of heat and vibration that creates specific patterns of energy. To help understand energy, think of it as the force behind one's actions and reactions. When referring to the chakras, imagine tiny energy points throughout the body that react to stimulation, whether it is chemically induced or physically initiated.

How does Energy Affect the Chakras?

Since our chakras are energy centers, they will respond very quickly to fluctuations in the environment such as temperature changes, air quality, sounds, sunlight and even physical activities. The chakras are sensitive to different vibrations surrounding the body, which means, change can occur without the person being consciously aware.

The changes in the chakras can impact a person emotionally, and physically at any given time. For instance, ever notice feeling tired in the winter or irritable in a hot room or unsettled by an anxious person? Since the body contains energy centers that become stimulated, excited or calmed by surrounding conditions such as temperature, fragrance, sound, and even by the mood of other people.

What makes energy change?

The neurotransmitters in the brain are easily stimulated by physical and emotional encounters, which in turn change the flow of energy. Almost any situation can create chemical changes; emotional responses, developmental changes, death, etc. Anything that uses energy has the potential to change energy patterns. When a person engages in exercise, conversations, works, eats or sleeps, they are using energy.

The chakras system retains all types of personal data and chemical imprints. Learning to tap into the chakras will allow an individual to tap into a history of events and reactions imprinted within the system. Different events such as childhood traumas, scary experiences, and pleasurable sensations leave chemical imprints within the chakra centers which serve as a roadmap into the background of any person.

Background on Different Energy Systems

The Western culture has adopted a chakra system strongly influenced by Hindu philosophies. The Hindu system used by Westerners is one of many used in the Hindu culture. There are a variety of energy systems utilized globally in healing and spiritual practices. To understand precisely how the various chakra systems, differ, it helps to do a comparative exploration of several energy systems. There is a sample outline of the Tao Chakra system, to give clinicians an opportunity to review more than one system, After the Tao Chakra, we will be reading about the Hindu Chakra system used by Western practitioners.

Taoist Chakra System

The Taoist energy system is primarily focused on the relationship between body, mind, and spirit, using chi to create a state of healing. The Taoists use the chakras as indicators of potential medical and spiritual problems. Taoist practitioners focus on the aspects of energy as related to the five elements in nature. In the Taoist system, numerous types of remedies are designed by combining the natural elements and their corresponding attributes.

The Taoist system is not as psychologically oriented as the Westernized Hindu system; however, it has an elaborate system of healing that creates a balance between the mind and body. The Taoist system is excellent, especially for practitioners in the medical or physical therapy profession. Below is a Taoist Energy System chart that provides a brief outline of different attributes.

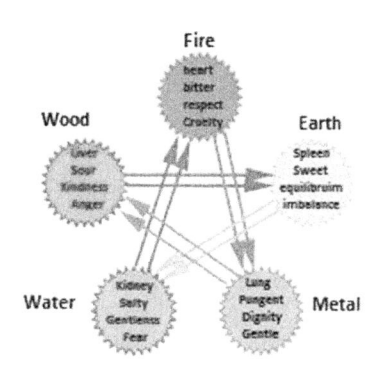

Taoist Energy Chart

Taoist Energy System

The 5 Chakras corresponding to the five organs

Energy Center	Element	Taste	Positive	Negative
Heart	Fire	Bitter	Respective	Cruelty
Lung	Metal	Pungent	Dignity	Grief
Kidney	Water	Salty	Gentleness	Fear
Liver	Wood	Sour	Kindness	Anger
Spleen	Earth	Sweet	Equilibrium	Imbalance

This system serves as a blueprint for designing diets, exercises, meditations and medical remedies. The Tao energy system is excellent for healthcare practitioners.

The Hindu Chakra System

Before beginning this section on the chakras, it is essential to understand why the Hindu system has been selected and used as a system for working with the chakras. First, the Hindu system is a spiritual system that was designed to help individuals evolve to their highest potential. This system has however been modified and adopted by Westerners, because of the way it allows one to tap into various emotional, physical and mental aspects.

The chakra system incorporates two dimensions one being the physical realm and the other the psychological realm (subtle body). (Sharma 2006) The subtle body contains over of 88,000 chakras, however traditionally, only 4 to 7 are utilized in most healing systems (Grimes 1996)

The Hindu chakra system focuses on seven centers. These centers correspond to 7 levels of development that allows an individual to evolve towards a spiritually enlightened path. The original Hindu system was modified to include a psycho-social approach that focuses on using the energy centers to maintain personal wellness and overall balance. (White)

The modified version of the Hindu Chakra System focuses on working through emotional and behavioral blockages to obtain a healthy lifestyle. In the traditional Hindu chakra system, one learns to overcome obstacles, to achieve spiritual enlightenment, while in the Western culture the system is used to work through personal blockages and achieve different goals

The 7 Chakra system deals with various aspects that affect the way we cope and deal with our daily lives and interact with the environment which consists of the following:

7th Chakra	This center connects us to our spiritual path
6th Chakra	Our ability to perceive and understand our environment
5th Chakra	Contains energy that enhances creativity and communication
4th Chakra	Connects us to others emotionally, and impacts relationships
3rd Chakra	Influences our ability to make decisions and achieve goals
2nd Chakra	Issues related to sexuality and sensuality
1st Chakra	This area influences the aspects of physical survival

Primary Function of the 7 Chakras

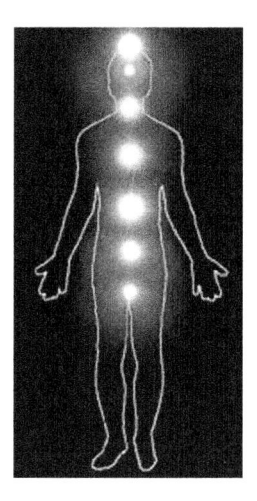

There are three types of functions for the chakras, mental, emotional and spiritual. Each chakra plays a specific role in how we handle our life daily. The seven chakras are similar to the organs in the body, where they are responsible for keeping the body working correctly. Though we focus on seven chakras, there are thousands of energy points (chakras) throughout the body. Again, in our physical body, we have our principal organs, then we have our sub-organs. The key is that our body is regulated and maintained in a healthy state by the principal organs. The energies within the chakras maintain our mental, emotional and spiritual system functioning in harmony with the environment.

When our chakras are working in harmony, there is energy exchanged between the environment and our system. Each chakra should have energy that's flowing in and out smoothly when they are working efficiently. However, the chakras are not always working smoothly, in the sense that the energy might be stuck or not circulating at which point problems begin to occur.

Energy provides us with the ability to perform specific tasks or engage in different activities. If the energy within the chakra system is blocked, there is a tendency to response sluggishly or with minimal effort. On the other hand, when there is excessive energy, we tend to have minimal control in handling the surplus of energy. In other words, the energy controls us, and we are often unable to manage or maintain a healthy balance. (Judith)

Reviewing the Chakra System

This section describes each chakra and how their specific function impacts us daily. The information provides us with material on how each chakra work when balance, as well as how it reactions when there are blockages or excessive amounts of energy. Also included are some therapeutic information that can be useful in mental health and healthcare treatment.

Though the focus is on the individual chakras, keep in mind, that a person may struggle with several issues at once which can also indicate that more than one particular chakra is off balance. In the event more than one chakra is off balance, the therapists or practitioner can do a combination of techniques.

Chakra # 1 - Survival (Muladhara)

The first chakra is located just below the tailbone of the spine. This area deals with the person's physical reality and how they interact with their world on a physical level. The energy in this area reflects the ability to survive and cope within the physical realm.

Attributes Associated with this Chakra

Issues related to making a living, dealing with the physical body and all areas linked to being able to feel safe and secure. The first Chakra allows us to handle financial matters, recover from illness and keep a roof over our heads.

Blockages: The issues found in the first chakra tend to create problems with making a living, obtaining finances, maintaining hygiene or health. The individual lacks the physical energy to engage in physical activities. There are problems with maintaining a stable home, job or health. Blockages in the first chakra can be mild or severe. However, the main issues are lack of stability, confidence, and security. **Personality Types:** The person is always struggling and unable to secure a job. There is a tendency to overeat when stressed and neglect their health. They seem to lack the skills to take proper care, might find themselves jobless, homeless or in poor health.

Excessive: When the energy is excessive in the first chakra it can reflect a person obsessed with money, physical appearance and material gains since they always fear to be broke. There is little satisfaction with material possessions, even when there is sufficient abundance. The person tends to reflect a greedy and needy nature. Another type of imbalance with excess energy is an obsession with their body. The person might lack a healthy outlook on their physical image. There is a tendency to see themselves as heavy, or they might have trouble maintaining a healthy weight. **Personality type:** This person may have obsessive traits, in which they hoard things or money. There is a tendency to have dysmorphic body issues since they may diet when in fact they are perfectly healthy in weight.

Key Treatment Focus

This chakra responds well to exercises that ground the energy. Some issues that related to the first chakra are **feelings of insecurity** and not believing in one's ability to endure stressful events or financial crisis. Guide the client through grounding meditations and visualization exercises to help them gain a sense of stability, and confidence to handle all situations. Colors to use during visualization are **reds, browns,** and **blacks** since they help ground energy and provide vitality. Red colors energize, brown and blacks stabilize, while **clear crystals** and **dark blues** have a calming effect. The meditations that work well with 1st chakra are as follows:

- **Grounding meditation** - Before doing any deep meditation techniques, grounding is useful in helping the person maintain calm and relax. It is essential that clients are comfortable in therapy otherwise their desires to share will become restricted due to anxiety and distrust.
- **Chakra visualization** - The visualization technique is valuable in obtaining information that can be used for developing treatment plans related to survival and feeling secure.
- **Inner Vision (Neiguan)** - This meditation is useful in reviewing the physical status of a client to help them understand issues related to their bodies and physical reality.
- **General chakra balance** – this guided meditation helps the client obtain balance and an energy boost. The general meditation is an excellent one to use for maintenance.

Chakra # 2 - Sacral Plexus Chakra (Svadisthana)

The second chakra is located below the navel. This chakra deals with energy used for sexual and sensual expression. It allows a person to enjoy their environment and relate to it emotionally and physically.

Attributes Associated with this Chakra

The energy in this chakra allows the person to engage in sexual activities and sensual pleasure. It dictates the person's ability to have fun, to enjoy pleasure and appreciate life. It influences emotional responses and interactions. This chakra makes it possible for a person to feel emotionally connected to a place of joy and pleasure.

Blockages: When blockages occur in the 2nd chakra it can prevent or limit a person from enjoying themselves sexually, emotionally and reduces sensual appreciation. When there is an indication of blockages, a person may become stoic, emotionally frigid, sexually disinterested or may find they lack interest in things that used to provide pleasure. **Personality type:** Sexually repressed and uncomfortable with the whole idea of being intimate, also struggles to relax and enjoy themselves in other areas as well.

Excessive: energy can create urgency for pleasure; overindulge in stimulating activities, such as overeating, drinking, and use of drugs, sexual promiscuity, and overspending. A person with excess energy is seldom satisfied with moderate pleasure; there is a need to fulfill an emptiness that never gets satisfied through ordinary means. Also, other issues consist of moodiness, over-sensitivity and having little control over emotional changes or reactions. **Personality type:** Very impulsive, tends to over-eat, drink too much or indulge in spending sprees. The fact is the over-consumption is about filling a void since they may feel empty or unfulfilled.

Key Treatment Focus

The imbalances in this chakra create excessive cravings and dissatisfaction with life. One of the general focuses should be to help a person find pleasure using techniques that are healthy. Clinicians should focus on helping the client find self-acceptance and joy without over-indulgence. Clients should be guided through a series of meditations using both breathing and visualization with colors. The colors to use during the visualization and with crystals are oranges and orange-reds to energize and create balance with blue tones.

- **2nd Chakra visualization** - The person is guided to explore issues related to sexuality and sensuality. Visualization can help a client imagine themselves enjoying things in balance and guilt free.
- **Vipassana meditation** - This meditation will help a person relax and obtain some balance by using breathing exercises and exploring whatever thoughts come up during the meditation.
- **Atma Vichara** meditation - This exercise allows the individual to explore their true nature without judgment or critical thoughts. The Atma vichara meditation helps individuals explore hidden sexual issues and how they impact their overall well-being.

Chakra #3 -Solar Plexus (Manipura)

The third chakra is located above the navel. The energy in this chakra allows us to obtain our goals, metabolize food and convert it into energy that can be used by the body. The energy within the 3rd chakra provides physical and mental endurance, the ability to complete goals, achieve potentials and maintain the motivation to move forward.

Attributes Associated with this Chakra

It motivates us to keep going, continue to pursue projects until they are complete. It gives us the energy to compete with others and complete task. It provides us with the energy to make decisions, take risks and face our fears. This center also allows us to connect intuitively to our surroundings (we recognize it as the gut feeling). We often **receive sensory information** through this center, which then we decipher through the 6th chakra where it becomes processed. The 3rd chakra can be described as the center of our gut feelings.

Blockages: When this chakra is blocked, it tends to make a person hesitate in making choices, trying a new task or even lacks the motivation to complete projects. It prevents a person from obtaining their goals, by making them feel unsure, tired or unmotivated. There is also, fear connected to this area that may make a person hesitate and become reluctant of not only taking a risk but also of achieving success. **Personality type:** The person is a procrastinator who waits so long to take action that they tend to miss out on great opportunities. This person has a lot of hang-ups and fears when it comes to making changes.

Excessive: The excess energy in the third chakra may make us more aggressive, ambitious and self-centered. We might take the risk without thinking of the consequences or dangers involved. We might even overlook others to move ahead. There is a need to become better than anyone else, in reality, there is a rejection of self, and one is often driven to become superior only to feed the fragile ego. The sense of importance or ego-driven behavior tends to mask fear, making the person appear more confident than what they are. **Personality type:** Overbearing, arrogant and competitive in a very unbalanced way.

Key Treatment Focus

The focus of treatment should be on helping a client develop awareness of their fears, tendencies to hesitate and self-sabotage. Meditations should help clients identify the fears that prevent them from obtaining goals and making confident decisions. Visualization techniques help develop courage, the mental clarity needed for making decisions, as well as improve the motivation required to complete tasks. Colors that can be useful in activating energy and creating proper motivation are in the yellow tones. Below are a few examples of techniques that can be used on the 3rd chakra.

- **Chakra visualization** -The person is guided to explore issues related to this chakra. This technique is valuable in obtaining information that can be useful in developing therapy goals.
- **Vipassana meditation-** This type of meditation incorporates breathing and learning how to control random thoughts that may cloud and impede decision making.
- **Mindfulness meditation-** This method is useful in helping a client focus on the moment, explore feelings and develop awareness

Chakra #4 - Heart Chakra (Anahata)

The fourth chakra vibrates within the heart region. The energy in this section serves as a connecting channel for the upper chakras and lower chakras. This chakra connects the energies of the upper with the lower to create a general state of balance. It also connects us to the outer world and connects the world to us.

Attributes Associated with this Chakra

This chakra also connects our energies to others. As a result, it serves as a relationship link, which allows us to connect emotionally, spiritually and mentally to others. This chakra influences our ability to receive and give love. Therefore, it can have either a positive or adverse effect on our ability to establish and maintain healthy relationships with others.

Blockage: Any type of block in the heart chakra can create many different types of problems in our ability to allow other people into our lives. It can make us very cautious and resistant to letting others into our emotional space. There is a tendency to lack trust, faith, and compassion for others. Our ability to have good relationships with others is impaired typically by the inability to open up and trust. **Personality type:** Cold and indifferent, often challenging to be around because they push people away

Excessive: When there is excessive energy in the 4th chakra, it can create a need to please and make others happy at the expense of our well-being. There is a tendency to lack proper boundaries and to know when to pull back. There is a compulsive need to be wanted and appreciated that is not healthy or fulfilling. **Personality type:** This is the people-pleaser and the type that lacks healthy boundaries. This person typically struggles to say no and tends to put others before themselves.

Key Treatment Focus

When this particular fourth chakra has a blockage, a person will struggle to trust and feel connected to others. The 4th chakra is a connecting center that provides a person with the ability to receive and give love. The general focus is to provide healing that will help a person overcome barriers to both receiving and giving. Some of the meditation exercises that are useful are **Metta meditation,** Atma Vichara, **Mindfulness** and **Vipassana techniques.**

The colors to use with this chakra are greens and pinks. The green provides balance, and the pink promotes healing. Use the colors during meditations or select crystals that match.

- **4th Chakra visualization** - The person is guided to explore issues related to relationships as well as self-love. Visualization can start by helping the person view themselves as being loving and love-worthy.
- **Metta meditation – Lovingkindness:** This meditation is useful in getting a person connected to others on a compassionate level. It helps promote self-love as well as loving connection to others.
- **Atma Vichara meditation** – It is a good meditation for individuals who have lost themselves in helping others, either through people-pleasing or simply as eternal caretakers.
- **Mindfulness meditation-** This very useful in exploring emotional states and developing inner awareness

Chakra #5 - Throat Chakra (Vishuddha)

The fifth chakra positioned in the throat area. (Darrah n.d.) This area affects our ability to communicate and express ourselves creatively. The fifth chakra is referred to as the creative center, through which we express our views of the world.

Attributes Associated with this Chakra

This center allows us to connect to the world through expressions and all forms of communication styles. Keep in mind that communication can take on many styles; we can communicate verbally, in writing, dancing, art, theater, photography, and teaching. Communication allows us to share with the world our thoughts and feelings, as well as the internal world.

Blockages: When the energy in the throat chakra area is blocked, it prevents freedom of expression. It can create speech problems, blocks in creativity and fear of expression. It may make a person resistant to share their feelings or even make them timid. It can also create anger, which can result from a collection of unexpressed feeling that has piled up over time. **Personality type:** This person is the human doormat who hesitates to speak their mind and stand up against abuse or poor treatment from others.

Excessive: Any time the energy is excessive it can make a person very talkative, to the point they are no longer able to listen to others or even to their own emotions. Talking becomes a tool to avoid feelings or hear unpleasant things. Creativity can be affected, in the sense that too much information can lead to confusion and not convey the right message. Also, rage can develop as a result of too much energy in the throat chakra. **Personality type**: This type of person can be aggressive or rude in their communication, or excessively chatty. There is poor impulse control which results in being insulting, rude or mean.

Key Treatment Focus

It can be difficult to communicate or express oneself when this chakra is blocked or has erratic energy. To help stabilize the chakra, clinicians should use visualization techniques to enable the client to let go of the fear and hesitations that prevent them from speaking with confidence. The therapist can help their client envision themselves as being assertive and capable of full expression. Use turquoise blue colors in crystals and visualizations techniques. The following are ideal meditations:

- **5th Chakra visualization** - The person is guided to explore issues related to communication and fears related to assertiveness. Visualization can help a client picture themselves being assertive and speaking eloquently.
- **Zuo Wang – emptiness meditation** - This meditation helps create inner quiet to help the person let go and regain clear thinking, especially when dealing with anger. Keep in mind, Emptiness meditation is not meant to keep a person silent about issues, but to help them think and process before communicating
- **Zhuangzi – Breathing meditation:** Another meditation designed to calm down the mind through breathing. Remember that a clear mind creates clear speech.

Chakra #6 - Third eye (Ajna)

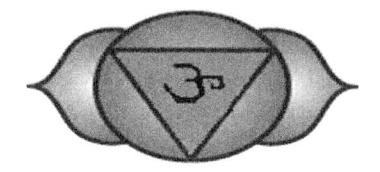

The sixth chakra located in the middle of the forehead. The sixth chakra is the center of visual perception, memories, thoughts and intuitive perception.

Attributes Associated with this Chakra

Through the 6th center, we can understand our world, others and ourselves. We develop awareness and understanding based on our ability to relate and perceive concepts. Through this center, we also gain an understanding of our world, intuitively. We can take the information we receive intuitively, process it and then translate it, to utilize the information productively.

Blockages: Any type of block in this chakra can create headaches, eye problems and trouble with visualizing. There may be a tendency to forget dreams or visualize during meditations. The person may not know how to interpret gut feelings or intuitive messages due to vagueness or inability to understand subtle concepts or ideas. There may be trouble in using the imagination or recalling memories.
Personality type: This person is often stubborn and inflexible. There is a tendency to be a bit close-minded and unwilling to see things that are different.

Excessive: The excessive energy within this area can create confusion and an inability to distinguish between fantasy and reality. There is confusion, irritability, as well as, lack of concentration, which is the result of not relaxing or resting enough. This person is often anxious to the point they cannot focus or sleep well. Also, the excess energy may contribute to reduced attention span and not be able to sit still for extended periods. **Personality type:** The person has trouble focusing because they are anxious and often easily distracted.

Key Treatment Focus

The key to helping restore this chakra back to balance is to help the person regain a sense of mental clarity and understanding. First, to achieve any clarity, the therapist must help a person obtain a peaceful state of mind and calmness. The therapist cannot work on any mental calmness or concentration until they help the person stabilize. A therapist can start out with simple breathing and then slowly introduce visualization techniques. The type of work that benefits this chakra would be, breathing exercises, Trataka, Vipassana, and Mindfulness meditations.

- **Trataka meditation** - helps calm the mind by using an object as a focal point. In this meditation the person keeps his/her eyes fixated on an object while breathing.
- **Vipassana meditation -** will teach the person to breathe deeply to relax their mind long enough to obtain insight
- **Mindfulness meditations** - will allow the client to learn to witness their life events without judgment.

Chakra #7 -Spiritual Center (Sahasrara)

The seventh chakra located in the crown area. The seventh chakra is our spiritual center. It connects us to our spiritual path and development. It allows us to stabilize our lives with a balance of hope, faith, and goodwill.

Attributes Associated with this Chakra

There is a blending of our actions and universal intervention working together. In this center, we can access information, understand and learn new ideas and concepts. We formulate thoughts and manifest them into realities.

Blockages: can create rigid and narrow-minded thinking. The person may have trouble accepting concepts that are different and new. There is a tendency to be stubborn and self-righteous. The person also lacks faith and tends not to believe in God/Goddess or Higher Power. Their faith is internal and believes only in themselves as being a source of Higher Being, rather than God or Goddess. **Personality type:** This person is the eternal skeptic, who cannot imagine or accept anything that they cannot see, hear or touch because at their core they do not trust anyone but themselves. They are excessively controlling and have little faith in anyone. The chances are strong that they will not want anything to do with intuitive techniques but might be willing to do meditation for stress and use aromatherapy.

Excessive: When the energy in this chakra is excessive, the person may not be very practical. There is a tendency to become fanatical, over-zealous and irrational; to have Christ-like thinking that is fragmented and not based on reality. A person with excessive energy can be easily confused, unaware and flighty; whose ungrounded energy can produce stress and anxiety. **Personality type:** This individual is often afraid to trust their thoughts. They do not take responsibility for their actions and often blame others for their issues.

Key Treatment Focus

The key is to help the client connect to their spiritual essence, which can be done using whatever spiritual or religious practice they are comfortable using. A therapist or practitioner can use either Western or Eastern tradition to help a person regain balance in this area. Also, the colors purple and white can be useful in visualizations to create a sense of balance and peaceful mindset. Some of the useful meditations can include:

- **Contemplative prayer -** The goal of using prayer is to allow the person to become connected spiritually to any source that provides them with comfort. This exercise is a personal one and culturally sensitive. As a therapist, if this does not feel comfortable, either explore with the supervisor or refer to someone who can provide this service.
- **Contemplative reading**- Spiritual readings are similar to prayers in which they are designed to help a person connect spiritually
- **Mantras -** They are words of empowerment, used with breathing helps a person relax and become centered.

Obtaining overall balance in energy can be a subtle but profound experience. The client can experience results but not notice them right away since the shift is often gradual and subtle. A therapist will know when the client is benefiting from meditation since they show improvements in attitudes and will report a shift in energy levels and feel relaxed.

Intuitive tools are not used to speed up outcomes, but to help a therapist tap into more inner core issues, and help a client relax without medication. Change, in general, is a process, and the results are a combination of efforts made by the client and the work done by the therapist. The changes are a combination of talk therapy, energy adjustments, and positive permissive attitudes. Studies in meta-analysis have demonstrated that meditation indeed reduces anxiety and stress, which contributes to overall improvement (Shear 2001). However, aside from the impact meditation may have, it is always essential to recognize the role the human mind plays on a person's ability to heal. According to Brann (2015), many techniques tend to work because individuals have an **approving mindset** which **facilitates positive outcomes**. In the case of therapy, when clients have a trusting relationship with their therapist, they typically are cooperative and willing to take direction unless the client has doubts about the efficacy of therapy itself.

Tools for Balancing the Chakras

There are different ways of creating balance within the chakra system. A person can obtain balance by using a variety of meditations and visualization techniques or energy tools such as crystals, aromatherapy or colors to name a few. The selection of healing techniques will depend on the needs of the clients since not every tool is user-friendly. For instance, a client with allergies will react poorly to aromatherapy treatments, while clients suffering from attacks with paranoia or anxiety might not feel comfortable using meditation.

The assortment of therapeutic techniques supplies a clinician with various choices which will provide their clients with a flexible arsenal for healing. There is never one way of doing things and being aware of the different tools will enable the clinicians to serve their clients well. In this section, there is a list of essential tools to help clinicians get started. (D'Angelo) The following are examples of useful healing tools for balancing the chakra energy centers.

Colors - can be used to balance and heal the energy centers. The colors are useful in visualizations, and in selecting crystals. Each chakra corresponds to a different color.

Crystals - are energizing and can be used to release blockages. The crystals can be placed upon the body in a pattern for chakra balancing or energy work.

Musical Notes - are useful for activating and calming the energy system. Meditation practice may include calming music or the sounds of gongs playing in the background.

Symbols - are suitable for meditations and visual focus combined with the specific chakra being worked scanned.

Herbs - great for healing, as well as balancing the energies. They can be taken internally in tea or dried and used with baths or powdered incense

Oils - used as an Aromatherapy tool for stimulating and calming the energies. Oils can be worn as a fragrance, added to candles, baths or powdered incense.

Elements - The elementals consist of Earth, Air, Water, Fire, and Ether, which are useful in designing healing plans. For issues related to physical conditions, elements related to the earth such as crystals or stones are beneficial, as well as grounding meditations.

Reiki Treatments: Reiki healings can be used in combination with aromatherapy and crystal layouts to balance the chakra centers. The therapist can use Reiki on a single chakra or provide treatment for the entire system depending on the nature of the session.

    The clinician can create a working combination of all the tools mentioned at their discretion. Alternatively, clinicians can use breathing, meditation, and visualizations techniques with each of the chakras associated with the client's existing problem. Also, when it comes to selecting healing tools, they do not need to be expensive or elaborate. The idea of using healing and intuitive tools is to enhance the senses and give them something that creates a mental anchor. (Bundrant 2013) Positive associations help set the stage for the majority of the healing journey, even if healing is the result of the **placebo effects** and a **permissive mindset.**

Practical Intuition for Therapeutic Practices

Quick Reference Guide

Chakra location & Sanskrit name	Element, color, mantra & music notes	Healing Essential Oils e = energizing c= calming	Healing Stones A= activate B-=balance C = calming
1st Chakra Muladhara	Earth, Red, LAM Deep C	(c) cedar, patchouli (e) musk, lavender, hyacinth	A= bloodstone, garnet B=Smoky quartz, black tourmaline, C= blue aventurine, blue agate
2nd Chakra Svadisthana	Water Orange VAM A	(c) musk, amber (e) rosemary, rose geranium	A=Carnelian, orange calcite, red jasper, B=aquamarine, kunzite, moonstone C= emerald
3rd Chakra Manipura	Fire Yellow RAM G	(c) vetiver; rose (e) Ylang-Ylang, Bergamot	A= tiger-eye, amber, Sunstone B= citrine C=sapphire, blue lace agate
4th Chakra Anahata	Air Green TAM F	(c) rose, sandalwood (e) pine, honeysuckle	A=peridot, rose quartz B=green aventurine, malachite, C=pink kunzite, rhodonite
5th Chakra Vishuddha	Ether Light Blue HUM F	(c) lavender, hyacinth (e) patchouli, musk, peppermint	A=Blue topaz, blue lace agate, B=turquoise, chrysocolla C= rose quartz
6th Chakra Ajna	Spirit Dark Blue OM D	(c) musk, hyacinth (e) rose, Star anise, geranium,	A=citrine, clear crystal B=blue agate, sodalite, lapis lazuli C=sapphire, kyanite, green aventurine
7th Chakra Sahasrara	Spirit Purple AUM C	(c) bergamot, rosemary (e) violet, amber, lotus	A=blue sapphire, B=Amethyst, clear quartz, diamond C=onyx, sugilite

Exploring One's Chakras

Learning to tap into the chakra system will allow a person to understand how the energy centers can influence and affect their lifestyle and overall well-being. The following exercise will allow the therapist to experience what it is like to tap into the chakra system and gather information.

When doing this exercise, remember visual information will appear as symbolic images or express itself as feelings or thoughts. The exercise is not designed to provide a person with details, but to help them get an idea of how to use guided meditations with clients and to experience first-hand how the process goes. If a person tends to struggle with visualizations, they should focus on the different sensations or thoughts. Not every person will get visual details since the individual sensory system will dictate how visualization will work for each person. If a person struggles to envision things, they should just think about them in their head, and this works just as well.

In the next section, there are a couple of meditations to explore. Try each exercise on separate occasions to give yourself a chance to process each one. After each exercise, write down whatever information was revealed, even if it does not make much sense.

Chakra Scanning Meditation exercise #1

Find a comfortable place to sit. Breathe in slowly. Relax the body, beginning with the face. Imagine your breath as a light breeze moving slowly down your head, neck, shoulders, and arms. Move the breeze down the chest, stomach and pelvic area. Now, let the warm breeze travel down the legs and feet; feel them relax. The entire body is in a comfortable, relaxing state.

Focus the attention on the first chakra, located on the lower level of the spine. Imagine looking inside the first chakra. How does this area feel physically? Pay attention to whatever comes up.

Imagine the first chakra as a screen revealing information. What images are reveal? There might be information that reveals itself as symbols, colors, pictures, or even as thoughts. Ask yourself; What issues affect the ability to survive, feel secure or maintain stability in life? Allow the answers to unfold and pay close attention regardless of how strange or obvious the information may be.

Next, focus on the energy vortex located above the pelvic bone, where the second chakra center lies. Let the inner eye scan the chakra for any information. Review all the messages or symbols revealed during the exercise. What is going on? Ask yourself what does the information mean and how does it affect the sexual and sensual energy? What are some of the issues within this area that affects daily existence? Wait for the answers.

Look inside the area above the navel, where the 3rd chakra energy rest. What type of information does this chakra reveal? What are some of the colors, symbols or messages that come up in this area? How does the information affect the ability to make decisions, achieve goals or judge issues in one's life? If there is any confusion, merely ask for clarity. All information is vital, so allow the process to unfold and accept whatever comes up.

Scan the energy vortex located in the center of the chest; this is the 4th chakra. Let the inner eye explore this area. What is going on? What type of messages or information is available? How does the information affect the ability to maintain or obtain close relationships? What are some of the issues that prevent the person from enjoying loving and caring interactions? Listen to whatever information appears without using critical judgment.

Next scan the area located in the throat area, this is the fifth chakra. Let the vision review all the symbols or messages that appear. What type of information was received? Listen, without judging. Ask what does it mean? How does the information affect the ability to express feelings, communicate with others or work with personal creativity?

Focus on the forehead area; this is the sixth chakra. What type of information was retrieved? Is it possible to see or hear any messages? How do they relate to the ability to perceive, understanding and intuitively connect to the environment? What are the blockages revealing and how do they affect a person's life?

Now scan the crown area, this is where the seventh chakra.

Permit your inner eye to scan for any information. What type of information did the chakra reveal? What does it mean? How does the information influence the spiritual needs or understanding of the beliefs? Listen without judgment.

Remain focused and review whatever was information presented. If necessary, go back to the areas that were either confusing or surprising in any way. Reflect, accept and try to understand the information received without critical judgment. Now allow white a light to fill all the chakras and aura. Allow this light to relax and balance the body completely. Now slowly open the eyes on 3; 1, 2, 3, open up the eyes.

When you have completed the exercise, make sure to document your experience. You can do this similar exercise with your clients and also use it as an ongoing check-in to review your energy centers. This meditation is useful in scanning the chakras for information that can provide insight and guidance useful for designing individualized treatment goals. Keep in mind that the energy in the chakra is constantly changing so the experiences will be different each time this exercise is done.

The next exercise is designed to help in balancing the energy system as a whole. This exercise is useful for both clinicians and clients.

Chakra Balancing Exercise # 2

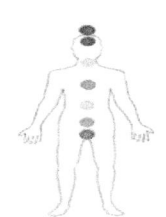

Find a comfortable position and breathe in slowly. Relax the body, beginning with the face. Imagine the breath as a light warm breeze that calms and soothes as it enters the body. Allow this breeze to relax the head, neck, arms, and hands, making them light and airy. Move the breeze down the chest, stomach, legs, and feet. The entire body is comfortable and completely relaxed.

Take a deep breath, feel it traveling down the body. Focus the attention on the spine, imagine it becoming long, and extending downward into the core of the Earth. Imagine the energy from the center of the Earth coming up and working its way up to the feet, legs, hips and pelvic making those areas feel revived. Continue to bring the energy up through the stomach, chest, and shoulders. Move the energy up to the neck, chin, and face. Completely cover the body from head to toes. Allow the energy to clear all tension from the body.

Focus the energy on the **first chakra**, located at the spine, allow it to clear away any unwanted energy. Place the energy on the **second chakra**, located below the navel. Once more allow the energy to release any tension. Next focus on the **third Chakra**, allow the energy to move to the front and back of the chakra, clearing away stagnated energy. Then, go to the **fourth chakra** located in the heart area, once more allow the energy to clear out blockages. Continue to move the energy up towards the **fifth chakra** located in the throat area, release blockages by just breathing in and out. Now, allow the energy to move up to the **sixth chakra** located on the forehead area, releasing any tension there. Move the energy up to the **seventh chakra** located on the crown area, let go of any tightness.

Next, imagine a **bright red** coming from the Earth's core and moving up throughout the body. Allow this red color to bathe every inch of the body, giving the body a sense of vitality and energy. Place the red color on **the first Chakra**, located in the lower part of the spine. As it fills the Chakra, affirm "I am stable, energized and secure." Repeat this at least three times.

Envision, a **vivid orange** color radiating throughout the body. Fill the entire body with orange, giving it passion, energy, and vitality. Concentrate on **the second Chakra,** located below the navel. Fill the chakra entirely with orange and affirm, "I am sensuous, fill with vitality and joy." Repeat this at least three times.

Imagine a **bright yellow** color coming from the core of the Earth and moving up every inch of the body. Let this color warm the body, making it feel light, healthy and joyous. Then, rest the color above the navel, **the third chakra**, where the solar plexus is located. Cover the chakra with yellow and affirm the following "I have an abundance of energy, willpower, and stamina." Repeat this about three times.

Think of a **forest green** color slowly covering the body, and making it relax. Take in the beautiful healing energy of green and place it on the **fourth chakra** located in the heart area. Allow the green color to remain on the chakra infusing it with a feeling of peace, balance, and love. Then affirm the following "I love myself, can love and receive love." Repeat this at least three times.

Next imagine a **silver-blue** color, moving up the entire body. Focus on the cooling and calming feeling the color induces as it covers the entire body. Allow the energy to relax and help calm the body completely. Place this beautiful color in the **fifth Chakra,** located in the throat area and say the following, "I am calm, clear and able to communicate all my thoughts, feelings and desires freely." Repeat this affirmation at least 3x.

Now think about a **deep indigo blue**, gradually coming up from the Earth and covering the body, making it feel peaceful and serene. Think about how serene and calm the body feel. Rest the color on the **sixth chakra** located in the forehead area and affirm the following, "I am serene, able to focus and perceive everything." Repeat this 3x.

Imagine a **bright violet** color going through the body and filling it with a sense of balance and harmony. Become aware of how comfortable the body feels and how the mind is relaxed and peaceful. Place this color in **the seventh chakra**, located in the crown area, and affirm the following "I live in harmony with life and the universe." repeat these three times.

Allow all the colors to radiate from the body evenly, creating a sense of balance and harmony. Affirm the following, "I am in harmony with myself and all that surrounds me." Repeat this three times. Once done, slowly open the eyes and count to one, two and three.

It is valuable to document whatever impressions or feeling came up during this exercise. This meditation is both useful for clinicians and clients to use whenever they are feeling stressed, overwhelmed or need to create an overall sense of harmony. The meditation is a wonderful exercise to use at the end of a stressful session, difficult week or basically for chakra maintenance.

Chapter Summary

As mentioned in previous chapters, the methods discussed in this particular chapter provides the therapist with options. The chakra system can be a valuable tool for creating balance, revealing hidden issues and creating new realities. The format in this chapter is one of many existing philosophies that cover the chakra system. The format selected in this chapter reflects the values of Western culture, but it does not mean that it is the only useful system. There is are a lot of different resources available on the chakra system which will provide more information as needed.

Chapter XII
Healing Regressive Techniques

People have motives and thoughts of which they are unaware. - Albert Ellis

Why This Chapter

Though the past is a completed chapter, its influence is continuously impacting the present. Diving into the past will not change the facts or remove the scars, but it will provide clarity and an opportunity for personal peace. Not everyone needs to dig into the dark corners of their mind to let go of the past; however, for many, the past holds the key to their present-day struggles. This chapter is for the mental health clinician and healthcare practitioner interested in learning how to incorporate regressive techniques into their therapeutic work.

What is Hypnosis?

The regressive techniques discussed in this chapter use hypnosis methods to induce the mindset required for the retrieval of unconscious information. Hypnosis is described as an induced state of relaxation created through a series of instructions provided by a hypnotist. (Cherry 2017)

History of Hypnosis in therapy

The techniques of hypnosis are not new and have been available for over 300 years. (Olson 2012). Throughout history, hypnosis has been utilized in both the medical and psychological field. In medicine, hypnosis has been used to help reduce pain during medical procedures while in therapy it was used to help clients uncover memories and unconscious patterns (Olson). Hypnosis is often considered the first form of psychotherapy since was an integral practice of therapeutic practice. (Jiang, White, Greicius, Waelde & Spiegel 2016)

Through the years, the clinical use of hypnosis became less prevalent, once it became popular with entertainers who used it to perform parlor tricks. (Potter 2004) However, various studies have proven the efficacy of hypnosis as an adjunct for treatment such as Psychoanalysis, Addiction therapy, Behavioral therapy, Cognitive Behavioral Therapy and pain management (Olson).

Hypnotic techniques are ideal for modifying behavior patterns, healing old wounds, creating new ways of thinking and diagnosing core issues. In this chapter, various techniques are explored and reviewed to provide information on the different styles of implementation.

Healing Regressions and Hypnosis Techniques

Hypnosis is a tool that helps a client become more receptive to uncomfortable questions and emotional recollections. A client in a state of hypnotic suggestion tends to be willing to explore issues and take directions, a lot more than someone who is fully conscious. Hypnotic techniques induce a mindset that allows the client to bypass **conscious critical thinking** that often makes them anxious, reactive and fearful of the unknown. Of course, not every person is "hypnotizable," which means that hypnosis might not be a useful tool for certain individuals. (Hilgard 1965).

Medical studies done with patients undergoing surgery using both local anesthesia and hypnosis as a supplement indicated that the combination provided significant results; Meantime, clients who were undergoing surgery with local anesthesia alone or only hypnosis did not yield a substantial outcome in comparison. (Faymonville, Fissetter, Mambourd, Roediger, Joris & Lamy 1995).

Hypnosis has been successful in helping clients reverse sensations and memories associated with pleasure and painful experiences, as well as alter cognitive functions. (Hilgard). Since hypnosis is successful in shifting emotional associations, it can be a significant tool in reducing self-sabotaging behaviors and negative patterns. Of course, hypnosis is not a replacement for therapeutic interactions, but a tool that can facilitate memory retrieval and behavior modification. Not all types of therapy modalities can benefit from hypnosis, especially if the sessions are focused on immediate needs.

There are areas in which hypnosis can be a valuable adjunct since it does help clients achieve relaxed states, which will allow them to engage in talk therapy with ease. Studies measuring the physiological responses to psychological stress under hypnosis reinforced its efficacy as a tool. (Freeman, Conway & Nixon 1986). In general, hypnosis can help clients become less anxious and tense when exploring painful memories without going into a severe crisis.

Conventional Therapy and Hypnosis

Though hypnosis might seem like an easy way to get to the core of a situation, it is not always the best technique to use in therapy. There are times when the information gathered through hypnosis might overwhelm the client emotionally; especially if they lack healthy coping skills.

Since clients often encounter sensitive memories, the therapist needs to be able to help them through the emotional process. The clinician is required to be adequately trained in hypnosis and has the therapeutic skills to handle a crisis. Also, it is essential for the clinician to know which therapeutic techniques are appropriate to use with hypnosis. Some recommended combinations of hypnosis and therapy are the following:

- **Aromatherapy** – Essential oils combined with hypnosis work together in triggering memory recall. The olfactory system has a memory bank that becomes activated whenever fragrances stimulate the senses. (Yun & Yazdanifard)
- **Art therapy** - art can be used to express whatever becomes uncovered under hypnosis. Through art, clients who are typically not very verbal can create pieces that represent whatever they experienced during their hypnotic state.
- **Addiction** - Hypnosis can be useful in creating new associations that can decrease desires or cravings. Clients can be taught new ways to view unhealthy cravings or desires with detachment or negative associations. (Potter)

- **Behavior therapy** – used for creating new beliefs and behavior patterns. Behaviors can be altered using hypnotic techniques that help clients envision new ways of engagement while pairing positive associations or anchors to those actions.
- **CBT (Cognitive Behavioral Therapy)** – works on exploring emotional states to develop new beliefs. With hypnosis, a client can trace emotional patterns and explore alternative ways to view them. In developing new ways to see old emotions, a client will learn new beliefs which will help create new thought patterns. (Kirsch, Montgomery, & Sapirstein 1993).
- **Holistic Coaching – a valuable** tool for exploring self-sabotaging patterns and obstacles to success. Hypnosis can allow a coach to review habits that sabotage clients and their ability to create positive changes and achieve success.
- **Pain Management** - Hypnosis has proven to reduce pain and has been used as an adjunct to pain management specifically for patients who had surgical procedures. (Faymonville et al.)
- **Psychoanalysis** – used for exploring the past and how it has formed current situations. Traditionally psychoanalysis has used hypnosis as a vital tool for helping clients uncover hidden emotional patterns and unresolved issues. (Bachner-Melman 2001)

Though hypnosis techniques offer valuable results, it is not a technique that should be utilized by every professional working with clients. Hypnosis techniques should be implemented only by professionals trained in the mental health field since the issues that may unveil during hypnosis may require proper emotional intervention.

Practical use of Hypnosis

The hypnotic process primarily focuses on past events in a symbolic sense. Our history is recorded in fragments that convert into symbolic tags. We seldom recall every single detail of our past. However, we tend to recall events that create strong emotional charges. Many events that create strong emotional reactions are paired off and stored away with our symbolic tags. The individual's emotional state contributes significantly to the construction of memories, which often taint the facts with subjective views. However, even if the experience is subjective and memories recalled are modified symbolic tags, the symbolism revealed remains a powerful ally in the healing process. (Read & Lindsay 2013)

Whenever an event occurs in the present that ignites emotional reactions, symbolic tags get activated, bringing to life the old emotional history. The past haunts everyone, because of the adverse emotional surges it reanimates, giving the impression, one is back in time. Hypnosis can reactivate old symbolic tags, which the therapist can use to help the client learn how to identify old emotional states and understand their role in current life situations.

Type of Client that can benefit from hypnosis

As mentioned before, not every client can benefit from hypnosis. When it comes to implementing hypnosis techniques, the following criteria can serve as a guideline:

1. The client should have a strong **therapeutic alliance** with the therapist
2. The issues being face are not an **immediate crisis**
3. There is **awareness of their own** PTSD or trauma history
4. There is **consistency** with therapy with both client and clinician
5. The client has **specific behavioral issues** that can benefit from modification
6. The **client is stuck** on issues related to the past
7. Useful in **reducing the symptoms** of specific mental health disorders: anxiety, depression, and OCD

8. Helpful in altering **self-sabotaging thoughts**
9. Improves the **flow of creativity**
10. Helps **athletic performance**
11. Useful for individuals in the **performance arts**

Hypnosis can be a fantastic aid in combination with traditional therapies; however, clinicians need to be aware of the limits as well as potentials. Hypnosis is excellent for gaining insight and reconstructing associations. Hypnosis can help clients develop ways to symbolically cope with their history of trauma or PSTD, as well as develop new emotional associations and behavior patterns. (Nathan & Gorman 2002)

When to Avoid Hypnosis

In any therapeutic relationship, the client needs to be ready and willing to participate in different aspects of therapy. A client who is not prepared to take on a specific task will not thrive and often drop out therapy when pushed too hard. There are few guidelines to follow when it comes to using hypnosis in treatment. The clinician should **not use** hypnosis for the following:

- There is **no signed a consent**
- The client is **in crisis**
- A Client who is **unstable**
- The client is **not comfortable** with the idea of hypnosis
- A client who **does not trust** their therapist
- The client is **not fully informed** or aware of the nature of hypnotic techniques
- The client is **intoxicated or under the influence** of drugs
- The Client has **current issues or crisis** that require immediate attention
- Clients with **poor memory recall**
- The therapist who is **not properly trained in hypnosis**
- Clients with an **active diagnosis** of delusions, dissociative disorders, psychotic or schizophrenia

- Clients with **inconsistent** attendance in therapy

Though there are limitations to hypnosis, it does not mean clinicians should avoid using it.
The key to the successful implementation of hypnosis depends on the needs of the client. (D'Angelo)

Implementing Healing Regressive Techniques

There are **numerous systems of hypnosis** that cater to a variety of therapeutic modalities making it challenging to decide which system to incorporate into therapy. (Olson) Knowing exactly how and when to use hypnosis is essential to produce effective outcomes. Hypnosis can be a valuable adjunct to therapy if used correctly and in combination with a treatment plan. (Kirsch, Montgomery, & Sapirstein). Using hypnosis without therapeutic goals is a waste of time and produces no necessary outcomes. Four regressive systems that help maximize the benefits of hypnosis consist of the following:

- **Exploratory technique** - **Utilizes hypnosis to assess core issues** for developing a productive plan of action.
- **Retrocognitive Review** – **Useful in reviewing memories** to obtain insight and understanding
- **Regressive Healing** - **Valuable in helping clients** work on trauma and emotional scars through release work
- **Regressive Recodification** – Used for **recodifying patterns** by reframing self-sabotaging thoughts and beliefs

The process of applying healing regression in therapy involves knowing how to combine hypnosis with treatment modalities that address the existing problems of the client. The different ways of using regressive techniques can be used gradually at different stages during the client's treatment process. Each technique uncovers a different component in the individual's life and should be utilized based on the therapeutic goals of each client.

Regardless of which **hypnotic technique is** in therapy, clients are in a trance-like state which permits them to be guided through a series of exercises. While in a trance, the person explores specific events or memories while remaining relatively calm.

The Hypnotic techniques used for **exploring, reviewing, healing** and **recodifying** use a sequence of suggestive instructions that take a client through a series of progressive stages. Each technique places the client in a trance-like state where they are relaxed and able to respond to suggestions. Each method will be explored separately and more thoroughly to provide both the clinician and practitioner with ideas on how to use hypnosis productively. Keep in mind that the four systems present for using hypnosis are **not a form of hypnosis** itself, but rather a concrete system in which to use hypnosis.

The Four Regressive Systems

The following systems can be used with most hypnotic techniques. The goal of each system is to allow the professional with a format that allows them to use their preferred hypnotic technique in their therapeutic practice.

Exploratory Tool
Primary Goal: This tool is for **exploring** and **uncovering the past.** The therapist can identify **core issues** that help direct treatment focus.

Exploring our past can be fascinating and seems to interest many people. There are countless reasons people are interested in their history. Some people want to reconnect with old memories and skills. While others want to heal old wounds or release old patterns that contribute to self-sabotaging behaviors

The past can hold the key to helping us to understand current behaviors and attitudes. We can regain confidence and the spark we might have lost throughout the years or even heal old wounds. Unlocking the core issues can be freeing for many individuals. Of course, some may struggle to face the past and might resist the process. At times specific events are locked away because we are not able to handle the memory emotionally, mainly if there is trauma or unbearable pain.

The past haunts us mostly because we tend to ignore the lessons it tries to teach us and because we repeat patterns. Also, history entraps us because of the unresolved issues that consciously affect us and often prevent us from obtaining specific goals. We hold onto the past like a weapon that we use for perpetual self-punishment. If we can learn from our past, we can also learn to let go of the pain and torment associated with it. Exploring the past does not need to be grim and painful, it can be uplifting and free when done correctly.

Our recollection of the past often occurs symbolically and not always in precise details. (Schacter et al.) If indeed what is a recall is only symbolic, it can still be helpful in developing an understanding of present issues or conflicts. However, in viewing a memory, what is the most vital aspect is not how disastrous the event was, but the usefulness of the information in helping the individual. The recollection of any memory can be beneficial in helping the client gain insight and tools for coping with patterns.

Limitations on Exploring the past

When it comes to using hypnosis, there is potential for the creation of false memories, which can be a problem when trying to undo negative associations that continuously impact the life of a client. (Schacter, Guerin, & Jacques, 2011). For example, in the case of dissociative disorders, clients cope by emotionally disconnecting from painful events. However, in trying to retrieve the memories, it can be tricky to determine which memories are real and which ones were created as part of the defense mechanism. Though hypnosis has been proven effective, it does have limits in reproducing specific memories. (Nathan & Gorman)

Complete memory recall is a problem with hypnosis since few individuals have precise recollections of their past. Memories can be distorted and poorly recorded, due to the intensity of an event and limited life experiences that influence the ability to develop cognitive understanding. Subjective interpretations of events create many false memories. Regardless how intelligent a child may be, they do not have the life experience to understand adult behaviors, and therefore their recollection of events will reflect their emotional state during the period of an event.

Experiences witnessed without proper cognitive understanding contribute to distorted memory patterns. For instance, children growing up with a working mom might assume the mother is never around because they do not like their kids. When in fact, the mother might be economically struggling to feed her kids but has kept the information to herself, because the kids are young and she does not want to burden them. Meantime, the kids grow up assuming that the mother did not like them, making their childhood memories tainted by misunderstandings and lack of complete awareness, sadly, this is the reality of many adult memories. Not having a complete understanding of the factual history can influence emotional states and beliefs for many individuals as well as create false memories.

Traumatic Emotional Imprints

Intense events like trauma and abuse, leave emotional scars that impact the individual throughout their lives. Whenever we face trauma, extremely emotional circumstances, our defense mechanism activates to protect us as best as possible. Individuals with trauma or PSTD, often develop dissociative disorders as a coping mechanism. As an outcome of using dissociation as a defense mechanism, many of the recorded memories have missing information and essential details. Dissociation protects individuals who might not have the proper coping skills to handle the intensity of the event. In the case of working with someone who lacks adequate coping tools, it is essential to help them develop proper skills before engaging them deeply with exploratory hypnosis techniques.

To survive both trauma and unpleasant circumstances, individuals learn how to diminish the pain. Many erase painful memories through defense mechanism and while others learn through reconstructing the realities based on cultural influences. Many memories can be influenced by a person's ability to cope and make sense of events that take place in their life. Moreover, depending on how well a person learns to survive in their environment, their recollection of their history will vary. (Read and Lindsey) Examples of how adverse conditions can influence the ability to cope are apparent in the behavior of kids who become rebellious, withdrawn or reckless after experiencing periods of abuse, trauma or personal crisis.

In essence, the ability to handle stressful or traumatic circumstances will influence how individuals react as well as form memories. Though memory patterns may have distorted details or missing pieces, the emotional residue is real. Most events in the past would create emotional imprints, even if the recorded history was based on misinterpretations or diluted by dissociative defense mechanisms.

Benefits of Hypnosis as an Exploratory Tool

In using hypnosis as an exploratory technique allows the clinician to **unlock core issues**. Though clients can benefit from hypnosis, not everyone is immediately responsive to the idea of uncovering deep core issues due to trust. Many individuals mistrust hypnosis due to its history of parlor tricks associated with show business. (Potter) Also, there may be clients who are willing to use hypnosis who might not be "hypnotizable." If the client is unable to achieve a hypnotic state, do not push the topic. Though hypnosis might have limits, there are **many benefits** associated with using exploratory techniques such as the following:

- **Reviewing** core emotions
- **Uncovering** negative associations
- **Exploring** old events
- **Tracing** old behaviors and how they influence the present

Clinicians can use **exploratory techniques** in a couple of ways depending on the nature of therapy. If a clinician wants to review a client's emotional history or trace old patterns and behaviors, hypnosis is an ideal tool.

Memories are gathered and created through a collection of historical events, which we piece together to form a cohesive plot that becomes our life story. However, it is essential to be aware that memories are recorded through a subjective interpretation of our past, creating natural limitations and several false memories. (Schacter et al.) There are a few things that impact memory collection and retention:

1. **Poor cognitive processing** – lacking full comprehension of events
2. **Misinformation** – not having access to entire facts, leads to false memories
3. **Defense mechanisms impact processing** – being in a state of shock impairs the processing of new accurate memory
4. **Poor attention skills** – not being able to focus impacts the ability to retain information
5. **Distraction created by chemical overstimulation** – too many activities overload the system
6. **Undiagnosed ADHD** – kids or even adults who struggle with concentration due to undiagnosed attention disorders may struggle to recall events
7. **Misdirection by over-protective adults** – being told false information to protect from pain
8. **Exaggerate impressions** – a tendency to perceive situations bigger than they are. (the big school desk in our childhood seems smaller when we visit as an adult)
9. **Cognitive Impairment** – Having limitations as the result of poor cognitive skills or disabilities
10. **Physical disabilities** – Individuals with the impaired sensory system will struggle to gather information through the senses. For instance, a person struggling with the olfactory system, will not recall what their grandmother's apple pie smells like; individuals lacking perfect sight will experience visual memory different than individuals a 20-20 vision.

Though memory recall may have limitations, the information retrieved can be **symbolically valuable** and useful in creating a new reality. False memories are tricky but are still useful in therapy. When working with hypnosis, the clinician is working with emotional memories, which are irrespective of its authenticity, can be recalled as being either painful or uncomfortable. The goal of hypnosis is not necessarily to "undo" the accuracy of history, but improve or modified the emotional connections to one's past by changing our views. In fact, what hypnosis is fundamentally doing is rewriting our perceptions.

Now the questions become, do we want to help a client revisit an event that they barely recalled and risk the possibility that the emotions will become intensified? In essence, the therapists should avoid placing a client in situations they can not handle emotionally and psychologically. As a therapist; they need to **know what they are doing** and **why they are doing it** because the client's well-being is at stake. Again, if **the therapist lacks the proper skills** to help the client cope with their Pandora's box of emotional demons; they should **not use hypnosis**.

Retrocognition Review

Primary Goal: The therapist uses this technique to get **insight and understanding of core issues**. This method allows a person to **gather information** from past events to improve **understanding** and **awareness** of hidden patterns, beliefs, and unresolved issues; it is also useful when doing regressive healing with clients.

This technique provides a person with the ability to tap into old memories and gather information that can be used in therapy, specifically with clients that are struggling to recall traumatic events. (Wagner 2017) This method allows a person to gather information from past events, which can be useful when doing regressive healing with clients. An individual's personal history can be both fascinating and painful, but it may not be readily accessible, especially if a client struggles with visualization or concentration abilities.

Many current situations are the result of unresolved issues from a person's past. Tapping into past events can help individuals develop insight into negative behavior patterns and begin to find ways to let go of old tapes. However, in viewing the personal history, the most vital aspect is not how one lived, but the usefulness of the information and what can be learned.

For many, the past holds the keys to freedom and overall healing. The past haunts many individuals mostly because there is a tendency to repeat old patterns and adhere to negative beliefs learned during painful events. Sometimes individuals hold onto the past as a weapon that gets used for perpetual self-punishment. If a person can learn from their past, they can also free themselves from its grip and torment. Past explorations do not need to be grim and painful; they can be uplifting and freeing if done correctly. If a person discovers that their recollection of past events was not meaningful or elaborate, they do not need to be alarmed. In the process of recollection, the information recalled is useful if it provides some insight and awareness.

Keep in mind whether theories are correct or not, one thing that seems consistent is that memories get stored in the form of symbols and with different types of associations. If indeed the experience only produces symbolic images, it still can be helpful in developing an understanding of the present issues or conflicts.

Symbolic recollection of the past is similar to the experience one has when trying to recall a dream. Whenever an individual wakes up from a dream, they often struggle to recall details. Sometimes the memory of a dream is entirely symbolic, and a person needs to decipher the meaning and sometimes its detailed enough where interpretation is relatively straightforward.

Limitations on Recognition Review

When working with clients in a regressive history session, it **can take time** to develop an understanding of a client's symbolic associations. The process of using Retrocognition can be tricky and will require knowing the client well enough to understand some of their associations.

Retrocognitive techniques are useful in cases that require intensive therapy but not often used since it requires some retrocognitive skills on behalf of the therapist. There are some specific limitations associated with recognition techniques which include some of the following:

- Both clinicians and practitioners need **training in hypnosis** techniques
- Clients need to have a **trusting therapeutic alliance**
- The client is **new to therapy**
- Some clients have **poor coping tools**
- Clients have **cognitive impairment**
- The client is **not sober enough** to handle old emotional triggers

- Active drug use can **impair experience and judgment**
- **Suicidal ideation** which requires priority

Recognition review can be challenging to do when a client does not trust the process of hypnotherapy or therapy in general. The client also needs to be in the proper state of mind to understand the process as well as the information obtained.

Benefits of Recognition Review

Before using regressive techniques, it is essential for the therapist to explore the exercise in advance to get comfortable with the process. Again, this skill is one used for **extreme cases** that require the intensive skill of therapy. For instance, the following situations would work well with retrocognitive techniques:

- Victims of rape, incest
- Post Trauma Stress Disorders
- Childhood traumas

The main reason to use retrocognitive techniques is to help facilitate the exploration of uncomfortable issues in a person's history. (Wagner) The therapist joins the client in the memory recall so that the client can feel safe and not entirely alone. Also, it helps in the exploration of topics that a client might not be comfortable verbalizing. The memory recall may have more symbolism for the therapist than the client; however, part of the process of therapy is to explore the meaning of the symbolic recall and help the client obtain meaningful understanding.

The following exercise is designed to help the clinician understand how hypnosis works and the benefits of using it. However, the exercise does not substitute for real training and should only be used in personal exploration.

Reviewing the past Exercise

Find a quiet place and get comfortable. Take a second to relax and let go of all thoughts. Take a deep breath and relax. Slowly, allow the thoughts and mental noise to quiet down. Close your eyes and imagine a white light above your head. Allow the light to gently enter through the top of the head, making it feel very calm. Allow the light to move down the face, neck, and shoulders. Gently let go of any tension.

Now relax the entire body, beginning with the head, shoulders, chest, stomach, legs, and feet. Relax and imagine a tunnel. Walk through the tunnel slowly – at the end, you will find a white room. In this room, there is a chair. Take a seat. Think about a specific issue to explore. While focusing on the issue, imagine a calendar in front of the chair and notice today's date on it. Allow the pages of the calendar to go back in time and then allow the calendar to stop wherever it may. The past is occurring now.

Visualize sitting in front of the screen, and see a movie playing based on the past. What is going on? What day is it? What is happening? Who is involved in this event? What type of feelings are you experiencing during the exercise? When did this event take place?

When satisfied, with the answers, allow the movie to end. Slowly allow the screen to vanish. The calendar replaces the screen. Let the calendar move forward until it stops on today's date. The calendar vanishes. See yourself standing in the white room and then begin to walk back through the tunnel, leaving behind the white room. Notice the chair. Focus on the body slowly waking up. Allow the legs, stomach, and chest to feel alert, neck and face. The entire body is awake and alert. Now slowly on the count of three, open the eyes; one, two, three.

Take a few seconds and mentally review the exercise. Before documenting the experience review the following questions:

- What type of images appeared?
- What type of thoughts did you have?
- How did your body respond to the energy?
- What type of colors did you see?
- Were there any shapes?

- Were there any symbols?

Once the questions are complete, document the outcome. Keep in mind the exercise was designed to provide an experience and not to evaluate performance. Each exercise is created to help the individuals explore and understand the experience.

It is essential to keep in mind that how an individual performs the exercise is essential. The exercise is designed to provide an opportunity to experience the process of **recognition review**. However, memory recall can be inaccurate due to lack of clarity and accuracy. Therefore the information should be treated as a **symbolic representation** and not an actual account of events.

The Regressive Healing Process

The" **regressive stage"** of hypnosis allows a client to be a "witness" while viewing their lives, merely to gain understanding. It does not necessarily mean, they will alter events or undo painful memories. However, they explore the past to learn how to heal. During the process of recalling the past, the client is merely gathering some facts and making sense of their history. Clients do not necessarily know how to create changes since the change is a process that requires modifying beliefs and attitudes.

During the regressive stage, the client goes through a series of exercises designed to help them review situations, so eventually, they can reformat how they view their past. Remember, as a therapist; hypnosis is not going to undo or remove the past; the task is to help the client review and understand what took place during hypnosis.

Regressive Healing Technique

The primary goal: The key to regressive work is to **learn ways to heal** that go beyond behavioral change. In regressive healing, the client reviews **harmful** and **self-sabotaging patterns** and then **learns ways to let go**. The therapist helps the client connect their current behavior with old patterns developed from their past to help break away from destructive actions.

The idea behind regressive healing is to guide an individual through a series of exercises designed to tap into past events to reframe their beliefs and associations. Through regressive healing exercises, an individual can **rebuild their views** on their past. Granted regression will not remove actual events nor undo the incidents that create painful memories. What regression can do, is help **review and reframe** how a person views **their past**. No one has power over old events regarding undoing them, but one does have the option on how one can examine his or her history and react emotionally to it.

Many of us have current beliefs that are rooted in our history which often keeps us stuck and unable to live fulfilling lives. Our views are often adaptations of the viewpoints of those that raise us and our environment. Our attitudes are influenced not only by beliefs we are exposed to but also our personal experiences. The combination of our inherited ideas and experiences, contribute to our abilities to function in the present.

Limitations on Regressive Healing techniques

All techniques in hypnosis can have their limitations and are never entirely suitable for all individuals. Many hypnotic techniques are useful in exploring issues, but not all techniques can help provide the healing clients require to live a fulfilling life. Several aspects restrict **Regressive healing** which includes the following:

- Insufficient Therapeutic training
- Lack of hypnosis training
- Client's mental status
- Immediate needs require attention
- Type of therapy is not compatible with hypnosis
- Agency policies do not permit the use of hypnosis
- Incorrect diagnoses

In order for regressive techniques to be effective, make any method relevant to therapy, the regressive technique needs to be proper for the treatment goals and the immediate needs of the client.

Benefits of Regressive Healing techniques

During the initial implementation stage, it is useful to have concrete information on what contributes to the existing problems. The attributes of regressive healing include **uncovering origins** of thought patterns and **emotional associations**, as well as **reduce defective thinking** and **self-sabotaging patterns**. Regressive healing can be beneficial for the following areas:

- PSTD
- Phobias or Fears
- Stress
- Grief and Loss
- Sexual dysfunction
- Anxiety
- Low-self esteem
- Self-sabotage
- OCD
- Depression
- Addictions

Though regressive techniques are useful in uncovering past issues and helping clients cope with painful memories by learning ways to let go, it does not remove the past events or the destructive personality patterns. Some patterns reflect personality traits and mental illnesses that regressive work cannot undo. For instance someone with a borderline personality disorder, dissociative disorders or schizophrenia will not benefit from regressive techniques. Therefore it is prudent to be clear about therapeutic goals when working with regressive techniques.

Regressive Recodification

This particular process of hypnosis allows individuals to **alter their views** on the past. It does not negate events that occurred, but it minimizes and **reframes** their significance in the person's life. The reason **recodification** is valuable has a lot to do with **reformatting** how the past impacts the present. Reframing the past does not mean an individual denies any occurrence took place, but what it does it lessen the value it plays in the present moment.

What is Regressive Recodification

Primary Goal: The key is **reframing self-sabotaging patterns** At this stage, the client learns how to develop **new associations** and create **new patterns.** The therapist uses this stage to teach the client new ways to handle situations by letting go of the past.

As we discussed, accurate recall is not always 100%. However, the ability to modified and reshape how we recall things is possible. Moreover, how we allow our "interpretation" of our history to influence us is also possible to alter.

Hypnotic recodifications work to undo negative associations, **learn new ways** to cope and **develop healthy beliefs**. Clients are guided through hypnosis to review old associations and modify them by placing their focus on healthier associations. The client is guided through a succession of progressive steps that help them redesign a new reality, using some standard associations that will help them relate. Suggestions are made to help the client learn how to view situations, feelings, and beliefs in a new and healthy manner. This type of hypnosis primarily focuses on changing old patterns, beliefs and creating new ones.

Limitations of Regressive Re-codification

Though the idea of recodifying patterns from the past is ideal, many individuals are not able to achieve changes. Individuals who struggle to achieve concrete results with any form of visualization will struggle with hypnosis. Also, individuals with the specific following issues will not benefit much from hypnotic re-codification:

- Cognitive impairment
- Active drug usage
- Uncomfortable with the process

The idea of re-modification allows individuals to alter how they perceive reality and how it impacts their behaviors and thinking patterns. However, not everyone can change their views on the past or feelings about past events regardless of how much time they are in therapy. These limitations go beyond the scope of many therapeutic techniques since impairments are not always tangible issues that have appropriate remedies. Though the goal of re-codification is about recreating the attitudes connected to the past, sometimes making peace with the past is healing.

Benefits of Hypnotic Recodifications

Recodification allows a client to undo old tapes, by rearranging their views on events that occurred in their past. The client can be guided to trace the origins of patterns and instructed to review the incident and then begin to view things differently. A client may be asked to see the incident through the eyes of the individual who cause them harm so that they can understand the situation from a fresh perspective. The incident does not need to be eliminated nor does a client need to deny the emotional impact it had on their lives. Critical elements in re-codifying the past consist of the following:

- Recognizing they are no longer a vulnerable person
- Recognizing their strengths
- Knowing that they are capable of handling present issues
- They have the right to let go
- They are not accountable for the behaviors of others
- They can stop blaming themselves
- They did not cause the incident
- They are presently not alone
- It is permissible to feel whatever feelings a person has
- It is ok to let go to make room for healthy emotions

Making peace with the past is crucial for many individuals struggling to move forward and live a fulfilling life. When an individual remains stuck in old patterns and feelings linked to old events, it becomes difficult to move forward and achieve personal goals. Though it is appropriate to have certain feelings regarding past events, remaining stuck in the past can be detrimental and stagnating.

Practical Guidelines

In this section, practical issues are reviewed to provide a productive experience when using hypnosis techniques. This section does not offer hypnotic techniques, but it covers issues such as:
- Hypnosis and Keywords
- Hypnosis and Culture Awareness
- Ethics and hypnosis

Hypnosis and Keywords

Words have power. The right selection of words, descriptions, and suggestions can make all the difference in how successful a hypnotic session will be. During hypnotic work, words regarded as negative or harsh will increase negative states. (Chooi, Nerlekar, Raju, & Cyna 2011) Words that are considered negative often reinforce negative conditions, while words that are considered positive will enhance and strengthen positive outlooks.

Though words hold personal meaning and often trigger everyone differently, certain keywords will improve or worsen conditions. (Chooi et al.) Words that induce a sense of well-being or invoke positive feelings are considered appropriate in hypnosis as well as in therapy. Words can be distracting, enhancing and create frustration. It is not enough to speak in a slow and soft pace. The words you select as a clinician will have the power to yield or limit results. For instance, words that represent empowerment, provide encouragement or motivation are preferred when doing hypnosis, meditation, visualization or therapy as a whole. For example, here is a brief list of words and statements that induce a positive state of mind:
- You enjoy
- You can
- You are able

- Release
- Let go
- Will create
- Imagine

The words provide the individual with having the ability to handle and do certain tasks. Though the words are simple, they are direct and reduce the opportunities for creating doubts or second-guessing oneself.

Hypnosis and Culture

Be mindful of the client's cultural or personal background when selecting specific words or phrases since they can trigger unwanted reactions. It is recommended that clinicians take courses on cultural sensitivity to help navigate the sessions as well as to learn about culturally rooted words that can create triggers. No one is suggesting that clinicians become a linguist, but it is vital that the therapist or practitioner become "aware" of the subtleness in language that provokes feelings specifically when using hypnotic suggestions.

The key when working with individuals from a different culture or background is to remain flexible and aware that the individual's personal experience with therapy will influence their ability to engage. The experience with hypnosis will reflect a personal reality for each regardless of their culture or belief system. According to Sapp 2016, hypnosis techniques permits culturally distinct individuals to experience the past in their unique way.

Ethics and Hypnosis

Historically hypnosis has been linked to theatrics and charlatans, which can make it difficult to consider as a useful tool for therapy. Many have seen shows in which the audience witnessed a few men and women behave like animals and entirely out of character, which is no wonder hesitate to take hypnosis seriously. Moreover, then there is the historical use of hypnosis by therapists who follow the teachings of Freud and primarily used it to trace back relationship issues with their mothers.

There is a middle ground, which has been evolving throughout the years giving hypnosis a seat upon the useful tools available in therapy. Of course, due to the number of misuses of hypnosis just like any other tool, a code of ethics has evolved providing practitioners with guidelines to protect the client and themselves from potential scandals and misconducts. The Hypnosis Training Academy (2015) cautions against unethical actions and has created some guidelines to help the therapist and practitioner maintain ethical standards. The ethical guidelines consist of the following:

1. **Informed consent:** All clients are entitled to informed consent, before administering hypnosis. A client needs to know and understands what hypnosis entails and what is the goal and purpose.
2. **Confidentiality:** Whatever information revealed under hypnosis, is between the client and clinician only. Client records are privileged information, and only the client has the privilege to reveal what they discuss in therapy.
3. **Misuse of Power:** A therapist cannot take advantage of a client under the state of hypnosis. There is to be no physical contact ever, either in a trance or while awake.
4. **Avoid making false Promises:** Therapist cannot claim nor promise results regarding the outcome of hypnosis. A therapist cannot guarantee results without knowing the entire state of the client's mental condition or physical state
5. **False Credentials:** Therapist cannot claim they have trained in any area when they have not. All therapists or practitioners who have not trained before should take a course or two courses or two in hypnosis. Do not lie to get a professional edge.
6. **Recycled Scripts**: Every client is unique and what works for one individual might not work for another. Avoid being lazy with clients; take the time to create an individualized hypnotic script.
7. **Poor Closure**: Nothing is worse than poor closure. Always make sure the client is out of their trance correctly or is ok emotionally. If a clinician is running late, they should not do a

hypnotic session, because clients need proper closure, time to process and they also need to be grounded to avoid going home in a vulnerable state.
8. **Avoid Ego**: The clinicians need to stop taking credit for fixing their clients. Everyone heals and improves on his or her own time and pace. Keep in mind, that hypnosis is a tool just like any other alternative or therapeutic technique. The real healing feature is the client, not the clinician or their technique

It is a professional obligation to maintain all sessions safe and free from harm. Every therapeutic effort needs to be approved by the client and their ability to participate. Effective therapy depends significantly on mutual respect and trust. Adherence to established ethical standards and codes provide individuals with a sense of safety and assurance in the practice of hypnosis. (Enea, & Dafinoiu, 2011)

Chapter Summary

Regarding learning how to do hypnosis, some of you may be wondering where are the instructions. The intentions of this chapter were not to supply a "how to do "hypnosis script since proper techniques should be learned. The thought of writing some scripts did occur to provide guidance was consider. However, the realization that some individuals would not bother to take proper training was the main reason for omitting a script. The lives of people are in the hands, of clinicians and we owe it to the clients to do an excellent job, without causing harm.

Chapter XIII
Intuitive Tarot and Psychotherapy

The true Tarot is symbolism; it speaks no other language and offers no other signs. - A. E. Waite

Intuitive Tarot and Psychotherapy

This section introduces the therapeutic benefits of utilizing the tarot deck in therapy. It is not a chapter on how to read the tarot since that would require additional material. The section reviews the role of symbolism, the benefits, limitations, and critical components for using the tarot. This chapter will not equip a clinician with the skills required to use the tarot therapeutically. However, it will help clinicians understand how the tarot can become a useful tool in therapy.

Integration of the Tarot in Psychotherapy

The possible integration of tarot readings in psychotherapy may seem contradictory to many. However, upon careful exploration, one can see the usefulness of using tarot cards in a therapeutic setting. The tarot deck when carefully examined without bias is a useful tool for free association, verbalizing thoughts and emotions that often elude the conscious mind and provides viable options for taking actions. An article in Psych Central (Dore 2017) compares the tarot deck to the Rorschach inkblot test, in which one can gain access to the unconscious mind through images. Though the tarot deck has no particular link to any school of psychology, its symbols are compatible with theories on symbolism used by Jung, Maslow, and Kelly (Semetsky 2005).

Throughout history, the tarot has been used primarily as a divination tool by psychics. However, authorities in the field of the psychoanalyst as well as psychology have explored divination tools, specifically the tarot due to their symbolism, personality archetypes, and personal constructs. Ralph Metzner (2008) explored various divination practices through his studies with groups and individuals, stated that divination is a method for obtaining knowledge. The tarot provides a reader, whether it is a psychic or therapist with a world of information through its **symbolism, archetypical figures, personal constructs**, as well as offering a system of navigating solutions through the **hierarchy of needs.**

The Value of Symbolism

Jung's theory of symbolism and its link to the unconscious mind provides us with insight into how the tarot represents our archetypes. (Adamski 2011) The cards provide a representation of our fears and hopes, as well as our potentials and personal roadblocks. A therapist can utilize the information displayed by the tarot spread to analyze hidden qualities and personal obstacles that can aid in the treatment of a client. For instance, if a card like "the Devil" card appears, one might assume it means terrible omens and evil events approaching, when in fact it indicates old patterns and a tendency to self-sabotage. (Wang)

Archetypical figures

Jung used archetypes to identify the various inner aspects of personality through symbolism. According to Adamski, he states that Jung used symbols to represent the inner world which consists of a multi-dimensional system that is best represented by archetypical types and symbolic associations connected with emotional temperaments.

The symbolism of archetypical figures relates to personality traits as well as temperaments that are represented by the tarot deck through the Major and minor arcana. The cards related to Major Arcane represents general roles and personality attributes. The Major Arcane allows the individual to access their inner guide or examine potential attributes that can assist them through difficult cycles in their lives.

The minor arcane consist of suits that represent the emotional temperaments of the individual. The minor arcane can be helpful in guiding the individual through emotional turmoil as well as provide them with options for coping and resolving conflicts. For instance, suits that represent swords, are often depictions of stressful states and anxiety, as well as indicating a need to handle situations logically. On the other hand, suits with cups can represent emotional well-being as well feeling emotionally vulnerable. The presence of any suit can indicate emotional states, in addition to providing guidance with handling stressful periods or find practical ways to cope.

Personal Constructs

Individuals have their unique way of constructing their realities. Psychologist George Kelly explains through his theories of personal constructs, that individuals have mental representations of experiences and observations that enable them to interact with society. (Cherry 2017). A therapist can tap into a client's construct to not only understand their reality but to decipher some of the negative patterns that create conflict and disharmony in the person's life.

Though Tarot readings, in general, can be a valuable instrument in therapy, as demonstrated by the rich symbolism, many therapists do not use them. The reason for the hesitation in using any divination technique is because many therapists are unsure how to integrate the tarot or divination tools into their practice legitimately without appearing eccentric or unprofessional. There are concrete ways to integrate the tarot deck into therapeutic sessions, but to do so, it helps to identify the benefits and most appropriate methods based on client needs.

Hierarchy of needs

Maslow's system of hierarchy of needs is a valuable format that suitable for both therapy and tarot readings. Maslow's system can be useful as a focal point when doing a tarot reading. A therapist can formulate a therapeutic game plan by reviewing what specific areas that require immediate attention in the client's life. According to Gilbert (2011), Maslow's system can be used to help a client grow through the different levels of their lives, and explore the essential aspects required for personal fulfillment.

Tarot and Visual Sensory

One of the central sensory system used in Tarot readings is the visual sensory system. The visual system offers tarot readers an opportunity to connect to visual symbols which activate the memory and intuitive insight. To develop the visual skills required to tap into the symbolic world of the tarot, the individual should focus on meditative and concentration exercises. Exactly how each exercise works in improving visual skills is as follows:

- **Meditation** – This allows the individual to enter a relaxed state and allow the unconscious mind to connect without the barriers created by overthinking and mental chatter. The meditation exercises will also help develop an internal connection to the tarot symbols, which will facilitate intuitive messages.
- **Concentration** – This trains both the eyes and mind to focus and reduces distracting thoughts from overwhelming the individual visually. Concentration exercises involve focusing on single objects or candles.

The tarot experience is facilitated through the visual senses, unlocking personal messages that reveal themselves through the vibrant colors, shapes, and images upon each tarot picture.

Benefits of Tarot Cards

Before using the tarot therapeutically, it is essential for clinicians to review the benefits. Not all divination techniques offer identical results or address issues in the same manner. Each client will have different experiences with divination tools since everyone has their constructs. However, regardless of the outcome, everyone will experience some benefit. Some of the benefits are the following:

- **Insight** - It provides insight into various situations, that talking alone does not provide.

- **Conscious connection** – It is a tool that offers the client an opportunity to explore areas they were not connected to consciously

- **Consequential processing** – It helps a client review actions and consequences before engaging in finalized behaviors

- **Empowerment** – It provides the client with a sense of options since it allows them to review possibilities rather than limitations

- **Evaluation** - It allows a client to review realities and unhealthy behavior patterns

- **Clarification** -An excellent tool for providing clarification on areas that may be confusing in the client's life

- **Assessment tool** -Great tool for exploring not only personal blind spots but personal limitations

- **Neutrally flexible** - A neutral system that does not subscribe to any one school of thought in either psychology or philosophy.

In understanding the benefits of the tarot deck, a therapist can create a proper game plan for working with clients. Everything presented in the symbolism of the tarot can help a therapist obtain understanding and clarity. However, a therapist will first need to understand the information and symbolism.

Limitations of Tarot cards

Though there are numerous benefits to using the tarot therapeutically, there are some limitations. Many individuals who read the tarot deck are not always qualified as a therapist. On the same note, there are therapists not trained to read the tarot or use divination techniques. As a result of limited training, it can be tricky for the therapist to implement the tarot in therapy. An example of limitations consist of the following:

- **Limited applications**– few therapists **know how to incorporate** tarot readings successfully with evidence-based practices.

- **Training** – Not many programs combine therapeutic modalities with divination techniques in their educational curriculum

- **Comprehending information** – It can be difficult for a therapist to analyze the psychological aspects of a reading

- **Therapeutic boundaries** – For some therapist, maintaining boundaries can be tricky if a client begins to turn the session into a psychic reading

- **Mainstream Acceptance** – it can be tricky to use divination techniques in facilities that maintain specific program regulations or adhere to evidence-based practices.

All tools have natural limitations regardless of their benefits. The deck offers the opportunity to expand beyond the limits of traditional techniques.

Critical Guidelines Utilizing the Tarot

For therapists that decide to utilize divination or tarot readings in their practice, it is essential that they adhere to some guidelines. The following are useful tips that will allow the therapist to achieve positive results when working with their clients in therapeutic sessions.

- It is essential to **know the difference between therapy and psychic readings**. Tarot reading uses the deck to help a client gain an understanding of their situations, but it does not offer guidance or psychological interpretations.

- When using the tarot deck or any divination tool, **be very specific** with the client about the goals and intentions behind selected tools.

- Practice **active listening skills** to avoid subjective guidance

- The therapist needs to **know their professional limits** when it comes to working with particular problems faced by clients. When in doubt seek guidance or refer to the proper sources.

- Keep in mind **tarot readings will not replace counseling**; they are only an assisting tool. A therapist will need to retain therapeutic goals and to use counseling techniques in their sessions.

- **Avoid vagueness** since it will continue to amplify the client's state of anxiety. Use the divination and deck correctly to interpret and obtain clarity as best as possible; if the method fails in providing clarity, the therapist will need to stop using it.

- **Do not engage in predictive readings**. Otherwise, the therapist will be doing psychic readings, and the client will not learn the skills needed for creating changes. Without using counseling skills to help the client change, a prediction is useless.

- Remember a **tarot deck is a tool** for clarification and not making negative judgments about a person's life or choices.

Regardless of how much a therapist reads about the benefits of using the tarot deck or how intuitive tools work, it is essential to seek proper training. Learning precisely how to fine-tune our skills enable proper implementation of intuitive tools and ensure productive outcomes.

Chapter Summary
The tarot deck is more than a tool for psychics, and fortune tellers. It is a valuable tool in providing insight and guidance for both

professionals and clients. This chapter demonstrated some of the practical uses of the tarot and how to integrate it as a guidance tool.

Chapter XIV
Using Reiki in Therapy

A single act of kindness can cause ripples of healing. – Author unknown

Reiki for Mental Health and Physical well-being

This chapter explores the benefits and practical applications of Reiki both mentally and physically. Reiki is a healing system which is therapeutically used by both mental health professionals and healthcare practitioners.

Healing Systems

There are many healing systems based on energy work, such as Qi Gong, acupressure, acupuncture, Prana healing, Chinese medicine, and a few other types which are hundreds of years old and currently used. (Altshul 2011) However, unlike the other styles of healing, Reiki is comparatively simple to learn and does not require as much intensive training as the other healing systems. Reiki's reasonably uncomplicated system of healing makes it ideal for most professionals to learn and assimilate into their working routine.

Though, many individuals report benefits from Reiki, the empirical data available has not provided sufficient evidence to support the claims (Lee, Pittler, & Ernest 2008). However, according to a study done on Nephrology patients, having a **permission-positive attitude** can be responsible for the efficacy of alternative therapies, such as Reiki and other hands-on-healing therapies (Ferraresi et al., 2013)

Researchers from Stanford Medical facilities have emphasized the value of a client's mindset, as an essential component to healing and recovering from illness (Shashkevich 2017). The fact is that illness and emotional distress is rooted in our beliefs and thoughts.

The ability to recover from illness relies on the individual's ability to trust a process, as well as a willingness to adhere to medical recommendations. The success of most medical procedures relies on the patient trusting medical advice. Healing systems such as Reiki, allow clients to relax and feel comfortable, creating the ideal mindset for healing to occur. Perhaps the benefits of Reiki may be linked to **permission positive** attitudes or a placebo effect; regardless of the core reasons, it does create the mindset required for healing to occur.

What exactly is REIKI?

Reiki is a simple type of healing system that uses energy transferred from the hands of the practitioner to the client, which can be applied both directly on or inches from the body. The focus of Reiki is to allow energy to move freely throughout the body with the intentions of releasing stagnated energy and improving its flow.

Reiki is a form of "laying-on-of-hands" technique originating from Japan and which worked its way to the Western alternative medicine culture. Reiki is a technique that according to some Reiki teachers incorporated Tibet scriptures, known as sutras used by monks in many of their spiritual practices. (Rand 2018). The Tibetan symbols, known as kanji were used in meditation for concentration, purifying thoughts, raising consciousness and balancing energies.

Reiki is used today in a variety of ways to promote healing, enhance concentration and obtain balance. It can be useful in working with emotional, physical and energy-related issues.

The Meaning of the word - REIKI

A simple method of remembering the name Reiki is to break down into two separate words:

- **Rei:** The word **Rei** is used to mean 'free passage' and 'spiritual consciousness or all-knowing wisdom from God.
- **Ki:** The word **Ki** refers to 'free passage' and 'universal life force' animating all living things.

History of Reiki

There has been much speculation about where Reiki came from, but there has been little confirmation of most of these theories. It is possible that is efficacy might have a lot to do with **permission-positive attitudes** or **placebo effect** in general. (Ferraresi et al.) However, despite the numerous theories regarding Reiki, it has gained popularity throughout the years

This word Reiki is not exclusive to the system of healing based on Mikao Usui Sensei's work. Reiki is a generic word to mean "Universe" and "Energy"; it is also used to describe many types of healing and spiritual work. The method of healing that evolved from Usui's teaching referred to as the Usui System of Natural Healing or Usui Reiki Ryoho.

Aside from Mikao Usui Sensei's healing system, there had been several energy-based systems practiced in Japan. (Rand). One particular method introduced in 1914 by a Japanese practitioner named Matiji Kawakami was called, Reiki Ryoho, along with a book called "Reiki Ryoho to Sono Koka (Reiki healing and its Effects). There were several other systems, which might have taken off, and perhaps introduced to the USA, had World War I or II not occurred. However, the energy system that became popular was Usui's System, since it was introduced to the United States by Hawayo Takata, a Hawaiian resident. (Rand)

Mikao Usui

Mikao Usui is credited as the founder of the Usui System of Reiki. He was born August 15, 1865, in the village of Yago in the Yamagata district of Gifu prefecture, Japan. (Rand) Usui Sensei had a keen interest in learning and worked hard at his studies. (Reiki Tree of Life). Usui Sensei was a Zen Buddhist practitioner that participated in various spiritual practices in Japan.

History indicates that Mikao Usui traveled throughout Europe and parts of Asia in his quest to further his education in the areas of psychology, philosophy, and religion. (Rand) In 1922 Usui Sensei rediscovered Reiki while researching various healing techniques from around the world. He traveled to places in the United States, Far East, India, and Tibet. During his stay in Tibet, he studied Tibetan ancient sutras used by the Tibetan monks in spiritual practices. Usui Sensei learned from the monks about the spiritual benefits of the "kanji symbols," also referred to as the "keys." (Rand) According to Usui Sensei, these keys were the symbols needed to prepare the body and mind for energy healing and meditation.

After his transformative spiritual period, Mikao Usui became the founder and president of the Usui System of Reiki organization in Japan. When Usui Sensei died, a succession of several presidents followed which included:

Mr. Ushida
Mr. Iichi Taketome,
Mr. Yoshiharu Watanabe,
Mr. Toyoichi Wanami
Ms. Kimiko Koyama and the successor to Usui Sensei as of 1998 is Mr. Kondo.

Opposing to what has been taught by some in the west; there is no "Grandmaster" or "exclusive lineage bearer" in the system of healing started by Usui Sensei, only the succession of presidents. (Rand)

Dr. Chujiro Hayashi

Mikao Usui Sensei taught the Master Attunement to 16 individuals, many of whom trained other students. One student who was influential in the spread of Reiki was Dr. Chujiro Hayashi. According to Reiki history, Usui Sensei passed the secret keys of Reiki before dying to his closest associate and friend, Dr. Chujiro Hayashi, a physician who ran a health clinic in Japan. (Rand)

Hawayo Takata

Dr. Chujiro worked on several patients throughout the years. It was one of his patients, Mrs. Hawayo Takata that brought Reiki to Hawaii in 1934. After recovering from years of illness, Mrs. Takata spent time in Japan studying Reiki healing techniques and a few years later was made a Reiki Master. In 1970, Mrs. Takata moved to

California and began to train others to become teachers.

The history of Reiki seems to have evolved with a variety of variations. The entire history might not ever reveal itself to the world. However, what is an actual component of Reiki is the numbers of individuals who reported benefits throughout the years. In the end, it is not the beginning history of Reiki that matters as much as the results and the benefits it produces.

How Does Reiki Work?

Reiki is an **energy facilitator**, and it **is not a cure,** but it will allow the mind to relax enough to let the body heal. The reason that many struggles to understand Reiki has a lot to do with false expectations and misunderstanding of how specifically energy healing works.

Many illnesses result from self-defeating beliefs and harmful behavior patterns. (Shashkevich 2017) A person, who thinks negatively and expect nothing but bad things, will eventually suffer physically and mentally. The mind is a dominant element in healing, and regardless of what medical treatment received, having a permissive positive attitude is essential for successful healing to occur.

When Reiki is working, a person tends to feel more relaxed, at ease and less frantic. In general, energy flows more naturally when the body is relaxed and not so tense. There are some specific ways in which Reiki works which consists of the following:

- Improving **energy flow** – when the energy throughout the body is flowing, it allows the body to recover and repair.
- Promotes **Permissive Mindset** – the right mindset is essential for any recovery to occur
- Provides **Emotional Nurturing** – feeling safe, nurtured and cared for promotes a positive mindset, while reducing the fears associated with illness

According to a study by Fish and Geddes (2009) electrical currents are conducted via the air, which impacts the body and its ability to function. The study by Fish and Geddes concluded that the electrical currents that travel throughout the body could impact anything from being accident prone to nerve stimulation. To understand how this is possible, imagine the impact x-rays have on the human body, which is why technicians must wear protective gear or leave the room when doing x-rays.

The sensation produced by physical contact and the warmth of having someone close creates an overall feeling of trust, comfort and general well-being (Williams 2015). The sensation of touch not only activates physical reactions but emotional ones as well. Studies reported by Keltner and Horberg (2010), strongly indicated that touch and nurturing behavior produces tremendous benefits that impact emotional well-being and overall health. Reiki treatments provide individuals with a **sense of being cared** for and **nurtured,** which is often lacking in the lives of many individuals.

The benefits of Reiki are not only based on assisting the release of stagnated energy; it provides a sense of comfort and emotional support. Individuals thrive on being cared for and supported emotionally and physically. (Konnikova 2015). Keep in mind the sense of touch is one of the first sensory systems to develop in infants. Our first introduction into the world is through touch. Studies done in Romania indicated that children who are home-reared vs. those living in institutions thrived better as the result of ongoing physical contact. (Field 2011) Also, studies with individuals suffering from infections indicated that the individual who had more support demonstrated a higher level of recovery. (Cohen, Janicki-Deverts, Turner & Doyle 2015).

Understanding Energy and Reiki

To understand how Reiki or any healing energy works, it helps to understand how energy itself works. Energy is the source of everything. In the **physical realm**, energy is manifested in three forms, the **electromagnetic field**, **brain waves**, and **energy fields** which affect brain activity (Feinstein 2012). The three forms of energy manifestation contribute to brain activities depending on environmental influences. The type of things that can trigger environmental changes which contribute to energy surges includes **temperature, physical activities**, and **chemical reactions**.

As discussed previously, Reiki is an energy facilitator. It creates slight heat changes that impact the body's surface even when treatment is applied a few inches above the skin. For instance, imagine heat coming from a heater, there is no need to touch it directly to feel the different degrees of heat. The body is susceptible to heat emissions and will respond to the slightest variation in temperature.

Reiki and the Sensory System

To fully comprehend how Reiki energy integrates with the body, it helps to review how the sensory system reacts to heat. There are different types of tactile sensations connected to the neurophysiology of the skin. (Ackerley et al. 2014) The skin is both a protective barrier against hazardous elements and a physical, sensory system. The nerve endings on the skin, allows the body to recognize weather changes, distinguish between pleasure and pain, as well as alert against dangerous chemicals.

The skin is a gateway not only for tactile sensations but also a portal for health and disease. For instance, our hands can collect different germs, while our skin is capable of benefiting from the vitamin D, through exposure to sun rays. The receptors located on the skin when activated, transmit sensory information that travels up the spinal cord and into the brain region. The sensory input triggers reactions that instruct the brain to produce neurotransmitters which release the chemicals needed to either excite or relax the individual. In excited states, the individual can become stressed, annoyed or anxious. In the relaxed state, the individual can become calm, relaxed or serene.

The body has **touch receptors**, known as Mechanoreceptors, throughout the surface of the skin that reacts to the slightest stimuli. Anything from temperature to physical contact will activate the touch receptors. (Bodytomy 2017) (Figure 1). The touch receptors consist of the following:

- **Meissner's corpuscles:** These receptors respond to **light touch** and lower frequency vibrations. **Fast adapting receptors**

- **Pacinian corpuscles:** These receptors are **extremely sensitive** to lightest vibrations and able to detect the slightest sensation.
- **Merkel's disks:** These receptors react to light sensations of touch. **Slow adapting** receptors. (Abraira & Ginty, 2013).
- **Ruffini ending:** These receptors respond to pressure that is felt on a deeper level than the other receptors (Bodytomy)

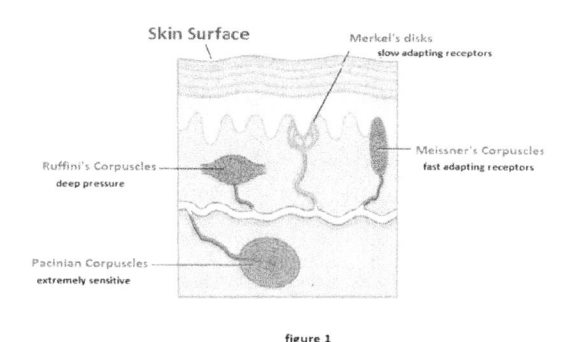

Figure # 1 The skin contains several types of receptors that react to stimuli

The skin can detect several sensations within the environment, from a cold wind to the gentle caress of a hand or a sharp object. The different environmental changes activate the receptors converting the stimuli into electrical nerve impulses, known as transduction. The skin contains receptors groups identified as the following:

- **Mechanoreceptors:** Reaction to **physical touches**, such as stroking or vibrations on the surface
- **Thermoreceptors:** Reaction to **temperature changes** from hot to cold.
- **Pain receptors**: Reaction to any **strong physical impact** that creates pain

The same sensory system that conveys messages to the brain allows the body to take in stimuli in the form of heat, touch or chemical reactions. In the case of Reiki or other healing systems, the energy received during healing is perceived by the body as heat. Once the body's sensory system detects the temperature changes produced by heat, it then stimulates the receptors, which in turn activates neurotransmitters in the brain. The type of neurotransmitters activated are the ones that produce a calm and relaxing state referred to as inhibitory and monoamine neurotransmitters, which consist of gamma-aminobutyric (GABA) and Serotonin. (Cherry 2018)

The sensation of calmness or peace is merely the body reacting to the temperature changes transmitted from the hands of a healer. In fact, it is no mystery that Reiki is just one of the several healing systems that generate heat producing energy that stimulates the inhibitory neurotransmitters that promote a sense of calmness and relaxation.

Training as Reiki Practitioner

There are many forms of healing in addition to Reiki. Each system of healing subscribes to its own philosophical and format of training its practitioners. To become a Reiki practitioner, the individual undergoes an energy attunement to Reiki energy, preparing them to work as a receiver of the Universal Life Energy or Energy source. The attunement prepares the body to allow energy to move through the body whenever a person decides to access it for healing oneself or others.

A Reiki Master (teacher) attunes your body by using the 'keys,' which facilitates the flow of Universal Life Energy. During the attunement process, a Reiki Master places the 'keys' above the crown and palm chakras, to permanently attune your body to the frequencies of the 'keys.' As the body is attuned, it becomes amenable to energy and a channel for Chi, also known as Universal Life Energy. These 'keys' and attunements can only be passed on by someone who knows the actual symbols for the 'keys' and attuned to them. The body's energy channel is aligned so that the hands can transmit the energy of Reiki. The process of attunement enables the person not only to provide healings but also to align the energy system in others, so they too can practice Reiki.

Only a Reiki Master can initiate the process of attunements to all levels since traditionally they are the only ones that know the activation keys. The role of a teacher (Master) in Reiki is one of significance but not one of ego. A teacher is of service to their students, and their role is to pass on knowledge and provide guidance.

Since the source of Reiki is Universal Life Energy, we can neither will it nor control it; At the same time, we <u>cannot</u> will others to take Reiki treatment without their consent. Application of Reiki energy requires mutual acceptance by individuals getting the healing. Keep in mind the Life Energy does not come <u>from</u> the person; *it comes through the person.*

Benefits of receiving Reiki attunements:

Though there many healing systems, there are wonderful reasons to become a Reiki practitioner.

- Permanent access to the Universal Life Energy because of the attunement process.
- Increases the flow of energy on a continuous basis
- Since the person cannot control it; the energy flow will not be interrupted by daily events: stress, mood changes, physical or mental fatigue.
- Unlike a person's natural energy reservoir, one does not need to work to maintain it at any level, since it passes through the person and remains within them forever.
- The Reiki symbols are imprinted for life.
- Great for working with others, oneself, animals, plants, crystals, ritual tools, water, and so on.
- An excellent complement to all types of bodywork, massage, and acupressure.
- Great for balancing chakras
- Good mood regulator
- Compliments all spiritual practices, yoga, meditation, prayer, and visualization.
- Respects free will
- Dogma-free, this meaning Reiki is not owned by any religious group.
- The rest is up to the individual's needs and imagination.

Limitations of Reiki Training

Though Reiki is a useful healing tool, it is hard to imagine any limitations or potential issues connected with it. However, there are some areas that professionals need to be informed about, that consist of the following:

- **New additions**: Since it is so flexible, many practitioners have included elements that are not at all part of the Reiki system. Not all systems are exactly alike
- **The Ego**: It is important to recognize that one cannot "heal" a person, but only facilitate the process
- **Remote Attunements**: Though reiki provides long distance healing, online courses do not provide physical attunements. Anyone claiming they can provide attunement via long distance is questionable and may want a person's money. Check the sources carefully.
- **Unnecessary Gimmicks**: There are many marketing gimmicks to attract students, so be aware
- **Expensive**: Some reiki courses can be expensive, depending which tradition the teacher follows
- **Unavailable local teachers**: There is a possibility that a person seeking training might have to travel to get their initial attunements which can be costly
- **Limited practice**: If you do not have other practitioners in your area, practicing can be tricky. Therefore, try to connect with others, even if it's an online distance healing group

Practical Applications for Therapist

The applications of Reiki will be determined by the type of therapy that the mental health professional or healthcare practitioner utilizes. When it comes to mental health, Reiki is useful for creating the proper mindset for creating change and healing to occur. In physical health, Reiki is helpful in creating a calmer state that will reduce stress-induced illness. The best way for mental health professionals and healthcare practitioners to determine how to use Reiki in therapy is to review the benefits. The list of benefits placed into two separate categories and labeled as follows: Mental health and Healthcare.

Mental health benefits:

The area of mental health consists of issues that impair a client's ability to function and establish a healthy lifestyle. When it comes to working with clients who have mental health issues, the ability to help them relax and focus is imperative for treatment success. Reiki does provide some improvement in therapy by helping in the following ways:

- Helps relax clients who are anxious (Cherry)
- Provides relief from stress
- Has a calming effect
- Excellent tool to use in regressive healing work
- Improves concentration by calming the mind

Health Care benefits:

The field of healthcare has a wide range of services that facilitate client recovery from ailments, help gain endurance and overall physical well-being. Reiki can assist the client to obtain the mindset needed for successful physical recovery. Some of the practical applications consist of the following:

- Helpful in pre and postsurgical care (Shashkevich)
- Useful in chakra therapy
- Pain management

- Increase relaxation
- Reduce illness induced stress
- Great component for stress management
- Ideal for charging crystals

The application of Reiki treatments will vary depending not only on the needs of the client but also the type of therapy used by the clinician. There are many situations in which a client needs to address specific issues and find concrete solutions that go beyond the scope of healing work. Changing behavior patterns and developing goals are areas that are outside the paradigms of Reiki since those areas require a proactive role. Reiki might indirectly help in changing behaviors and development of goals, by helping the individual become less stressed over decision-making tasks. However, when it comes to change and goal attainment, taking direct actions is paramount.

Treatment expectations

The Reiki experience is a personal process. Different individuals will report having a wide range of sensations and emotional reactions, which can vary in intensity and duration. Many individuals report positive experiences while some do not. Every session may produce different results and reactions; it often depends on the mindset and personal expectations of the individual. The mind is a significant component of healing and mental health regardless of the efficacy techniques or the expertise of the clinician.

The fact is that individuals preset the stage of healing often based on personal expectations and beliefs. Different types of beliefs contribute to false benefits as well as create barriers to healing. As stated previously, **permissive positive attitudes** contribute to healing, just as much as negative attitudes. According to hospital studies, Patients who received Reiki treatments consistently reported positive outcomes and noticeable improvement in both mental health and medical issues. (Bier 2014)

The various experiences reported vary from person to person. Therefore, there is no one definitive manner to experience the healing sensations of Reiki. According to reports on Reiki studies, individuals have reported a variety of experiences, of different intensities. (Lenoy 2010). Both, the Reiki practitioner and the client have reported experiences that include the following:

- Healing sensations
- Tingling
- Coughing
- Emotional recollection
- Overall good feelings
- Relaxed
- peaceful
- Nausea
- Sleepy
- General heaviness
- Also, sadness and intense emotions can surface

Then there are occasions in which a person will not experience anything significant or noticeable. The lack of sensation does not imply that the procedure did not produce benefits since there are individuals who will not recognize certain sensations, especially if they are apprehensive and closed to the experience. Then again, there are instances in which a person will not experience anything, and that is perfectly normal.

Steps in Reiki Treatments:

These are sample preparation procedures, to help the therapists or practitioner provide the most benefit during the Reiki session.

1. Make sure that the working space is comfortable and as pleasant as possible. (Minimize noise, distractions; turn off the phone and make sure no one disturbs the session.)
2. Remove your jewelry, especially bangles and wash your hands.
3. Be aware of offensive body odor, bad breath or strong perfume
4. Ask the client to remove their jewelry, loosen up belts and remove shoes
5. Have the client to sit upright on a chair or lay on a

massage table if one is available
6. Begin the treatment at the client's head.
7. Standing straight, assume Kanji Hand position #1, #2 or #3 to center yourself.
8. Disconnect from any outcome. As the session begins, focus on the roof of your mouth gently press the tongue against it and at the same time contract the HUI YIN (the buttock muscles) a few times. As you squeeze your HUI YIN and touch the roof of your mouth with your tongue, bring your hands together by interlocking the fingers and thumbs.
9. Then slowly place your hands above the client's head without touching the client directly.
10. Prepare to proceed with the energy application, beginning with the head, then working downward to each location accordingly. (See section on Reiki Treatment Guide)

Practical Intuition for Therapeutic Practices

Reiki Treatment Guide

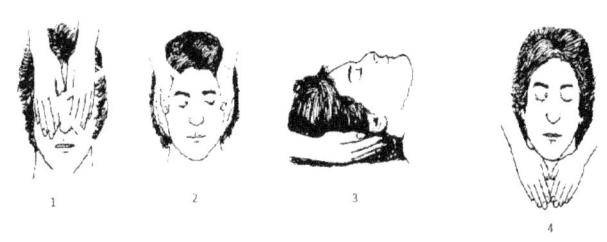

Begin with the head and work yours hands downwards

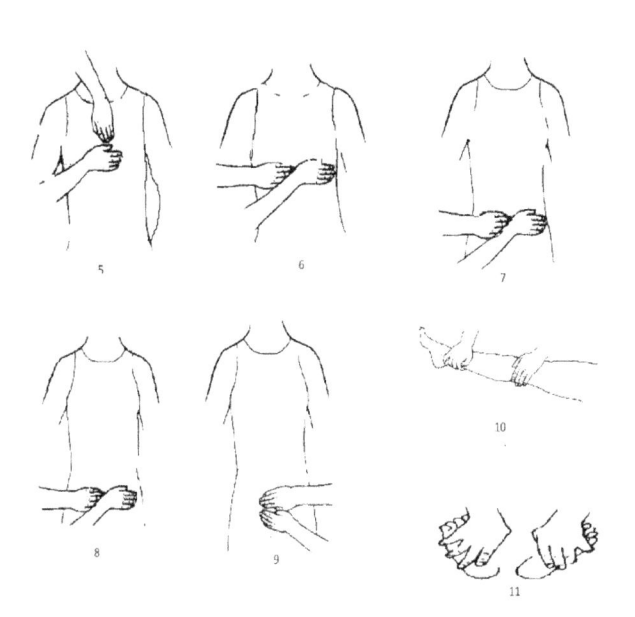

Remember to keep hands slightly above the body and move slowly between each area

Self-treatment for Practitioners

When working with others, regardless of what role we play, whether it is a physical therapist, psychotherapist, coach or bodywork, we do get depleted and can benefit from an energy boost. To you guide through self-treatment, please refer to the Reiki self-treatment chart below:

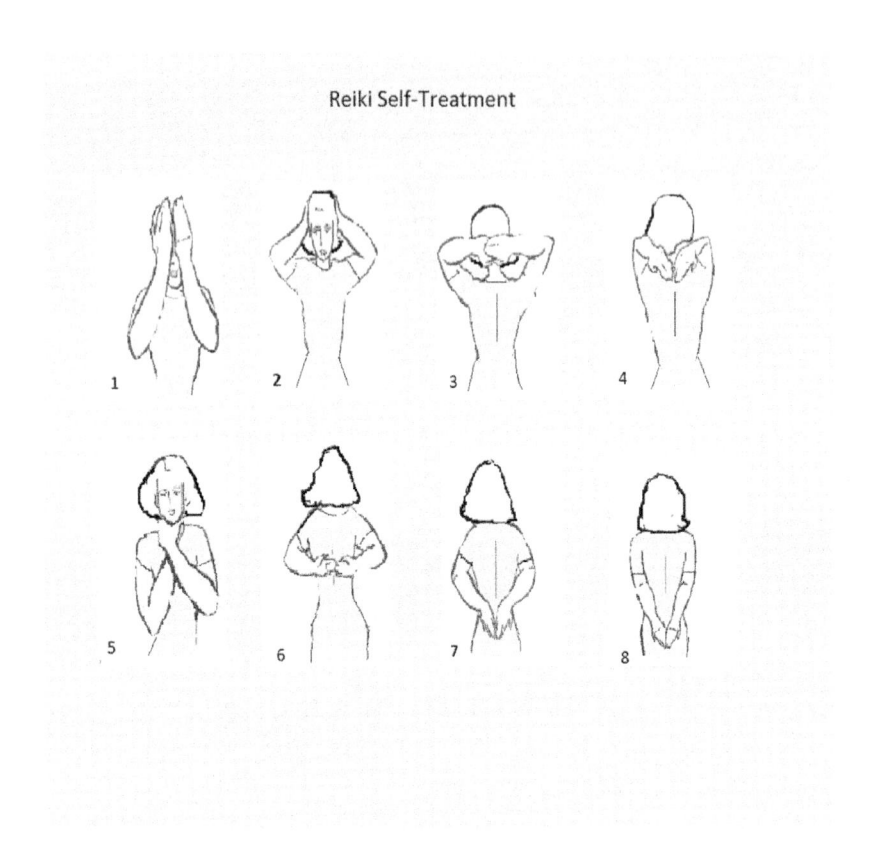

Practical Things to think about

Though Reiki is not a religion, it has a spiritual component. Reiki is not a religious or dogma-based practice, but it does entail being comfortable and tolerant of its spiritual inclinations. Therefore, if a therapist finds working with energy to be not within their scientific comfort zone, then Reiki is not for them.

Energy work can be draining, especially if the professional forgets to replenish and disconnect. It is essential to let go of the need to fix individuals. Otherwise, it can become exhausting and produce to burn-out. There are a few things to reflect on when doing energy work that will facilitate the experience for both the professional and the client, which consist of the following:

- Reiki will not cure clients; it only facilitates the flow of energy which promotes healing
- Reiki will not replace therapy
- Reiki does not require direct touch

The Efficacy of Reiki

Reiki is a system of healing that is **not evidence-based** but rather a **practice-based** practice which relies on the intuitive skills of the practitioner. Even though scientific research has provided mixed data, Reiki has demonstrated benefits, though some may argue that the results are nothing more than a placebo effect. The human mind response significantly to what it trusts and views as having merit, which is the source of healing for many. However, there a lot of areas science has yet to understand, which is why it is essential to keep an open mind. Remember science relies on research and research relies on man's ability to design test and systems for measuring theories.

According to a study presented by Barkham and Mellor-Clark (2003), practitioners do not necessarily engage in evidence-based practices exclusively. Though many facilities might have a mission statement based on evidence-based practice, the reality is that therapeutic practices often step outside the lines since no two clients behave the same even when facing similar issues. The fact is, people, have fluid personalities, and as much as they may have traits that follow a pattern, no two individuals handle situations in the same way.

Though Evidence-based data is limited, studies have reported benefits, but it is possible that it may be due to two things: **placebo effect** or a **permission-positive attitude.** Keep in mind; even if something occurs based on the placebo effect, it still has merit, since the healing process always begins with the cooperation of the mind, especially once a person has decided to get help.

Chapter Summary

When using Reiki, remember, it is a source of energy that one is tapping into, not created by intentions or desires. The person is merely a conduit that allows Reiki energy to travel through. The process of Reiki works by moving chi (energy) through a person or an object. Now, many will not feel the power of chi going through them, which is similar to not experiencing anything when taking vitamins, yet the benefits still occur.

It is essential to remember that mastering Reiki itself does not mean that a person can heal every issue wrong with an individual. Reiki is a tool for facilitating the healing process, but not a panacea for everything that ails a person. If a person has a medical or severe mental health condition, they need immediate attention. Though Reiki is an exceptional energy system, useful in helping clients struggling with emotional imbalances, and stress it is not a replacement for medical or psychiatric care. In general, always remember, when using intuitive techniques, the real validation is the outcome and the results that create change or enhances someone's life.

SECTION III

Professional Preparation

Chapter XV
Professional Integration

Researchers should always consider ethical concerns in scientific research and disclose their data to the public. Scientists also need to discuss issues surrounding their research with those who are concerned. - Shinya Yamanaka

Preparing for Professional Integration

The integration of various techniques may seem daunting and confusing at first since traditional treatment modalities do not often incorporate intuitive methods. However, once the clinician or practitioner has reviewed what each system consists of, they can select what feels most comfortable and suitable for the needs of the clients they serve. It is essential that the clinician or practitioner also seek proper training and guidance in how to utilize intuitive techniques since knowing about **the benefits** and **practical uses** are not sufficient for practical integration.

For successful integration, it is essential that professionals are prepared both educationally and mentally to handle the task of intuitively working with clients. Some fundamental areas require attention which consists of three main groups with subcategories in the following:

Professional Expectations

- Professional Conduct
- Skills Maintenance

Training Requirements

- Intuitive Training
- Training Expectations

- Training Duration

Professional Maintenance

- Natural Barriers
- Elements of Burnout
- Empathic Experience
- Self-Care

Professional Management

- Organizing
- Schedules
- Documentation
- Appointments vs. Drop-ins

Professional Fee

- Payment
- sliding scale
- insurance
- payment schedule
- cancellations

Each area will be carefully reviewed, to assist the individual in learning how to integrate intuitive techniques into their professional work.

Professional Expectations

Professional Conduct

Working with clients as a mental health professional and healthcare practitioner requires the right attitude in addition to professional training. There many reasons individuals enter the field of mental health and healthcare, which range from pure altruistic beliefs to unresolved childhood conflicts. Regardless of the initial motivations for being a helping professional, there is a need to maintain the right attitude when working with clients in need of mental health and healthcare services.

In the field of mental health, not all professionals possess the same professional skills nor the experiences. However, regardless of professional training, when it comes to working with clients, there are some necessary skills a professional should possess which consist of flexibility, empathy, and advocacy. (Shallcross 2012) In addition to the necessary skills, Wright and Davis (1994) suggest several approaches that enhance the quality of therapy and therapeutic alliance, which consist of the following:

- Maintain a safe and professional setting
- Treat patients with respect
- Do not minimize concerns
- Provide undivided attention.
- Be professionally trained
- Provide practical resources as needed
- Do not impose your personal values on the client
- Allow clients to experience their process
- Seek cultural sensitivity training
- Follow up on recommendations

Depending on the treatment style of therapy, some attributes and qualities may differ from professional to professional. Nevertheless, some qualities are necessary regardless of personal preference or personality type which consist of the following:

- **Respect** – for relationships of any kind to flourish, individuals need to treat each other with respect, which means respecting boundaries and not talking down to the individual

- **Retain Professionalism** – The client is not a peer and deserves professional services.
- **Mindfulness** – being aware of one's behavior and how one speaks to clients. Words have power and can sometimes trigger individuals, especially clients with mental health issues
- **Active listening skills** – listening means paying attention and learning about the person behind the words.
- **Cultural sensitivity** – many therapists are trained in therapeutic systems based on Western ideals and cultural values. It is essential to be aware that not everyone has had good experiences with Westernized beliefs, specifically minorities. Avoid imposing personal or cultural beliefs on clients,
- **Self-awareness** - As a clinician or practitioner know your limits and ask for help whenever necessary.
- **Safe space** – Clients need to know that they can talk freely without judgment or breach of privacy.

Not all helping professionals possess an outgoing personality. However, they still manage to provide excellent services. Professional services are often a reflection of personal work ethics and training. A professional who is well-prepared will deliver excellent services even if they are not charming or sociable in therapy.

Skills Maintenance

In the field of mental health and counseling, there is a recertification process that occurs with most licenses or certifications. The reason for recertification is to keep the mental health professionals current and maintain relevant therapeutic skills. (Isaac, 2016) Both in the mental health and healthcare field, there are constant changes due to new research and therapeutic approaches evolving in the field.

What was once prevalent in the world of mental health 30 years ago is not necessarily relevant in the present. For instance, the DSM IV was revised in 2015, and now it's referred to as the DSM V. The changes in the DSM V were due to updates in mental health terminology and new diagnostic criteria. As new theories surface, new research outcomes give birth to new evidence-based practices, which means therapists need to update their skills to remain professionally relevant.

Regarding intuitive skills, therapists need to practice and remain sharp. Intuitive skills can be

maintained a lot easier than mental health skills since intuition will always respond to ongoing practice. Some of the essential tools to keep intuition sharp are simple and consist of the following:

- Regular meditation practice
- keeping a journal of intuitive experiences
- Practicing some intuitive technique a few times a week such as tarot readings, chakra scanning or aura readings.
- Exercising since it gets the body healthy and able to handle work stress
- Eating well since food is fuel
- Detachment exercises to keep a person from burning out:
- Relaxing is essential for also preventing burn-out

In maintaining sharp, one should not only focus on learning or staying updated, but they should also include self-care. A professional who takes care of themselves has a better chance of having a satisfying career with positive outcomes not just for the client, but also for themselves.

Training Requirements

Intuitive Training

Mental Health Professionals and healthcare practitioners need to understand the nature and the format of intuitive techniques fully, so they can logically incorporate them into their professional practice. Though the process of learning intuitive techniques appears difficult, it's no harder than learning CBT, RET or any other therapeutic technique.

There are vital factors to consider when learning intuitive methods which consist of the **introductory phase**, **practice drills**, and **guidance** from a mentor or teacher. Regardless of the field, all professions require some preparation and training. Whether an individual is naturally intuitive or not, it is wise to seek professional courses and teachers to help them **fine-tune their skills** and learn **how to incorporate techniques** into their professional work.

All professionals in the mental health and healthcare field are required to obtain specific training and testing to qualify for a license or certification in their field. Training ensures that the professional is adequately qualified and has the knowledge required to do the work. Though testing for a license or certification is not required for practicing intuitive techniques, proper training is still recommended. Though the area of intuitive development is relatively new, and accreditation is not available, there are a variety of courses available.

Selecting a Teacher or Mentor

Individuals who want to use intuitive skills in a professional setting, need to learn from a teacher. When selecting a teacher, it is recommended that you seek someone who is familiar with your professional background since they will know how to help you incorporate the material you learn into your professional practice.

If there are no teachers in your area, there are many available online courses, with teachers who are available via Skype. Keep in mind that developing your psychic skills on your own is perfectly fine when working as a psychic, but it is not advisable in the field of mental health or healthcare. A mental health clinician and healthcare practitioner have to deal with different degrees of responsibilities that are not faced by psychics. The role of a psychic is to provide clients with a reading that offers clarification and guidance in personal life issues. Psychics are not trained to provide **psychological advice**, perform **mental health assessment**s or **engage in psychoanalyzing** a client. Though there are many brilliant psychics, the typically psychic training does not cover mental health issues. Therefore, it is advisable that clinicians and practitioners seek proper training, from someone who is trained in the same field and knows how to teach intuitive techniques in coordination with therapeutic protocols.

In summary, there are many reasons to take courses from an actual teacher with a background in therapy, rather than just learning with a book or YouTube videos. There are several reasons to train with a teacher with a mental health background which includes the following:

- The person has a background in mental health counseling, psychotherapy or coaching.
- Teaches offers courses that relevant to the professional needs of the individual
- Provides opportunities for supervision
- Offers assignments and practice drills
- Gives the student feedback on their progress
- Helps the student develop their career goals
- Is available to answer questions

It is possible to develop intuitive skills independently. However, for individuals working with clients in a professional setting, it is both a necessary and ethical to learn techniques for successful implementation.

Training Expectations

Not every instructor teaches the same course in the same fashion. Some classes are more detailed than others, and some are simple and to the point. It is wise to select a teacher that offers the individual not only **what they need to learn**, but also will help them **achieve their learning goals**. Many instructors and even some books teach mostly in theoretical terms and do not offer much regarding practical applications or hands-on practice. It is advisable to take courses that allow students the opportunity to practice, not just by doing assignments, but by finding time to utilize the exercises on others.

Individuals need to practice, regardless of how much information they get from books or other sources. A person can fill in the gaps with reading material, but they cannot engage in intuitive work with just literary knowledge. For instance, if a person wants to learn to cook, they can read a couple of books on tips and methods for cooking, but they only fully learn to cook once they work with the ingredients.

Reading alone will not develop the person's skills until they put their knowledge to the test. The individual can become well-informed in almost any area by reading, but until they practice and make mistakes; they will not develop their practical knowledge. The following are reasons for taking a structured course:

- There is an opportunity to **practice with direct guidance** from the instructor
- Students can **ask questions directly** on any topic and get clarification
- There is a chance to **see firsthand** how things operate
- The person can get **feedback on their performance**
- There is an opportunity for a **performance evaluation**, which will help the individual determine which areas need improvement.
- A person can **try out techniques** and **fine-tune** them before using them with clients
- There is an opportunity to try out techniques with **minimum risk to clients**
- The experiential process **will help develop confidence** which will reduce mistakes at the expense of the client
- Practice will enable the **individual to gain the knowledge** needed to make proper decisions
- The teacher will help **students fine-tune their skills** so that they can handle any crisis or issues that may occur
- There are many **opportunities to ask questions** that pertain to mental health specifically
- Students have an opportunity to do **hands-on work** with other students who have similar backgrounds before using techniques on clients
- **Class participation** enriches the learning experience

The expectations differ for each type of course and teacher, but the key is to be aware of what is in store when seeking training in intuitive development. Learning from an individual will always be different than learning through a book or a YouTube channel. Though courses can be beneficial, it can be challenging for students who worry about falling behind or do not enjoy class settings.

Training Duration

Depending on what type of therapy the individual provides; their training goals will vary. When it comes to learning how to use intuitive techniques, it does not take an eternity to learn the basics. Intuitive techniques like chakra balancing, guided meditations, energy and sensory work do not necessitate a long time to master since they do not require strong intuitive abilities to utilize them. Most techniques do not require long periods to learn. However, techniques like tarot reading, aromatherapy, regressive work, aura or chakra scanning require a bit more time, practice and patience.

Professional Maintenance

Natural Barriers

There are various obstacles that one can face as a therapist. Some obstacles impede the professional relationship and limited therapeutic results. It is essential that professionals find ways to identify and counteract the barriers so that they can have a successful practice. Examples of barriers that impede professional outcomes consist of:

1. Limited **Cultural awareness**
2. **Subjective ideas** that clash with clients
3. Inappropriate **boundaries**
4. Poor **listening skills**
5. Inadequate **training**
6. Not having **a mentor or supervisor**
7. Inadequate **supervision**
8. Having a **big ego**

9. Poor boundaries that **lead to burn-out**
10. Trying to be the **super healer**
11. Thinking they **what is best**
12. Violating **confidentiality**
13. **Poor bookkeeping** skills
14. **Canceling appointments** with clients
15. **Multi-tasking** during a session
16. Poor **skills maintenance**
17. **Personal life** interfering with work

Sometimes staying out of one's way can be difficult. Not addressing the barriers will reduce the success rate of a person's practice and impact their client's motivation to maintain treatment. Professionals need to be aware of their limits and the barriers that prevent them from being adequately productive in their work with clients. (Shallcross 2013) Therefore, it is wise to keep the skills up-to-date and address the issues with a neutral individual such as a mentor or supervisor who specializes in the same type of professional field.

For a clinician to provide their client with the best level of care, they need to do a proper assessment and then decide if they have the skill sets to proceed with treatment. If the therapist finds that a client is not a suitable candidate for treatment, they will need to refer them to someone else. Keep in mind that it will be unethical to try to help someone who suffers from issues that the clinician is not equipped to handle. Therefore, the clinician needs to make sure they have proper referral sources at hand in their practice. Once the clinician determines what level of care the client needs, they can then proceed to create an appropriate treatment plan to assist the client in obtaining the optimum benefits from therapy.

Elements of Burnout

Mental health and healthcare professionals often burn out from the stress of working with individuals who are in constant crisis. There is a tendency to feel responsible for outcomes, and when the results are not favorable, professionals can become overwhelmed and emotionally drained

There are key factors that contribute to the different levels of burnout:

- Countertransference
- Hero Complex
- Parental tendency
- Poor training
- Inadequate supervision
- Professional insecurity
- No time to rest
- Poor self-care
- Lack of sleep or poor diet
- Undiagnosed illness (mental or physical)
- Secondary Trauma Syndrome

The key to surviving burnout is maintaining an ongoing routine of self-care and emotional maintenance. It is essential and necessary that all professionals take care of themselves. (Shallcross 2011) It not only helps demonstrate healthy life skills to the client, but it also helps the therapist remain emotionally stable and enjoy their work longer.

Self-Care for Clinicians

Self-care is a personal process, but a necessary one for all working individuals. (Barnett 2014). The idea behind self-care is to maintain a lifestyle that not only includes time for personal care but also incorporates mindfulness that enhances both personal and professional life. Self-care should not be an activity that occurs after the damage of stress has taken over, but should be used as a preventive life plan. Barnett wrote an article for the Society for Psychotherapist highlighting specific strategies for self-care which include the following:

- Schedule regular breaks throughout the day
- Engage in hobbies or enjoyable activities often
- Learn to say "no."
- Know about the limitation and stop playing superhero
- Avoid isolation

- Be watchful for potential burnout
- Seek support
- Keep a journal to help track stress and significant changes
- Accept human limitations
- Avoid trying to "fix" people
- Practice keeping work and home separate
- For individuals who work at home, create a workspace used only for work
- Maintain professional supervision and peer support
- Take vacation "time."
- Avoid working six days straight
- Keep Organized
- Make home a personal sanctuary
- Exercise and eat a clean diet
- Meditate regularly

Many professionals working in the field of mental health and healthcare, forget to take care of themselves. In the process of caring for others, many individuals forget that in practicing self-care they are also modeling healthy behaviors for their clients. By watching how a clinician maintains balance, clients also learn how to take care of themselves. Self-care not only prevents burn-out but enhances the energy needed to maintain professional services.

The Empathic Experience

There is a propensity to get overwhelmed by energy work and as a result become emotionally drained. Though many will regard the overwhelming experience as an empathic one, it tends to go beyond empathy. Some factors contribute to the feelings of being overwhelmed and emotionally depleted. Many individuals who perform energy healing and intuitive techniques become enmeshed in the process of working and often forget to let go. The tendency to want to help and improve the lives of individuals can create a symbiotic relationship that leaves the professional vulnerable and eventually leads to burnout.

There are times when the therapist experiences

countertransference in the process of doing healing or therapeutic work, in which they over-identify with the client. Therapists who typically came from households, in which they played a parental role as the result of being the oldest child or having a sick parent, often become a parentified therapist. (Weisshaar, 2007) Many parentified professionals often tend to become overly invested in helping their clients, specifically those that trigger countertransference for the therapists.

In the process of over identifying, the therapist will begin to experience what is known as Novoa (2011) calls **secondary trauma syndrome**. Therapists find themselves experiencing emotional overloads after dealing with clients who face trauma, especially if the therapist had a similar history to the client.

Professional Management

Stress and burn-out are sometimes the results of having too much paperwork, unmanageable schedules and dealing with payment issues. To avoid becoming overwhelmed, professionals need to learn to manage their practice with efficacy and develop proper strategies. Though many individuals in the helping profession have a strong dislike for paperwork, certain routines and tasks are necessary for professional success.

The key to surviving in one's professions has a lot to do with preventive actions and being mindful. There are professional practices that minimize stress and burn-out which consist of the following:

- **Get Organized** – create a system that helps maintain some order and is easy to maintain
- **Create Schedules** – keep a schedule of appointments, task, and follow-up. Assign a day for paperwork, treatment plan updates, follow-up calls and filing. Make sure to schedule treatment plans as a session with the client; this will prevent paperwork overload and also includes the client in the process of doing their treatment plan.

- **Documentation** – Make sure to write the session notes immediately after each session to avoid forgetting essential details and having paperwork pile-up. Make sure to include 5 minutes to the end of each session for documenting session notes.
- **Appointment vs. Drop-in** - Keeping a scheduled is helpful for both the clients and the professional. For starters, professionals can manage their schedules more effectively when there are continuity and less last-minute appointments. Schedules help clients develop a routine and increase stability. Also, if an emergency takes place, appointments are easier to manage than drop-ins.

Professional Fee

Not everyone is great at collecting debts and managing their bookkeeping. However, many independent practitioners and clinicians are faced with the task of completing insurance forms, collecting and charging treatment fees. Though many agencies handle the bookkeeping, there are some areas which are handled by the clinicians and practitioners directly. Examples of areas often managed by the professionals consist of the following:

- ❖ **Sliding scale** – This fee adjustment is designed for individuals who do not earn enough to pay full price for treatment. Typically, the fee is adjusted according to the client's weekly pay rate and can be revised as financial situations improve.
- ❖ **Insurance** – Coverage varies depending on the insurance company. Each insurance company has their policies regarding **how much coverage**, treatment **duration** and type of service provided. The fact is, insurance companies can deny full coverage and prefer treatment that is short term rather than long extended periods. (Knickman, et al. 2016)
- ❖ **Payment schedule** – Collecting payment can be tedious since it can require additional paperwork. Maintaining a payment schedule keeps things simple and manageable.

- ❖ **Cancellations** – Last minute cancellations can be economically frustrating, especially for professionals who get paid "fee for service" or in private practice. Some professionals charge for the missed session, especially if cancellations are less than 24 hours.

Keep in mind, though many professionals enjoy the idea of helping others, it does not mean they should undercut their worth. The payment is not just about making money, but about getting paid for time and energy, because those are valuable commodities.

Chapter Summary

Many professional in the mental health and healthcare have an innate ability and desire to be of service to others, which is an admirable quality. However, many professionals forget that to be effective in their field of work they have to have the energy and the mental clarity to continue working.

This chapter was written to remind individuals that self-care is just as essential as taking care of others. Taking care of oneself is necessary and not an indication of failure or weakness. In taking care of oneself, one is acting as a role model for clients, as well as ensuring against professional burnout. Whenever a professional encounters burned-out or stress, the people who suffer the most are the very clients being served. Being stressed or burned out contributes to poor judgment, irritability and lack of mental clarity.

Remember, self-care allows the body and mind to rejuvenate, reflect and recharge, which makes it easier to continue the journey of helping others.

Chapter XVI
Ethics and Intuitive work

Ethical decisions ensure that everyone's best interests are protected. When in doubt, don't. - Harvey Mackay

Intuitive Work and Ethics

There are no established organizations that formally overlook the conduct of psychics or individuals who utilize intuitive skills. Therefore the ethics explored in this chapter reflect the codes established by the mental health profession. However, individuals who work in the mental health and healthcare field are often licensed and certified by organizations that monitor professionals and uphold them accountable for professional conduct. The ethical principles are designed to protect clients who seek services from mental health clinicians and healthcare professionals.

The value of Ethical Conduct

Most therapists sincerely believe that their way of working is moralistic and beneficial for the population they serve. (Barnett 2017). However, as much as we all assume that we have the best interest of our clients at hand; there are times when clinicians fail ethically. There is a tendency to dismiss our natural inclinations as potential issues when it comes to working with people.

Many individuals come from painful and traumatic backgrounds that enter the mental health and healthcare professions with the intentions of helping others overcome their pain. Moreover, there some individuals who become clinicians because of a mixed bag of assumptions about the field. In general, the reasons for becoming a clinician vary from individual to individual, even though there might be a few universal common grounds.

Many clinicians due to their professional background might not be aware that specific behaviors are detrimental to the clientele they serve. For many being a therapist or a health care professional provides both satisfaction and joy knowing individuals are getting better. However, sometimes good intentions come with an ego and an underlying assumption that we might know what is best for our clients. In truth, working with individuals who struggle, and face specific challenges can be both rewarding and frustrating. The reward sometimes comes from feeling good about helping and believing someone took our advice, which changed their lives. The frustration comes from clients resisting change and not taking sage advice. The fact, getting better or remaining stuck is not for the clinician to determine. Many professionals take credit for the failures and successes of their client.

In truth, our role is designed to be one of a facilitator and emotional translator. Clinicians are not Demi-gods that brings light or darkness into the lives of our clients. There are times we do contribute to the demise of our clients, by making decisions and recommendations that are detrimental and go beyond the scope of our therapeutic role.

In developing an ethical practice, it is necessary for every clinician, whether they are a licensed mental health worker, a coach or healthcare practitioner; they need to adhere to explicit ethical codes. Depending on the field the individual might be licensed under, the codes might vary. However, there are standard ethical codes which professionals should follow to protect their clientele and themselves.

There are fundamental guiding principles that pertain to all individuals working in the mental health and healthcare industry, which ensure that both the clinician and the client retain appropriate balance. (Benov 2013) The ethical principles consist of the following:

Ethical Principles

1. **Respect for Autonomy**: This **fosters self-determination** and **freedom** for the client to choose their directions in therapy. The principle of having respect is designed to keep the clinician from inheriting the role of the decision maker or behaving against the

client's free will or right to choose.

2. **Beneficence**: This ensures the responsibility of **promoting what is right** and contributing to the welfare of the client. A clinician is expected to provide the best intervention possible for the **well-being** of the client.

3. **Non-maleficence**: This is about taking actions in a manner that **produce no harm** or wrongdoing. A clinician has the responsibility to ensure that their therapeutic interventions produce no harm to their clients.

4. **Justice:** This is about conducting therapy in a fair and just manner. The clinician is expected to **behave in a non-discriminatory** manner towards the individuals they serve. In an attempt to prevent inappropriate misconduct due to cultural insensitivity, the therapist should become informed about the culture of their clientele.

5. **Fidelity:** This principle is about the trust between client and clinician. The **needs of the client c**ome before the needs of the clinician. The client needs to be able to trust the clinician will not take advantage of their relationship and will do what is best for their well-being.

In any field that provides a person with a license, they need to be aware of their ethical codes, to avoid infractions that might cause them to lose their license. However, aside from the agency that provides the individual with licensing, some general codes serve as an umbrella for all professionals who work in the helping professions. Some basic standards will protect both the clinician and practitioner regardless if an individual is in private practice or works for a treatment facility. The American Psychological Association recommends the following specific code of ethical guidelines to ensure that clinicians and the individuals they treat remain protected; the recommendations consist of the following:

Dual relationships- it is advisable that the clinician maintains healthy boundaries. One way to avoid crossing professional boundaries is by maintaining a strictly professional relationship and avoid any casual contact. Of course, refraining from nonprofessional contact can be difficult if the clinician provides other services outside of therapy or if the client works in a related service industry. The only type of relationship that is not permissible while a client is currently engaged in therapy is a romantic one. After two years of non-professional contact, romantic relationships are permitted, however, be mindful that relationships with ex-clients are not always healthy, specifically if the client continues to struggle with mental health issues.

Informed Consent – Clients need to be aware of the nature of their treatment and know what to expect from treatment. Clients need to know about the limits of confidentiality, the nature of documentation, what services the clinician is providing whether its evidence-based, experienced-based or alternative. Informed consents are about respecting the client's autonomy regarding their freedom to choose therapy according to their needs

Confidentiality – Client records and participation in treatment is privileged information and not one to be shared randomly or freely outside of treatment. Upon entering therapy, a client needs to be informed about confidentiality issues and what it entails. Clients should know the limits of confidentiality and the requirements for disclosing any clinical information. The only way a therapist can share information is based on the following legal restrictions:

- The therapist is required to report a client if they are a danger to themselves or others.
- The Therapist can discuss client's enrollment in treatment if they are dealing with insurance companies.
- Incidents involving abuse, neglect or violence towards children, the elderly or people with disabilities require reporting. Therapists are mandated -reporters and have a duty to report.
- There is a court order requesting information on the mental stability of a client. However, a client has the right to deny access to information, since the privilege to disclose belongs to the patient only (Tanford 2001)

Expertise- It is vital that the clinician conduct therapy within the scope of their expertise and they are not offering services that they are not trained to provide. If a person is an intern or new to the field, a client has the right to know about their professional limitations

Billing – A therapist must charge the client accordingly, as well as the insurance company if they charge the insurance for payment. It is essential to maintain good records of all the appointments to bill accurately. Record keeping prevents discrepancies with bill collections.

Internet – some guidelines need to be established when working on the internet to ensure confidentiality when working with clients. (Barnett, 2009) The therapist needs to use systems that do not compromise privacy and identity. The internet is a viable method for conducting sessions, but caution needs to be taken to avoid recording any information that can potentially leak through hacking or identity theft.

Keep in mind the **code of ethics** not only protects the client, but it also protects the professional providing services. Some basic concepts help retain the integrity of the work done and provide overall consistency and mindfulness for all parties concerned. If a person wants more information on the details of the code of ethics, they should review the following websites:
http://www.apa.org/ethics/code/code-1992.aspx

The **conduct of ethic** and the **ethical principles** are designed to maintain the integrity of therapy and protect both the client and therapist from unnecessary hardships that can be triggered by improper conduct. (Pope & Vetter n.d.) Also, remember, though some clinicians might be practicing intuitive techniques that do not require specific licenses, they are still responsible for their conduct and how they engage in therapy.

Another way for professionals to maintain professionally clear of unethical practices is to remain current on changes that impact professional and legal guidelines. Engaging in training updates not only maintain skills sharp but also provide information on current and outdated practices. (Isaac 2016)

Chapter Summary

Adhering to ethical codes is an essential element in all professional fields. However, in the field of mental health and healthcare, it is vital since the emotional and mental well-being of the client relies on the upholding ethical practices that ensure professionalism.

The time has come to formulate guidelines for the ethical conduct of scientist, perhaps in the form of a voluntary Hippocratic Oath. - Joseph Rotblat

Conclusion

This book is the end product of years of working in mental health and recovering from brain surgery on April 27, 2017. My recovery journey involved efforts that combined intuition and practical skills. I did things to heal that often made no logical sense, but somehow managed to contribute to my healing.

My healing journey allowed me to test some personal theories and uncover resources that were valuable. In this book, I have shared several intuitive techniques I used personally to help me deal with depression and physical issues I encountered during my recovery.

My recovery made me realize that some of the techniques I used are truly valuable and useful adjunct to therapy and healthcare. I do understand that some of the methods go beyond traditional evidence-based practices and are more effective as practice-based knowledge which honestly means proficiency will evolve through practice.

I will not tell you that every method or system I used is appropriate for every type of clinician or healthcare practitioner. However, I will tell you, that the techniques will help you get outside the box and expand your therapeutic horizons to levels beyond what you can only imagine.

Always remember, the journey of **Intuitive Development** is personal and only as limited as your willingness.

Reference

(2013). How the brain processes auditory signals. Hear it. Retrieved from https://www.hear-it.org/How-the-brain-processes-auditory-signals

(2015). The 10 deadly sins you should never commit as a professional and ethical hypnotherapist. Hypnotherapy. Retrieved from https://hypnosistrainingacademy.com/10-things-a-hypnotherapist-shouldnt-do/

(2017). Carl Rogers' Client-Centered Therapy: Definition, Techniques, and Goals. Psychology Program. Retrieved from https://positivepsychologyprogram.com/client-centered-therapy/

(2017). Carl Rogers' Client-Centered Therapy: Definition, Techniques, and Goals. Psychology Program. Retrieved from https://positivepsychologyprogram.com/client-centered-therapy/

Abraira, V.E., & Ginty, D.D. (2013). The sensory Neurons of touch. Retrieve from https://www.cell.com/neuron/pdf/S0896-6273(13)00710-1.pdf?code=cell-site

Ackerley, R., Carlsson, I., Wester, H., Olausson, H., & Wasling, H.B. (2014). Touch perceptions across skin sites: differences between sensitivity, direction discrimination, and pleasantness. *Frontiers in Behavioral Neuroscience*. Retrieved from https://hal.archives-ouvertes.fr/hal-01470589/document DOI: 10.3389/fnbeh.2014.00054

Adamski, A. (2011). Archetypes and the collective unconscious of Carl G. Jung in the light of Quantum Psychology. *NeuroQuantology*, 9 (3), 563-571. Retrieved from http://citeseerx.ist.psu.edu/viewdoc/download?doi=10.1.1.921.5519&rep=rep1&type=pdf

A. E. Waite- Brainy Quotes. (n.d.). Retrieved from https://www.brainyquote.com/topics/tarot

AIPC. (2010). Ethical Decision-making process. Retrieved from http://www.aipc.net.au/articles/ethical-decision-making-process/

Albert Einstein – Brainy Quote (n.d.). Retrieved from https://www.brainyquote.com/authors/albert_einstein

Alexis Carrel Quotes - Brainyquote. (n.d.). Retrieved from https://www.brainyquote.com/quotes/alexis_carrel_158388

Alfred A. Montapert Quotes – Brainyquote. (n.d.). Retrieved from
https://www.brainyquote.com/authors/alfred_a_montapert

Altshul, S. (2011). How energy works healing works. *Prevention*. Retrieved from
https://www.prevention.com/mind-body/natural-remedies/how-energy-healing-works

American Music Therapy Association. (2011). What is music therapy? Retrieved from https://www.musictherapy.org/about/musictherapy/

American Psychological Association: APA: Retrieved from
http://www.apa.org/ethics/code/code-1992.aspx

Bachner-Melman, R. (2001). Freud's relevance to hypnosis: a reevaluation. *American Journal of Clinical Hypnosis*,44, 1. Retrieved from
http://www.asch.net/portals/0/journallibrary/articles/ajch-44/bachner.pdf

Barkham, M., & Mellow-Clark, J. (2003). Bridging Evidence-based practice and practice-based evidence: Developing a rigorous and relevant knowledge for the psychological therapies. *Clinical Psychology and Psychotherapy*, 10, 319-327. Retrieved from
https://is.muni.cz/el/1423/podzim2008/PSY494/um/Barkham___Mellor_Calrk_2003_EB_practice.pdf

Barnett, J. E. (2009). Ask the ethicist: The role of technology in psychotherapy. Retrieved from http://www.societyforpsychotherapy.org/ask-ethicist-role-technology-psychotherapy

Barnett, J. (2014). Distress, burnout, self-care, and the promotion of wellness for psychotherapists and trainees: Issues, implications, and recommendations. Retrieved from http://www.societyforpsychotherapy.org/distress-therapist-burnout-self-care-promotion-wellness-psychotherapists-trainees-issues-implications-recommendations

Barnett, J. E. (2017). Being an ethical psychotherapist: Five easy steps. Retrieved from http://www.societyforpsychotherapy.org/being-ethical-psychotherapist-5-steps

Bartgis, J., & Bigfoot, D. (2010). Evidence-Based Practices and Practice-Based Evidence. *National Indian Health Board Edition, Healthy Indian Country Initiative Promising Prevention Practices Resource Guide*. Retrieved from
https://www.ncuih.org/krc/D_bigfoot_EBP_PBE

Beck, A.T., & Haigh. E.A.P. (2014). Advances in Cognitive theory and therapy generic cognitive model. *Annual Review of Clinical Psychology*, 10, 1-24. Retrieved from https://www.annualreviews.org/doi/10.1146/annurev-clinpsy-032813-153734

Benov, E. (2013). The five general principles. APA guidelines Retrieved from http://blog.efpsa.org/2013/08/15/apas-five-general-principles-of-ethics/

Beystehner, K.M. (2001). Psychoanalysis: Freud's Revolutionary Approach to Human Personality. Retrieved from http://www.personalityresearch.org/papers/beystehner.html

Bier, D. (2014). Reiki healing and mental health: what the research shows. *PsychCentral*. Retrieved from https://psychcentral.com/lib/reiki-healing-and-mental-health-what-the-research-shows/

Boals, G.F. (1978). Toward a Cognitive Reconceptualization of Meditation. *Journal of Transpersonal* Psychology, 10:14382

Bodytomy. (2017). How does the sense of touch work in humans? Retrieved from https://bodytomy.com/how-does-sense-of-touch-work-in-humans

Brann, L., Owens, J., & Williamson, A. (2015). The Handbook of Contemporary Clinical Hypnosis Theory and Practice. *Wiley Blackwell*, 416-418.

Bundrant, M. (2013). NLP anchoring: 5 steps to make it work. NLP Personal Development. Retrieved from https://inlpcenter.org/nlp-anchoring/

Butje, A., Repede, E., & Shattell, M. (2008). Healing scents: An overview of clinical aromatherapy for emotional distress. *Journal of Psychosocial Nursing and Mental Health Services*, 46(10), 46-52.

Cahn, B.R., & Polich, J. (2006). Meditations states and traits: EEG, ERP and neuroimaging studies. *Psychological Bulletin*, 132 (2), 180-211. DOI: 10.1037/0033-2909.132.2.180

Carolina Herrera Quotes – Brainyquote. (n.d.). Retrieved from https://www.brainyquote.com/quotes/carolina_herrera_534395

Castro, R. (2017). What is Holistic Coaching? Retrieved from https://holisticcoachingsite.wordpress.com/2017/08/23/what-is-holistic-coaching/

Chaffey, L., Unsworth, C.A., & Fossey, E. (2011). Relationship between intuition and emotional intelligence in occupational therapists in mental health practice. *American Journal Occupational Therapy*, 66 (1)88-96. Retrieved from https://www.ncbi.nlm.nih.gov/pubmed/22389943

Chakra: Religion, Encyclopedia Britannica. Retrieved from https://www.britannica.com/

Chen, M., Floridi, L., & Borgo R., (2013). What is visualization really for? 1-11. Retrieved from https://arxiv.org/ftp/arxiv/papers/1305/1305.5670.pdf

Cherry, K. (2017). Adrenal glands and the endocrine system. Retrieved from https://www.verywell.com/what-are-the-adrenal-glands-2794816

Cherry, K. (2017). George Kelly's theory of personal constructs. *Very Well*. Retrieved from https://www.verywell.com/what-is-personal-construct-theory-2795957

Cherry, K. (2017). Piaget's theory: the 4 stages of cognitive development. *Very Well Mind*
Retrieved from https://www.verywellmind.com/piagets-stages-of-cognitive-development-2795457

Cherry, K. (2017). What is hypnosis? Hypnosis applications, effects, and myths. *Verywell mind*, Retrieved from https://www.verywellmind.com/what-is-hypnosis-2795921

Cherry, K. (2018). Identifying a neurotransmitter. *Brain Health*. Retrieved from: https://www.verywellmind.com/what-is-a-neurotransmitter-2795394

Cherry, K. (2018). How cognitive biases influence how we think and act. *Very well*. Retrieved from https://www.verywell.com/what-is-a-cognitive-bias-2794963

Cholle, F.C. (2011). What is intuition, and how do we use it. *PsychologyToday*. Retrieved from https://www.psychologytoday.com/blog/the-intuitive-compass/201108/what-is-intuition-and-how-do-we-use-it

Chooi, C.S.L., Nerlekar, R., Raju, A. & Cyna, A.M. (2011). The effects of positive or negative words when assessing postoperative pain. *Anesthesia and Intensive Care*. 39(1) 102-106. Retrieved from
https://www.researchgate.net/profile/Allan_Cyna2/publication/50286336_The_effects_of_positive_or_negative_words_when_assessing_postoperative_pain/links/546b29f40cf2397f78314fe5/The-effects-of-positive-or-negative-words-when-assessing-postoperative-pain.pdf?origin=publication_detail

Cohen, S., Janicki-Deverts, D., Turner, R.B., & Doyle, W.J. (2015). Does hugging provide stress-buffing social support? A study of susceptibility to upper respiratory infection and illness. *Psychological Science*, 26 (2) 135-147. Retrieved from http://www.psy.cmu.edu/~scohen/Does%20Hugging.pdf

Coleman, C.R. (2014). Systematic research supporting psychoanalytic and psychodynamic treatments. *Contemporary Psychoanalysis*, 50 (1-2), 34-42. DOI:10.1080/00107530.2014.880295

Conway, B. R., Soumya Chatterjee, S., Field, G.D., Horwitz, G.D., Johnson, E.N., Koida, K., & Katherine Mancuso, K. (2010). Advances in color science: from Retina to Behavior. *The Journal of Neuroscience*, 30 (45), 14955-14963. Retrieved from http://www.lsrweb.net/Assets/NEIPages/BevilConway/pdfs/Conwayetal_2010.pdf

Corton, G. (1985). Can East and West Meet in Psychoanalysis? *American Journal of Psychiatry*, 142,122627.

Creath, K. (2004). Measuring effects of music, noise, and healing using see germination bioassay. *The Journal of Alternative and Complementary Medicine*, 10 (1), 113-122.

Dane, E., Baer, M., Pratt, M.G., & Oldham, G.R. (2011). Rational versus intuitive problem solving: How thinking "off the beaten path" can stimulate creativity. *Psychology of Aesthetics, Creativity and the Arts*, 5(1) 3-12.

D'Angelo, R. (2002). *Aromatherapy. In S. Shannon (Ed.), Handbook of complementary and alternative therapies in mental health*, (71-92). San Diego, CA: Academic Press.

Darragh, I. (n.d.). Chakra Balancing. Retrieved from http://www.ingriddarragh.com/Chakra-Balancing.php

David Lynch- BrainyQuote. (n.d.). Retrieved from https://www.brainyquote.com/search_results?q=david+lynch

Davidson, R.J., Kabat-Zinn, J., Schumacher, J., Rosenkranz, M., Muller, D., Santorelli, S.F., Urbanowski, F.,
Harrington, A., Bonus, K., & Sheridan, J.F. (2003). Alternations in brain and immune function produced by mindfulness meditation. *Psychosomatic Medicine*, 65, 564-570.

De la Fuente-Fernandez, E., Lidstone, S., & Stoessl, A.J. (2006). Placebo Effect and dopamine release. *Journal Neural Transmission*, 70,415-418.

Dermody, M., Martin, J., Reid, S., Corbett, P., Ward, K.., & Dorter, J. (2017). Balance the challenges of mental health claims in insurance. Retrieved from https://www.actuaries.asn.au/Library/Events/SUM/2017/SUM17MartinEtAlPaper.pdf

Dienstmann, G. (2015). Types of meditation – an overview of 23 meditation techniques. Retrieved from https://liveanddare.com/types-of-meditation

Dore, J. (2017). Using Tarot in Psychotherapy. *Psych Central Professional*. Retrieved from https://pro.psychcentral.com/using-tarot-in-psychotherapy/0020437.html

EIA, US Energy Information Administration. (2018). What is energy? Retrieved from https://www.eia.gov/energyexplained/index.cfm?page=about_home

Enea, V., & Dafinoiu, I. (2011). Ethical principles and standards in the practice of hypnosis. *Romanian Journal of Bioethics*, 9(3), 110-116. Retrieved from http://bioetica.ro/index.php/arhiva-bioetica/article/download/207/343

Falk, E.B., O'Donnell, M.B., Cascio, C, N., Tinney, F., Kang, Y., Lieberman, M.D., Taylor, S.E., Lawrence, A., Resnicow, K., & Strecher, V. J. (2014). Self-affirmation alters the brain's response to health messages and subsequent behavior change, *PNAS Early Edition*. Retrieved from
http://www.pnas.org/content/pnas/early/2015/01/29/1500247112.full.pdf

Faymonville, M., Fissetter, J., Mambourg, P.H., Roediger, L., Joris, J. & Lamy, M. (1995). Hypnosis as adjunct therapy in conscious sedation for plastic surgery. Regional; Anesthesia American *Journal of Psychiatry*, 20(2),145-151. Retrieved from
https://orbi.uliege.be/handle/2268/26764

Feinstein, D. (2008). Energy Psychology: A Review of the Preliminary Evidence. Psychotherapy: Theory, Research, Practice, Training. 45(2), 199-213. Retrieved from
http://citeseerx.ist.psu.edu/viewdoc/download?doi=10.1.1.485.7433&rep=rep1&type=pdf

Ferraresi, M., Clari, R., Moro, I., Banino, E., Boero, E., Crosio, A., & Piccoli, G. B. (2013). Reiki and related therapies in the dialysis ward: An evidence-based and ethical discussion to debate if these complementary and alternative medicines are welcomed or banned. *BMC Nephrology*. Retrieved from: https://bmcnephrol.biomedcentral.com/articles/10.1186/1471-2369-14-129

Field J. (2011). Touch for socioemotional and physical well-being. Retrieved from http://rolfing.nyc/wp-content/uploads/2016/06/Touch-for-socioemotional-and-physical-well-being-A-review.pdf

Fischer, J. (2015). The role of intuition in Science. Retrieved from https://ideas4sustainability.wordpress.com/2015/06/01/the-role-of-intuition-in-science/

Fish, R.M., & Geddes, L.A. (2009). Conduction of electrical current to and through the human body: a review. Retrieved from
https://www.ncbi.nlm.nih.gov/pmc/articles/PMC2763825/

Flexer, C. (2017). The ears are doorways to the brain. Phonak Insight. Retrieved from https://audiologyblog.phonakpro.com/ears_are_doorways_to_the_brain/

Fonareva, I. (2013). Physiological, cognitive and expectancy effects of aromatherapy follow acute stress. *Oregon Health & Science University*. Retrieved from https://digitalcommons.ohsu.edu/cgi/viewcontent.cgi?article=1903&context=etd

Franquemont, S. (2006). How does intuition speak to me? Taking Charge Retrieved from https://www.takingcharge.csh.umn.edu/explore-healing-practices/intuition-healthcare/how-does-intuition-speak-me

Freeman, L.J., Conway, A., & Nixon, P.G. (1986). Physiological responses to psychological changes under hypnosis in patients considered to have the hyperventilation syndrome: implications for diagnosis and therapy. *The Royal Society of Medicine*, 79

Gibb, B. (ND). The chemicals of the brain. The Big Picture. Retrieved from https://bigpictureeducation.com/chemicals-brain

Gilbert, T. (2011). Using Tarot to map your developmental journey. Retrieved from https://tarotelements.com/2011/01/20/maslows-hierarchy-of-needs-pyramid/

Goel, A. (N.D.). Trataka – A Meditation Practice for Everyone Retrieved from http://www.healthandyoga.com/html/news/meditation/trataka.aspx

Goleman, D. (1976). Meditation and Consciousness: An Asian Approach to Mental Health. *American Journal of Psychotherapy*, 30,41-54.

Goyal, M., Singh, S., Sibinga, E.M.S., Gould, N.F., Roland-Seymour, A., Sharma, R., Berger, Z., Sleicher, D., Maron, D.D., Shihab, H.M., Ranasinghe, P.D., Linn, S., Saha, S., Bass, E.B., & Haythornthwaite, J.A. (2014). Meditation programs for psychological stress: A systematic review and meta-analysis. *JAMA Internal Medicine*, 174(3) 357–368. DOI:10,1001/jamainternmed.2013.13018

Grimes, J.A. (1996). *A Concise Dictionary of Indian Philosophy: Sanskrit Terms Defined in English*. State University of New York Press. Pp. 100–101. ISBN 978-0-7914-3067-5.

Green, C. D. (2000). Classics in the history of psychology. Retrieved from http://psychclassics.yorku.ca/Rogers/therapy.htm

Hagger, M.S. (2017). Changing behavior using mental imagery & mental stimulation. *Ministry of Health Malaysia*. Retrieved from http://www.infosihat.gov.my/index.php/multimedia/garis-panduan/item/mental-changing-behaviour-using-mental-imagery-mental-simulation

Harding, J. (2008). *The essential oils handbook*. London, UK. Duncan Baird Publishers, p 2

Harrower-Erickson, M. (1945). *Large-scale Rorschach techniques: a manual for the group Rorschach and multiple-choice test"*. Springfield, Illinois: Charles C Thomas Publisher, Ltd.

Harvey Mackay Brainy -Quotes (n.d.). Retrieved from https://www.brainyquote.com/authors/harvey_mackay

Hatfield, H. (2005). The Science Behind How We Taste. Retrieved from https://www.webmd.com/diet/features/science-how-we-taste#1

Hazelgrove, J. (1998). What is integrated therapy? William & March School of Education. Retrieved from http://education.wm.edu/centers/ttac/resources/articles/consultcollaborate/integratherapy/index.php

Hellerstein, D.J. (2008). Practice-based evidence rather than Evidence-based practice in psychiatry. *Medscape Journal of Medicine*. Retrieved from: https://www.ncbi.nlm.nih.gov/pmc/articles/PMC2491680/

Helsel, P.B. (2014). Witnessing the body's response to trauma: Resistance, ritual and nervous. Retrieved from www.ictg.org/uploads/1/2/9/5/12954435/phil_helsel_dec_2014_article.pdf

Henri Poincare Brainy Quotes (n.d.). – Retrieved from https://www.brainyquote.com/authors/henri_poincare

Hilgard, E.R. (1965). *Hypnotic Susceptibility*, New York. Harcourt, Brace & World.

History of Reiki. Retrieved from: https://iarp.org/history-of-reiki/

Introduction to Taoism. Tao Healing Center. Retrieved from http://www.taohealing.com/introduction.html

Isaac, H. (2016). Ethical considerations for psychotherapy in natural settings. Retrieved from https://www.liebertpub.com/doi/abs/10.1089/eco.2016.0008?journalCode=eco doi.org/10.1089/eco.2016.0008

Jackson, R.N. (n.d.). The effect of stimulating and soothing smells on heart rate and memory. *McNair Scholars Journal*, 11. 97-110. Retrieved from http://www.csus.edu/mcnair/_all-scholars-articles-photos-webpage/11_2009_2010/journal_2009-10/rachanee_jackson_csus_mcnair_2010-11.pdf

Jalil, N.A., Yunus, R.M., & Said, N.S. (2012). Environmental Colour Impact upon Human Behaviour: A Review. *Procedia – Social and Behavioral Sciences*, 35, 54-62. Retrieved from: http://renketkisi.com/docs/eng/environment%20color%20effect%20on%20human.pdf

Jiang, H., White, M.P., Greicius, M.D., Waelde, L.C. & Spiegel, D. (2016). Brain activity and functional connectivity associated with hypnosis. *Cerebral Cortex*. Retrieved from http://farehypnosis.com/wp-content/uploads/2017/04/Stanford-Research.pdf

Joelson, R.B. (2017). Locus of control. *Psychology Today*. Retrieved from https://www.psychologytoday.com/blog/moments-matter/201708/locus-control

Jo, H., Rodiek, S., Fujii, E., Miyazaki, Y., Park, B.J., & Ann, S.W. (2013). Physiological and psychological response to floral scent. *HortScience*, 48(1)82-88. Retrieved from http://hortsci.ashspublications.org/content/48/1/82.full.pdf

Joseph Rotblat Brainy -Quotes (n.d.). Retrieved from https://www.brainyquote.com/search_results?q=Joseph+Rotblat

Judith, A. (1987). *Wheels of life, a user's guide to the chakra system*. St Paul, Mn, Llewelyn's New Age Series

Jung, C. (1967). *Collected works of C.G. Jung*, (207-273). Princeton University Press,

Jung, C. G. (1964). *Approaching the unconscious: In C. G. Jung (Ed.), Man and his symbols* (18–103). London, England: Aldus.

Jung, C. G. (1964). *Man, and his symbols*. New York, NY: Anchor Press Double Day

Jurik, V. (2015). How Body Influences Memory: The embodied aspects in the retrieval of autobiographical memories. *Annales Psychologici*, 1, 28-38.

King, G. (2018). Intuition and psychic development, everyone can be psychic. *The Aetherius Society*. retrieved from https://www.aetherius.org/intuition-and-psychic-development/

Kirsch, I., Montgomery, G., & Sapirstein, G. (1993). Hypnosis as an adjunct to Cognitive-behavioral Psychotherapy: A meta-analysis. *Journal of Consulting and Clinical Psychology*, 63(2) 214-220. Retrieved from https://pdfs.semanticscholar.org/c270/0ff934d2c39213699d62b3fc210bfd24963f.pdf

Knickman, J., K.R.R. Krishnan, H.A. Pincus, C. Blanco, D.G. Blazer, M.J. Coye, J.H. Krystal, S.L. Rauch, G.E. Simon, and B. Vitiello. (2016). Improving Access to Effective Care for People Who Have Mental Health and Substance Use Disorders. Discussion Paper, Vital Directions for Health and Health Care Series. *National Academy of Medicine*, Washington, DC. Retrieved from. https://nam.edu/wp-content/uploads/2016/09/improving-access-to-effective-care-for-people-who-have-mentalhealth-and-substance-use-disorders.pdf

Konnikova, M. (2015). The power of touch. Retrieved from https://www.newyorker.com/science/maria-konnikova/power-touch

Krapp, M. (1999). Empirical Research in psychoanalysis and analytic psychotherapy. 556-586

Kutz, I., Borysenko, J.Z., & Benson, H. (1985). Meditation and Psychotherapy: A Rationale for the Integration of Dynamic Psychotherapy, The Relaxation Response, and Mindfulness Meditation. *American Journal of Psychiatry,* 142,18

Lanoy, T.L. (2015). Reiki: application as a modality of integrative therapy for treating post-traumatic stress disorder and other wounded warrior issues. Air War College.

Lao Tzu, Brainy Quotes. Retrieved from
https://www.brainyquote.com/quotes/lao_tzu_137138

Lee, M. S., Pittler, M. H., & Ernst, E. (2008). Effects of reiki in clinical practice: a systematic review of randomized clinical trials [Abstract]. *International Journal of Clinical Practice, 62*(6)947-954. Retrieved from http://www.ncbi.nlm.nih.gov/pubmed/18410352

Leung, M.K., Lau, W.K.W., Chan, C.C.H., Wong, S.S.Y., Fung, A.L.C., & TMC, L. (2017). Meditation-induced neuroplastic changes in amygdala activity during negative affective processing. *Social Neuroscience,* 10,1-12. DOI: 10.1080/17470919.2017.1311939. Retrieved from
https://www.ncbi.nlm.nih.gov/pubmed/28393652

Lieberman, M.D., Jarcho, J.M., & Satpute, A.B. (2004). Evidence-based and intuition-based knowledge: an FMRI study. *American Psychological Association,* 87(4)421-435. DOI:10.1037/0022-3514.87.4.421

Lilienfeld, S.O., Lynn, S.J., Ruscio, J., & Beyerstein, B.L. (2010). *50 Great Myths of popular psychology. Shattering widespread misconceptions about human behavior.* Malden, MA. Wiley-Blackwell.

Lillehei, A.S. (2014). Effect of Lavender Aromatherapy via Inhalation and Sleep Hygiene on Sleep in *College Students with Self-Reported Sleep Issues.* Retrieved from
https://conservancy.umn.edu/bitstream/handle/11299/165750/Lillehei_umn_01 30E_14869.pdf;sequence=1

Lucian Freud - Brainy Quote (n.d.). Retrieved from:
https://www.brainyquote.com/search_results?q=aura

Lufityanto, G., Donkin, C., & Pearson, J. (2016). Measuring Intuition: Nonconscious Emotional Information Boosts Decision Accuracy and Confidence. *Psychological Science.* DOI: 10.1177/0956797616629403

MacDonald, C. (n.d.). Health psychology center presents: What is health psychology? Retrieved from http://healthpsychology.org/what-is-health-psychology/

MacIntyre, B., Hamilton, J., Fricke, T., Ma. W., Mehle S., & Michel, M. (2008). The Efficacy of Healing Touch in Coronary Artery Bypass Surgery Recovery: A Randomized Clinical Trial. *Alternative Therapies,* Jul/Aug,14(4)24-32.

MacWilliam, B. (n.d.). Creative Arts Therapies. Retrieved from https://brianamacwilliam.com/art-therapy/

Magnetic imaging (2009). Magnetometers, x-rays and more: airport security technology. Retrieved from http://www.foxnews.com/tech/2009/12/29/magnetometers-x-rays-airport-security-technology.html

Magnetic Resonance Imaging (MRI). Science Education. Retrieved from https://www.nibib.nih.gov/science-education/science-topics/magnetic-resonance-imaging-mri

Mahershala Ali – Brainy Quotes. Retrieved from: https://www.brainyquote.com/search_results?q=chakras

Martin, B. (2018). In-depth: Cognitive Behavioral Therapy. *PsychCentral*. Retrieved from https://psychcentral.com/lib/in-depth-cognitive-behavioral-therapy/

Martinez-Conde, S., & Macknik, S. L. (2014). How the color red influences our behavior. *Scientific America*. Retrieved from https://www.scientificamerican.com/article/how-the-color-red-influences-our-behavior/

McLeod, S. (2008). Visual Perception Theory. *Simply Psychology*. Retrieved from https://simplypsychology.org/perception-theories.html

McLeod, S. (2015). Humanism. Simply Psychology. Retrieved from https://www.simplypsychology.org/humanistic.html

Metzner, R. (1998). Hallucinogenic drugs and plants in psychotherapy and shamanism. *Journal of Psychoactive Drugs*, 30(4) 1-10.

Metzner, R. (2008). *Alchemical divination. Accessing your spiritual intelligence for healing and guidance*. Green Earth Foundation & Regent Press.

Miller, A. (2006). *The body never lies: the lingering effects of cruel parenting*. New York, NY: W. W. Norton & Company.

Miller, J.J., Fletcher, K., & Kabat-Zinn, J. (1995). Three-year follow-up and clinical implications of a mindfulness meditation-based stress reduction intervention in the treatment of anxiety disorders. *General Hospital Psychiatry*, 17, 192-200.

Milner, A. D., & Goodale, M. A. (1998). The visual brain. *PSYCHE*, 4 (12) http://psyche.cs.monash.edu.au/v4/psyche-4-12-milner.html

Milner, A. D., & Goodale, M. A. (2008). Two visual systems reviewed. *Neuropsychologica*, 46, 774–785.

Moreno, A. (1967). Jung's Collective Unconscious. *Laval theologique et philsophyique*, 23 (2)174-195. Retrieved from https://www.erudit.org/fr/revues/ltp/1967-v23-n2-ltp0971/1020110ar.pdf

Morgan, K. (2018). What are the benefits of attending seminars? Retrieved from http://education.seattlepi.com/benefits-attending-seminars-1929.html

Munger, D. (2007). What we hear and how it affects what we see. Retrieved from http://scienceblogs.com/cognitivedaily/2007/01/09/what-we-hear-and-how-it-affect/

Nathan, P.E., & Gorman J.M. (2002). A guide to treatments that work. *Oxford University Press*. 2nd 478-480

NCCIH- National Center for Complementary and Integrative Health. (2016). Meditation. U.S. Department of Health & Human Services. *National Institute of Health*. Retrieved from https://nccih.nih.gov/sites/nccam.nih.gov/files/Meditation_04-25-2016.pdf

Neal, D., Vujcic, J., Hernandez, O., & Wood, W. (2015). The science of habit: creating disruptive and sticky behavior, change in handwashing behavior. *Catalyst Behavioral Sciences*. Retrieved from https://www.healthynewbornnetwork.org/hnn-content/uploads/habits-neal2015.pdf

Newell, B. (2013). Explainer: what is intuition? Retrieved from http://theconversation.com/explainer-what-is-intuition-13238

NIDA (2018). Treatment approaches for Drug addiction. Retrieved from https://www.drugabuse.gov/publications/drugfacts/treatment-approaches-drug-addiction

NIDCD (2017). Recent advances in taste and smell research. Transduction Mechanism. *National Institute on Deafness and other Communication Disorders*. Retrieved from https://www.nidcd.nih.gov/about/strategic-plan/2017-2021/recent-advances-taste-and-smell-research

Nierenberg, C. (2016). The Science of Intuition: How to Measure 'Hunches' and 'Gut Feelings'

Live Science. Retrieved from https://www.livescience.com/54825-scientists-measure-intuition.html

NIH. (2017). Smell Disorders. NIH National Institute on Deafness and other Communication Disorders. Retrieved from https://www.nidcd.nih.gov/health/smell-disorders#2

NIH. National Institute of Mental Health (1999). Bridging Science and Service. *A Report by the National Advisory Mental Health Council's Clinical Treatment and Services*

Research Workshop. Retrieved from https://www.nimh.nih.gov/about/advisory-boards-and-groups/namhc/reports/bridging-science-and-service-a-report-by-the-national-advisory-mental-health-councils-clinical-treatment-and-services-research-workgroup.shtml

NIMH. (2005). Treatment Research in Mental Illness: Improving the Nations' Public Mental Health Care through *NIMH funded Interventions Research*. Retrieved from https://www.nimh.nih.gov/about/advisory-boards-and-groups/namhc/reports/interventions-research_33825.pdf

Novoa, M.P. (2011). The effects of Reiki treatment on mental health professionals who are at risk for secondary traumatic stress. *LSU Doctoral Dissertations.* 2183. Retrieved from https://digitalcommons.lsu.edu/cgi/viewcontent.cgi?article=3182&context=gradschool_dissertations

O'Connell, C. (2016). What is energy? *Comos the Science of Everything.* 9-12-2016. Retrieved from https://cosmosmagazine.com/physics/what-is-energy

Olson, A. (2012). Hypnosis in clinical social work practice: What contributes to its under-utilization. *Master of Social Work Clinical Research*, 136. Retrieved from https://sophia.stkate.edu/cgi/viewcontent.cgi?article=1136&context=msw_papers

Oswalt, A. (2008). Early childhood cognitive development: intuitive thought. Retrieved from https://www.mentalhelp.net/articles/early-childhood-cognitive-development-intuitive-thought/

Pettijohn, J.F., Brenneman, M.M., Glass, J.N., Brito, G.R., Terranova, A.M., Kim, J., Meyersburg, C.A., & Piroch, J. (n.d.). College student perceptions of psychology as a science as a function of psychology course enrollment. *College Student Journal. Project Innovation Inc.* 461-465.

Pope, K.S., & Vetter, V.A. (n.d.). Ethical dilemmas encountered by members of the American Psychological Association a national survey. Retrieved from https://kspope.com/ethics/ethics2.php

Potter, G. (2004). Intensive therapy: Utilizing hypnosis in the treatment of substance abuse disorders. *American Journal of Clinical Hypnosis*, 47(1). 22-28. Retrieved from https://pdfs.semanticscholar.org/3b24/6c0182daa4748ae0e2cf5753ddd3b5ec080e.pdf

Privitera, A.J. (2018). Sensation and perception. Retrieved from http://nobaproject.com/modules/sensation-and-perception

Psychometry. (n.d.). In Merriam-Webster Dictionary Online. Retrieved from https://www.merriam-webster.com/dictionary/psychometry

Rand, W. L. (n.d.). What is the history of Reiki? Retrieved from
http://www.reiki.org/FAQ/HistoryOfReiki.html

Rea, S. (2016). Neurobiological change explains how mindfulness meditation improves health. Retrieved from
https://www.cmu.edu/news/stories/archives/2016/february/meditation-changes-brain.html

Read, J.D. & Lindsay, D. S. (2013). Recollections of Trauma. Scientific evidence and clinical practice. *Series A: Life Sciences*, 291, 50-52.

Redstone, L. (2015). Mindfulness meditation and aromatherapy. *Archives of Psychiatric Nursing* 29, 192-193. Retrieved from
https://pdfs.semanticscholar.org/6268/f2d539d17cf06b2c48a7e346a2f9a8b97593.pdf

Reitan, A. (2013). Humanistic theory and therapy Applied to psychotic individual. Retrieved from http://brainblogger.com/2013/02/24/humanistic-theory-and-therapy-applied-to-the-psychotic-individual/

Rennie, L., Uskul, A.K., Adams, C., & Appleton, K. (2012). Visualization for increasing health intentions. Retrieved from
http://eprints.bournemouth.ac.uk/21330/4/RennieUskulAdamsAppleton_PHinpress.pdf

Roseler, C. (2013). Evidence for the effectiveness of Jungian psychotherapy: a review of empirical studies. *Behavioral Science*. 3, 562-575. DOI: 10.3390/bs3040562

Sahoo, A. (2014). The scientific evidence of human aura. Retrieved from
https://www.speakingtree.in/allslides/the-scientific-evidence-of-human-aura/119276

Sapp, M. (2016). Hypnosis and Postmodernism: Multicultural Applications. *Sleep and Hypnosis*, 18 (1)19-25. Retrieved from
http://www.sleepandhypnosis.org/ing/Pdf/9405bd31c83e41fd9847a94d9ced51f8.pdf

Sayers, W.M., Creswell, J.D., & Taren, A. (2015). The emerging neurobiology of mindfulness and emotion processing. Retrieved from
http://repository.cmu.edu/cgi/viewcontent.cgi?article=2410&context=psychology

Schacter, D.L., Guerin, S.A., & Jacques, P.L. (2011). Memory distortion: an adaptive perspective. *Trends in Cognitive Science,* 15(10)467–474. Retrieved from:
https://www.ncbi.nlm.nih.gov/pmc/articles/PMC3183109/
DOI: 10.1016/j.tics.2011.08.004

Schredl, M. (2008). Freud's interpretation of his own dreams in "The interpretation of dreams: A continuity of hypothesis perspective. *International Journal of Dream*

Research, 1(2)44-47.

Semetsky, I. (2005). Integrating tarot readings into counseling and psychotherapy. *Spirituality and Health International*, 6(2) 1-14.

Shallcross, L. (2011). Taking care of yourself as a counselor. Retrieved from https://ct.counseling.org/2011/01/taking-care-of-yourself-as-a-counselor/

Shallcross, L. (2012). The recipe for truly great counselors. Retrieve from: http://ct.counseling.org/2012/12/the-recipe-for-truly-great-counseling/

Shallcross, L. (2013). Multicultural competence: A continual pursuit. Retrieved from https://ct.counseling.org/2013/09/multicultural-competence-a-continual-pursuit/

Sharma. A. (2006). A Primal Perspective on the Philosophy of Religion. *Springer*, 193–196. ISBN 978-1-4020-5014-5.

Shashkevich, A. (2017). Patient mindset matters in healing matters and deserves more study, experts say. *Medical Stanford Medicine*. Retrieved from https://med.stanford.edu/news/all-news/2017/03/health-care-providers-should-harness-power-of-mindsets.html

Sherwood, K. (1988). *Chakra Therapy: for personal growth and healing*. St. Paul, MN: The Llewellyn New Times.

Shiny Yamanaka Brainy Quotes (n.d.). Retrieved from https://www.brainyquote.com/authors/shinya_yamanaka

Snow, A.L., Hovanec, L., & Brandt, J. (2004). A controlled trial of aromatherapy for agitation in nursing home patients with dementia. *The Journal of alternative and complementary medicine*, 10(3)431-437. Retrieved from https://www.liebertpub.com/doi/pdf/10.1089/1075553041323696

Solar Energy Pros and Cons - 1990 Words | Bartleby. (n.d.). Retrieved from https://www.bartleby.com/essay/Solar-Energy-Pros-and-Cons-FKRVG3EKRZYA

Srikanth, N. J. (2017). Pre and post experiences of viewing human aura: An exploratory study. *International. Journal of Research. Ayurveda Pharmacy*, 8(2):51-55. Retrieved from http://www.ijrap.net/admin/php/uploads/1750_pdf.pdf

Tanford, J.A. (2001). The therapist-patient privilege: a brief guide for mental health professionals. Retrieved from http://www.law.indiana.edu/instruction/tanford/web/archive/Psypriv.html

Tang, Y.Y., Hölzel, B.K., & Posner, M.I. (2015). The neuroscience of mindfulness meditation. *Nature Review, Neuroscience*, 16, 213-225. Retrieved from http://www.awakeatwork.net/sites/default/files/Tang_1426855548_1%20-final.pdf

Taren, A.A., Gianaros, P.J., Greco, C.M., Lindsay, E.K., Fairgrieve, A., Brown, K.W., Rosen, R.K., Ferris, J.L., Julson, E., Marsland, A.L., Bursley, J.K., Ramsburg, J., & Creswell, J.D. (2015). Mindfulness meditation training alters stress-related amygdala resting-state functional connectivity: a randomized controlled trial. *Social Cognitive and Affective Neuroscience*, 10(12)1758-1768. Retrieved from http://www.psy.cmu.edu/~creswell/papers/Taren%20et%20al%20(2015),%20mindfulness%20training%20amygdala%20resting%20state%20functional%20connectivity,%20SCAN.pdf

Taylor, T. (n.d.). Muscles of the eye. Retrieved from http://www.innerbody.com/anatomy/muscular/head-neck/muscles-eye

Than, K. (2016). How the human eye works. Retrieved from https://www.livescience.com/3919-human-eye-works.html

The Visible Body. (2017). How the Human Eye Works. *Visible Body*: Retrieved from https://www.visiblebody.com/learn/nervous/five-senses

Titus, S., & Horsman, E. (2009). Characterizing and improving spatial visualization. *Journal of Geoscience Education*, 57(4) 242-254. Retrieved from https://files.eric.ed.gov/fulltext/EJ1164746.pdf

Tummala-Narra, P. (2013). Psychoanalytic Applications in a diverse society. *American Psychological Association*, 30(3)471-487. DOI: 10.1037/a0031375

Turner, K. (2014). The Science behind intuition. *Psychology Today*. Retrieved from https://www.psychologytoday.com/blog/radical-remission/201405/the-science-behind-intuition

Tyrrell, M. (2017). 3 core hypnotherapy techniques that every therapist should now. Retrieved from https://www.unk.com/blog/3-hypnotherapy-techniques-every-therapist-should-know/

Valvano, L. (2017). Easy Everyday Exercise - Isometrics - The Stress. Retrieved from http://www.stress.org.uk/easy-everyday-exercise-isometrics/

The University of Rochester. (2005). Color Perception Is Not in The Eye of The Beholder: It's in *The Brain*. *ScienceDaily*. Retrieved April 23, 2018, from www.sciencedaily.com/releases/2005/10/051026082313.htm

Wang, R. (1990). *Tarot psychology. A Handbook for Jungian Tarot*. Urania Verlag's AG. Germany

Wagner, S. (2017). Understanding Retrocognition. *Thought Co*. Retrieved from https://www.thoughtco.com/what-is-retrocognition-2593962

Wallis, C. (n.d.). The six most important things you never knew about the Chakra system. Tantric Yoga. Retrieved from http://tantrikstudies.squarespace.com/blog/2016/2/5/the-real-story-on-the-chakras

Wanjek, C. (2013). Left brain vs. right: It's a myth, research finds. Retrieved from https://www.livescience.com/39373-left-brain-right-brain-myth.html

Warner, L., & McNell, E. (1988). Mental Imagery and its potential for physical therapy. 68(4) 517-521. Retrieved from: http://citeseerx.ist.psu.edu/viewdoc/download?doi=10.1.1.840.3750&rep=rep1&type=pdf

Way, B.M., Creswell, D.J., Eisenberger, N.I., & Lieberman, M.D. (2010). Dispositional mindfulness and depressive symptomatology: correlations with limbic and self-referential neural activity during rest. *Emotion. American Psychological Association*, 10(1)12-24. DOI:10.1037/a0018312

Weisshaar, D.L. (2007). The therapist's experience of feeling in too deep with a client. Retrieved from https://scholarworks.gsu.edu/cgi/viewcontent.cgi?article=1037&context=psych_diss

White, D.G. (2012). Yoga in Practice. *Princeton University Press* 2012, 14-15.

Wikipedia, Symbolic representation. Retrieved from https://en.wikipedia.org/wiki/Symbolic_representation

Williams, R. (2015). 8 reasons why we need human touch more than ever. Retrieved from https://www.psychologytoday.com/blog/wired-success/201503/8-reasons-why-we-need-human-touch-more-ever

Wilson, K.R., Havighurst, S.S., & Harley, A. E. (2012). Tuning in to Kids: An effectiveness trial of a parenting program targeting emotion socialization of preschoolers. *Journal of Family Psychology*, 26(1) 56-65.

Witteman, C., Van den Bercken, J., Claes, L., & Godoy, A. (2009). Assessing rational and intuitive thinking styles. *European Journal of Psychological Assessment*, 25(1)39-47.

Wong, C. (2017). 9 most popular types of massages. Retrieved from https://www.verywell.com/most-popular-types-of-massage-89741

Wong, T.H., Chang, J.H.W., Chee, F.P., & Dayou, J. (2017). Effects of string tensions to the fundamental frequency of sound and body vibration of shape. *Transactions on Science and Technology*, 4(4) 437-441.

Wood, K.C., Smith, H., & Grossniklaus, D. (2001). Piaget's Stages of cognitive development. *Dept of Psychology and Instructional Technology, University of Georgia.* Retrieved from http://projects.coe.uga.edu/epltt/

Woojan, L., & Pachmayer, A. (2016). The Impact of Visualization and Expectation on Tourists' Emotion and Satisfaction at the Destination. Tourism Travel and Research Association: *Advancing Tourism Research Globally*, 12. http://scholarworks.umass.edu/ttra/2012/Oral/12

Yun, O.W., & Yazdanifard, R. (2013). Correlation between ambient scent and the brand position within consumers' unconscious self. *Global Institute for Research and Education*, 2(6)12-15. Retrieved from http://www.southcentralav.com/wp-content/uploads/2017/02/research-ambient-scent-12-15-vol-2-6-13-gjcmp.pdf

Ziegler, M., Kemper, C.J., & Lenzner, T. (2015). The issue of fuzzy concepts in test construction and possible remedies. *European Journal of Psychological Assessment*, 31(1)1-4. DOI: 10.1027/1015-5759/a00025

Index

A

Addiction Counseling, 37
alternative techniques, 1, 7
analytical thinking, 26
Aromatherapy, 10, 67, 68
Art therapy, 37
Aura reading, 71

C

Chakra Scanning, 71
Chakra therapy, 35, 37, 38
client-centered therapy, 28, 36
Cognitive Behavioral therapy, 34
Cognitive therapy, 34, 38
cultural norms, 27

E

Eclectic Therapy, 39
Effectiveness Research, 25
Efficacy Research, 25
emotional intelligence, 9, 10
energy balancing, 36
ethical codes., 31
evidence-based practices, 5, 9, 10
experienced-based, 5

H

hard science, 9
healer, 5
Holistic Coaching, 38

Humanistic therapy, 38
Hypnotherapy, 38
Hypnotic Regressive Therapy, 35

I

Integrated Therapy, 39
intuition, 3, 5, 6, 8, 10, 11, 12, 13
intuitive awareness, 7, 9
intuitive development, 3, 12
intuitive interpretive reading, 36
intuitive methods, 10
intuitive mind, 7
intuitive skills, 2, 4, 7, 8, 10, 12

J

Journaling, 46, 47, 49, 50, 51, 52, 54, 55, 57, 60, 71

L

lateralization, 6
lateralization,, 6

M

Maslow's system, 242
meditation, 3, 4, 5, 11, 13, 22, 32, 34, 37
meditation., 4
memories, 18, 27, 28, 29, 30, 35, 44, 45, 46, 47, 60, 67, 68, 73
memory, 21, 22, 27, 28, 30
mental health, 1, 5, 7, 9, 11, 12, 20, 24,

25, 26, 30, 31, 32, 33, 39, 41, 52, 53, 55, 56, 57, 58, 63, 64, 66, 67, 72, 75, 99, 103, 107, 108, 109, 128, 138, 140, 142, 155, 159, 214, 218, 219, 247, 259, 260, 266, 269, 270, 271, 273, 274, 275, 279, 283, 288, 289, 292, 302, 304
modalities, 24, 31, 33, 36, 38, 39, 41, 42, 44, 54, 63, 75
Music therapy, 39

O

olfactory., 21

P

positive attitude, 100
practical applications, 4, 5, 12
Practice Research, 25
psychic reader, 5
psychoanalysis, 2, 17, 27, 35, 36
Psychoanalysis, 39
Psychometry, 71

R

rational approach, 18
Regressive Hypnosis, 35
Regressive Recodification, 221
Regressive therapy, 46, 47
Reiki, 4, 11
reiki energy, 5
Reiki Healing, 36
Reiki treatments, 36
retrieval, ii, 7, 16, 20, 30, 34, 71, 73, 82, 85, 87, 158, 216, 298
retrieval techniques, 71

Retrocognition, 71
Rorschach test, 28

S

subconscious, 6
substance abuse, 1, 7, 10, 302
symbolism, 16, 20, 21, 27, 30, 35
symbols, 2, 13, 27, 29
systematic desensitization, 37

T

tarot deck, 3, 28, 30, 35, 45, 59, 71, 73, 74
Tarot Guidance, 71
tarot meditations, 38
Tarot Therapy, 35
Therapeutic Meditation, 68
therapist, 1, 3, 5, 7, 10, 11
treatment modalities, 2, 5

U

unconscious, 14, 16, 17, 18, 22, 26, 29, 30, 32, 34, 38

V

visual sensory system, 142, 242
visualization. *See*
Visualization, 34, 37, 48, 50, 51, 52, 54, 55, 57, 59, 61, 63, 71

W

Western culture, 35

ABOUT THE AUTHOR

Rosa Castro, PsyD, is a Psychotherapist, Intuitive Coach, Intuitive teacher, and Reiki Master. She has over 39 years' experience in the Mental Health and Addiction field. She has worked in hospitals, schools and private clinics providing individual and group therapy. She has taught workshops and classes in coping with addictive problems, stress management, self-empowerment, as well as intuitive development courses. In her private practice, she combines her professional background with her intuitive talents to bring balance, clarity, and healing in her sessions. She also teaches Reiki and Intuitive development classes. Ms. Castro is a well-known psychic and intuitive teacher who hosted Psychic Sundays on WEVD Radio as Psychic Phoenix Rose did several guest appearances on Cable shows and lectures at both the New Life and Whole Life Expos.

Endnote

Thank you for taking the time to read this book. If you have comments or additional questions, feel free to email me at

DrRosaCastro@gmail.com

Always Ro